Human, All Too Human:
A Book for Free Spirits
Part One and Part Two

Human, All Too Human: A Book for Free Spirits
Part One and Part Two

by Friedrich Nietzsche

Translated by Alexander Harvey and Paul V. Cohn, B.A.

Table of Contents

Part One
Translated by Alexander Harvey

Preface.

1. It is often enough, and always with great surprise, intimated to me that there is something both ordinary and unusual in all my writings, from the "Birth of Tragedy" to the recently published "Prelude to a Philosophy of the Future": they all contain, I have been told, snares and nets for short sighted birds, and something that is almost a constant, subtle, incitement to an overturning of habitual opinions and of approved customs. What!? Everything is merely–human–all too human? With this exclamation my writings are gone through, not without a certain dread and mistrust of ethic itself and not without a disposition to ask the exponent of evil things if those things be not simply misrepresented. My writings have been termed a school of distrust, still more of disdain: also, and more happily, of courage, audacity even. And in fact, I myself do not believe that anybody ever looked into the world with a distrust as deep as mine, seeming, as I do, not simply the timely advocate of the devil, but, to employ theological terms, an enemy and challenger of God; and whosoever has experienced any of the consequences of such deep distrust, anything of the chills and the agonies of isolation to which such an unqualified difference of standpoint condemns him endowed with it, will also understand how often I must have sought relief and self-forgetfulness from any source–through any object of veneration or enmity, of scientific seriousness or wanton lightness; also why I, when I could not find what I was in need of, had to fashion it for myself, counterfeiting it or imagining it (and what poet or writer has ever done anything else, and what other purpose can all the art in the world possibly have?) That which I always stood most in need of in order to effect my cure and self-recovery was faith, faith enough not to be thus isolated, not to look at life from so singular a point of view–a magic apprehension (in eye and mind) of relationship and equality, a calm confidence in friendship, a blindness, free from suspicion and questioning, to two sidedness; a pleasure in externals, superficialities, the near, the accessible, in all things possessed of color, skin and seeming. Perhaps I could be fairly reproached with much "art" in this regard, many fine counterfeitings; for example, that, wisely or wilfully, I had shut my eyes to Schopenhauer's blind will towards ethic, at a time when I was already clear sighted enough on the subject of ethic; likewise that I had deceived myself concerning Richard Wagner's incurable romanticism, as if it were a beginning and not an end; likewise concerning the Greeks, likewise concerning the Germans and their future–and there may be, perhaps, a long list of such likewises. Granted, however, that all this

were true, and with justice urged against me, what does it signify, what can it signify in regard to how much of the self-sustaining capacity, how much of reason and higher protection are embraced in such self-deception?—and how much more falsity is still necessary to me that I may therewith always reassure myself regarding the luxury of my truth. Enough, I still live; and life is not considered now apart from ethic; it will [have] deception; it thrives (lebt) on deception ... but am I not beginning to do all over again what I have always done, I, the old immoralist, and bird snarer—talk unmorally, ultramorally, "beyond good and evil"?

2. Thus, then, have I evolved for myself the "free spirits" to whom this discouraging-encouraging work, under the general title "Human, All Too Human," is dedicated. Such "free spirits" do not really exist and never did exist. But I stood in need of them, as I have pointed out, in order that some good might be mixed with my evils (illness, loneliness, strangeness, acedia, incapacity): to serve as gay spirits and comrades, with whom one may talk and laugh when one is disposed to talk and laugh, and whom one may send to the devil when they grow wearisome. They are some compensation for the lack of friends. That such free spirits can possibly exist, that our Europe will yet number among her sons of to-morrow or of the day after to-morrow, such a brilliant and enthusiastic company, alive and palpable and not merely, as in my case, fantasms and imaginary shades, I, myself, can by no means doubt. I see them already coming, slowly, slowly. May it not be that I am doing a little something to expedite their coming when I describe in advance the influences under which I see them evolving and the ways along which they travel?

3. It may be conjectured that a soul in which the type of "free spirit" can attain maturity and completeness had its decisive and deciding event in the form of a great emancipation or unbinding, and that prior to that event it seemed only the more firmly and forever chained to its place and pillar. What binds strongest? What cords seem almost unbreakable? In the case of mortals of a choice and lofty nature they will be those of duty: that reverence, which in youth is most typical, that timidity and tenderness in the presence of the traditionally honored and the worthy, that gratitude to the soil from which we sprung, for the hand that guided us, for the relic before which we were taught to pray—their sublimest moments will themselves bind these souls most strongly. The great liberation comes suddenly to such prisoners, like an earthquake: the young soul is all at once shaken, torn apart, cast forth—it comprehends not itself what is taking place. An involuntary onward impulse rules them with the mastery of command; a will, a wish are developed to go forward, anywhere, at any price; a strong, dangerous curiosity regarding an undiscovered world flames and flashes in all their being. "Better to die than live here"—so sounds the tempting voice: and this "here," this

"at home" constitutes all they have hitherto loved. A sudden dread and distrust of that which they loved, a flash of contempt for that which is called their "duty," a mutinous, wilful, volcanic-like longing for a far away journey, strange scenes and people, annihilation, petrifaction, a hatred surmounting love, perhaps a sacrilegious impulse and look backwards, to where they so long prayed and loved, perhaps a flush of shame for what they did and at the same time an exultation at having done it, an inner, intoxicating, delightful tremor in which is betrayed the sense of victory—a victory? over what? over whom? a riddle-like victory, fruitful in questioning and well worth questioning, but the first victory, for all—such things of pain and ill belong to the history of the great liberation. And it is at the same time a malady that can destroy a man, this first outbreak of strength and will for self-destination, self-valuation, this will for free will: and how much illness is forced to the surface in the frantic strivings and singularities with which the freedman, the liberated seeks henceforth to attest his mastery over things! He roves fiercely around, with an unsatisfied longing and whatever objects he may encounter must suffer from the perilous expectancy of his pride; he tears to pieces whatever attracts him. With a sardonic laugh he overturns whatever he finds veiled or protected by any reverential awe: he would see what these things look like when they are overturned. It is wilfulness and delight in the wilfulness of it, if he now, perhaps, gives his approval to that which has heretofore been in ill repute—if, in curiosity and experiment, he penetrates stealthily to the most forbidden things. In the background during all his plunging and roaming—for he is as restless and aimless in his course as if lost in a wilderness—is the interrogation mark of a curiosity growing ever more dangerous. "Can we not upset every standard? and is good perhaps evil? and God only an invention and a subtlety of the devil? Is everything, in the last resort, false? And if we are dupes are we not on that very account dupers also? must we not be dupers also?" Such reflections lead and mislead him, ever further on, ever further away. Solitude, that dread goddess and mater saeva cupidinum, encircles and besets him, ever more threatening, more violent, more heart breaking—but who to-day knows what solitude is?

4. From this morbid solitude, from the deserts of such trial years, the way is yet far to that great, overflowing certainty and healthiness which cannot dispense even with sickness as a means and a grappling hook of knowledge; to that matured freedom of the spirit which is, in an equal degree, self mastery and discipline of the heart, and gives access to the path of much and various reflection—to that inner comprehensiveness and self satisfaction of over-richness which precludes all danger that the spirit has gone astray even in its own path and is sitting intoxicated in some corner or other; to that overplus of plastic, healing, imitative and restorative power which is the very sign of vigorous health,

that overplus which confers upon the free spirit the perilous prerogative of spending a life in experiment and of running adventurous risks: the past-master-privilege of the free spirit. In the interval there may be long years of convalescence, years filled with many hued painfully-bewitching transformations, dominated and led to the goal by a tenacious will for health that is often emboldened to assume the guise and the disguise of health. There is a middle ground to this, which a man of such destiny can not subsequently recall without emotion; he basks in a special fine sun of his own, with a feeling of birdlike freedom, birdlike visual power, birdlike irrepressibleness, a something extraneous (Drittes) in which curiosity and delicate disdain have united. A "free spirit"—this refreshing term is grateful in any mood, it almost sets one aglow. One lives—no longer in the bonds of love and hate, without a yes or no, here or there indifferently, best pleased to evade, to avoid, to beat about, neither advancing nor retreating. One is habituated to the bad, like a person who all at once sees a fearful hurly-burly beneath him—and one was the counterpart of him who bothers himself with things that do not concern him. As a matter of fact the free spirit is bothered with mere things—and how many things—which no longer concern him.

5. A step further in recovery: and the free spirit draws near to life again, slowly indeed, almost refractorily, almost distrustfully. There is again warmth and mellowness: feeling and fellow feeling acquire depth, lambent airs stir all about him. He almost feels: it seems as if now for the first time his eyes are open to things near. He is in amaze and sits hushed: for where had he been? These near and immediate things: how changed they seem to him! He looks gratefully back—grateful for his wandering, his self exile and severity, his lookings afar and his bird flights in the cold heights. How fortunate that he has not, like a sensitive, dull home body, remained always "in the house" and "at home!" He had been beside himself, beyond a doubt. Now for the first time he really sees himself—and what surprises in the process. What hitherto unfelt tremors! Yet what joy in the exhaustion, the old sickness, the relapses of the convalescent! How it delights him, suffering, to sit still, to exercise patience, to lie in the sun! Who so well as he appreciates the fact that there comes balmy weather even in winter, who delights more in the sunshine athwart the wall? They are the most appreciative creatures in the world, and also the most humble, these convalescents and lizards, crawling back towards life: there are some among them who can let no day slip past them without addressing some song of praise to its retreating light. And speaking seriously, it is a fundamental cure for all pessimism (the cankerous vice, as is well known, of all idealists and humbugs), to become ill in the manner of these free spirits, to remain ill quite a while and then bit by bit grow healthy—I mean

healthier. It is wisdom, worldly wisdom, to administer even health to oneself for a long time in small doses.

6. About this time it becomes at last possible, amid the flash lights of a still unestablished, still precarious health, for the free, the ever freer spirit to begin to read the riddle of that great liberation, a riddle which has hitherto lingered, obscure, well worth questioning, almost impalpable, in his memory. If once he hardly dared to ask "why so apart? so alone? renouncing all I loved? renouncing respect itself? why this coldness, this suspicion, this hate for one's very virtues?"—now he dares, and asks it loudly, already hearing the answer, "you had to become master over yourself, master of your own good qualities. Formerly they were your masters: but they should be merely your tools along with other tools. You had to acquire power over your aye and no and learn to hold and withhold them in accordance with your higher aims. You had to grasp the perspective of every representation (Werthschätzung)—the dislocation, distortion and the apparent end or teleology of the horizon, besides whatever else appertains to the perspective: also the element of demerit in its relation to opposing merit, and the whole intellectual cost of every affirmative, every negative. You had to find out the inevitable error[1] in every Yes and in every No, error as inseparable from life, life itself as conditioned by the perspective and its inaccuracy. Above all, you had to see with your own eyes where the error[1] is always greatest: there, namely, where life is littlest, narrowest, meanest, least developed and yet cannot help looking upon itself as the goal and standard of things, and smugly and ignobly and incessantly tearing to tatters all that is highest and greatest and richest, and putting the shreds into the form of questions from the standpoint of its own well being. You had to see with your own eyes the problem of classification, (Rangordnung, regulation concerning rank and station) and how strength and sweep and reach of perspective wax upward together: You had"—enough, the free spirit knows henceforward which "you had" it has obeyed and also what it now can do and what it now, for the first time, dare.

7. Accordingly, the free spirit works out for itself an answer to that riddle of its liberation and concludes by generalizing upon its experience in the following fashion: "What I went through everyone must go through" in whom any problem is germinated and strives to body itself forth. The inner power and inevitability of this problem will assert themselves in due course, as in the case of any unsuspected pregnancy—long before the spirit has seen this problem in its true aspect and learned to call it by its right name. Our destiny exercises its influence over us even when, as yet, we have not learned its nature: it is our future that lays down the law to our to-day. Granted, that it is the problem of classification[2] of which we free spirits may say, this is our problem, yet it is only now, in the

midday of our life, that we fully appreciate what preparations, shifts, trials, ordeals, stages, were essential to that problem before it could emerge to our view, and why we had to go through the various and contradictory longings and satisfactions of body and soul, as circumnavigators and adventurers of that inner world called "man"; as surveyors of that "higher" and of that "progression"[3] that is also called "man"—crowding in everywhere, almost without fear, disdaining nothing, missing nothing, testing everything, sifting everything and eliminating the chance impurities—until at last we could say, we free spirits: "Here—a new problem! Here, a long ladder on the rungs of which we ourselves have rested and risen, which we have actually been at times. Here is a something higher, a something deeper, a something below us, a vastly extensive order, (Ordnung) a comparative classification (Rangordnung), that we perceive: here—our problem!"

8. To what stage in the development just outlined the present book belongs (or is assigned) is something that will be hidden from no augur or psychologist for an instant. But where are there psychologists to-day? In France, certainly; in Russia, perhaps; certainly not in Germany. Grounds are not wanting, to be sure, upon which the Germans of to-day may adduce this fact to their credit: unhappily for one who in this matter is fashioned and mentored in an un-German school! This German book, which has found its readers in a wide circle of lands and peoples—it has been some ten years on its rounds—and which must make its way by means of any musical art and tune that will captivate the foreign ear as well as the native—this book has been read most indifferently in Germany itself and little heeded there: to what is that due? "It requires too much," I have been told, "it addresses itself to men free from the press of petty obligations, it demands fine and trained perceptions, it requires a surplus, a surplus of time, of the lightness of heaven and of the heart, of otium in the most unrestricted sense: mere good things that we Germans of to-day have not got and therefore cannot give." After so graceful a retort, my philosophy bids me be silent and ask no more questions: at times, as the proverb says, one remains a philosopher only because one says—nothing!

Nice, Spring, 1886.

Of the First and Last Things.

1. Chemistry of the Notions and the Feelings.—Philosophical problems, in almost all their aspects, present themselves in the same interrogative formula now that they did two thousand years ago: how can a thing develop out of its antithesis? for example, the reasonable from the non-reasonable, the animate from the inanimate, the logical from the illogical, altruism from egoism, disinterestedness from greed, truth from error? The metaphysical philosophy

formerly steered itself clear of this difficulty to such extent as to repudiate the evolution of one thing from another and to assign a miraculous origin to what it deemed highest and best, due to the very nature and being of the "thing-in-itself." The historical philosophy, on the other hand, which can no longer be viewed apart from physical science, the youngest of all philosophical methods, discovered experimentally (and its results will probably always be the same) that there is no antithesis whatever, except in the usual exaggerations of popular or metaphysical comprehension, and that an error of the reason is at the bottom of such contradiction. According to its explanation, there is, strictly speaking, neither unselfish conduct, nor a wholly disinterested point of view. Both are simply sublimations in which the basic element seems almost evaporated and betrays its presence only to the keenest observation. All that we need and that could possibly be given us in the present state of development of the sciences, is a chemistry of the moral, religious, aesthetic conceptions and feeling, as well as of those emotions which we experience in the affairs, great and small, of society and civilization, and which we are sensible of even in solitude. But what if this chemistry established the fact that, even in its domain, the most magnificent results were attained with the basest and most despised ingredients? Would many feel disposed to continue such investigations? Mankind loves to put by the questions of its origin and beginning: must one not be almost inhuman in order to follow the opposite course?

2. The Traditional Error of Philosophers.—All philosophers make the common mistake of taking contemporary man as their starting point and of trying, through an analysis of him, to reach a conclusion. "Man" involuntarily presents himself to them as an aeterna veritas as a passive element in every hurly-burly, as a fixed standard of things. Yet everything uttered by the philosopher on the subject of man is, in the last resort, nothing more than a piece of testimony concerning man during a very limited period of time. Lack of the historical sense is the traditional defect in all philosophers. Many innocently take man in his most childish state as fashioned through the influence of certain religious and even of certain political developments, as the permanent form under which man must be viewed. They will not learn that man has evolved,[4] that the intellectual faculty itself is an evolution, whereas some philosophers make the whole cosmos out of this intellectual faculty. But everything essential in human evolution took place aeons ago, long before the four thousand years or so of which we know anything: during these man may not have changed very much. However, the philosopher ascribes "instinct" to contemporary man and assumes that this is one of the unalterable facts regarding man himself, and hence affords a clue to the understanding of the universe in general. The whole teleology is so planned that

man during the last four thousand years shall be spoken of as a being existing from all eternity, and with reference to whom everything in the cosmos from its very inception is naturally ordered. Yet everything evolved: there are no eternal facts as there are no absolute truths. Accordingly, historical philosophising is henceforth indispensable, and with it honesty of judgment.

3. Appreciation of Simple Truths.—It is the characteristic of an advanced civilization to set a higher value upon little, simple truths, ascertained by scientific method, than upon the pleasing and magnificent errors originating in metaphysical and æsthetical epochs and peoples. To begin with, the former are spoken of with contempt as if there could be no question of comparison respecting them, so rigid, homely, prosaic and even discouraging is the aspect of the first, while so beautiful, decorative, intoxicating and perhaps beatific appear the last named. Nevertheless, the hardwon, the certain, the lasting and, therefore, the fertile in new knowledge, is the higher; to hold fast to it is manly and evinces courage, directness, endurance. And not only individual men but all mankind will by degrees be uplifted to this manliness when they are finally habituated to the proper appreciation of tenable, enduring knowledge and have lost all faith in inspiration and in the miraculous revelation of truth. The reverers of forms, indeed, with their standards of beauty and taste, may have good reason to laugh when the appreciation of little truths and the scientific spirit begin to prevail, but that will be only because their eyes are not yet opened to the charm of the utmost simplicity of form or because men though reared in the rightly appreciative spirit, will still not be fully permeated by it, so that they continue unwittingly imitating ancient forms (and that ill enough, as anybody does who no longer feels any interest in a thing). Formerly the mind was not brought into play through the medium of exact thought. Its serious business lay in the working out of forms and symbols. That has now changed. Any seriousness in symbolism is at present the indication of a deficient education. As our very acts become more intellectual, our tendencies more rational, and our judgment, for example, as to what seems reasonable, is very different from what it was a hundred years ago: so the forms of our lives grow ever more intellectual and, to the old fashioned eye, perhaps, uglier, but only because it cannot see that the richness of inner, rational beauty always spreads and deepens, and that the inner, rational aspect of all things should now be of more consequence to us than the most beautiful externality and the most exquisite limning.

4. Astrology and the Like.—It is presumable that the objects of the religious, moral, aesthetic and logical notions pertain simply to the superficialities of things, although man flatters himself with the thought that here at least he is getting to the heart of the cosmos. He deceives himself because these things have power to

make him so happy and so wretched, and so he evinces, in this respect, the same conceit that characterises astrology. Astrology presupposes that the heavenly bodies are regulated in their movements in harmony with the destiny of mortals: the moral man presupposes that that which concerns himself most nearly must also be the heart and soul of things.

5. Misconception of Dreams.—In the dream, mankind, in epochs of crude primitive civilization, thought they were introduced to a second, substantial world: here we have the source of all metaphysic. Without the dream, men would never have been incited to an analysis of the world. Even the distinction between soul and body is wholly due to the primitive conception of the dream, as also the hypothesis of the embodied soul, whence the development of all superstition, and also, probably, the belief in god. "The dead still live: for they appear to the living in dreams." So reasoned mankind at one time, and through many thousands of years.

6. The Scientific Spirit Prevails only Partially, not Wholly.—The specialized, minutest departments of science are dealt with purely objectively. But the general universal sciences, considered as a great, basic unity, posit the question—truly a very living question—: to what purpose? what is the use? Because of this reference to utility they are, as a whole, less impersonal than when looked at in their specialized aspects. Now in the case of philosophy, as forming the apex of the scientific pyramid, this question of the utility of knowledge is necessarily brought very conspicuously forward, so that every philosophy has, unconsciously, the air of ascribing the highest utility to itself. It is for this reason that all philosophies contain such a great amount of high flying metaphysic, and such a shrinking from the seeming insignificance of the deliverances of physical science: for the significance of knowledge in relation to life must be made to appear as great as possible. This constitutes the antagonism between the specialties of science and philosophy. The latter aims, as art aims, at imparting to life and conduct the utmost depth and significance: in the former mere knowledge is sought and nothing else—whatever else be incidentally obtained. Heretofore there has never been a philosophical system in which philosophy itself was not made the apologist of knowledge [in the abstract]. On this point, at least, each is optimistic and insists that to knowledge the highest utility must be ascribed. They are all under the tyranny of logic, which is, from its very nature, optimism.

7. The Discordant Element in Science.—Philosophy severed itself from science when it put the question: what is that knowledge of the world and of life through which mankind may be made happiest? This happened when the Socratic school arose: with the standpoint of happiness the arteries of investigating science were

compressed too tightly to permit of any circulation of the blood—and are so compressed to-day.

8. Pneumatic Explanation of Nature.[5]—Metaphysic reads the message of nature as if it were written purely pneumatically, as the church and its learned ones formerly did where the bible was concerned. It requires a great deal of expertness to apply to nature the same strict science of interpretation that the philologists have devised for all literature, and to apply it for the purpose of a simple, direct interpretation of the message, and at the same time, not bring out a double meaning. But, as in the case of books and literature, errors of exposition are far from being completely eliminated, and vestiges of allegorical and mystical interpretations are still to be met with in the most cultivated circles, so where nature is concerned the case is—actually much worse.

9. Metaphysical World.—It is true, there may be a metaphysical world; the absolute possibility of it can scarcely be disputed. We see all things through the medium of the human head and we cannot well cut off this head: although there remains the question what part of the world would be left after it had been cut off. But that is a purely abstract scientific problem and one not much calculated to give men uneasiness: yet everything that has heretofore made metaphysical assumptions valuable, fearful or delightful to men, all that gave rise to them is passion, error and self deception: the worst systems of knowledge, not the best, pin their tenets of belief thereto. When such methods are once brought to view as the basis of all existing religions and metaphysics, they are already discredited. There always remains, however, the possibility already conceded: but nothing at all can be made out of that, to say not a word about letting happiness, salvation and life hang upon the threads spun from such a possibility. Accordingly, nothing could be predicated of the metaphysical world beyond the fact that it is an elsewhere,[6] another sphere, inaccessible and incomprehensible to us: it would become a thing of negative properties. Even were the existence of such a world absolutely established, it would nevertheless remain incontrovertible that of all kinds of knowledge, knowledge of such a world would be of least consequence—of even less consequence than knowledge of the chemical analysis of water would be to a storm tossed mariner.

10. The Harmlessness of Metaphysic in the Future.—As soon as religion, art and ethics are so understood that a full comprehension of them can be gained without taking refuge in the postulates of metaphysical claptrap at any point in the line of reasoning, there will be a complete cessation of interest in the purely theoretical problem of the "thing in itself" and the "phenomenon." For here, too, the same truth applies: in religion, art and ethics we are not concerned with the "essence of the cosmos".[7] We are in the sphere of pure conception. No

presentiment [or intuition] can carry us any further. With perfect tranquility the question of how our conception of the world could differ so sharply from the actual world as it is manifest to us, will be relegated to the physiological sciences and to the history of the evolution of ideas and organisms.

11. Language as a Presumptive Science.—The importance of language in the development of civilization consists in the fact that by means of it man placed one world, his own, alongside another, a place of leverage that he thought so firm as to admit of his turning the rest of the cosmos on a pivot that he might master it. In so far as man for ages looked upon mere ideas and names of things as upon aeternae veritates, he evinced the very pride with which he raised himself above the brute. He really supposed that in language he possessed a knowledge of the cosmos. The language builder was not so modest as to believe that he was only giving names to things. On the contrary he thought he embodied the highest wisdom concerning things in [mere] words; and, in truth, language is the first movement in all strivings for wisdom. Here, too, it is faith in ascertained truth[8] from which the mightiest fountains of strength have flowed. Very tardily—only now—it dawns upon men that they have propagated a monstrous error in their belief in language. Fortunately, it is too late now to arrest and turn back the evolutionary process of the reason, which had its inception in this belief. Logic itself rests upon assumptions to which nothing in the world of reality corresponds. For example, the correspondence of certain things to one another and the identity of those things at different periods of time are assumptions pure and simple, but the science of logic originated in the positive belief that they were not assumptions at all but established facts. It is the same with the science of mathematics which certainly would never have come into existence if mankind had known from the beginning that in all nature there is no perfectly straight line, no true circle, no standard of measurement.

12. Dream and Civilization.—The function of the brain which is most encroached upon in slumber is the memory; not that it is wholly suspended, but it is reduced to a state of imperfection as, in primitive ages of mankind, was probably the case with everyone, whether waking or sleeping. Uncontrolled and entangled as it is, it perpetually confuses things as a result of the most trifling similarities, yet in the same mental confusion and lack of control the nations invented their mythologies, while nowadays travelers habitually observe how prone the savage is to forgetfulness, how his mind, after the least exertion of memory, begins to wander and lose itself until finally he utters falsehood and nonsense from sheer exhaustion. Yet, in dreams, we all resemble this savage. Inadequacy of distinction and error of comparison are the basis of the preposterous things we do and say in dreams, so that when we clearly recall a

dream we are startled that so much idiocy lurks within us. The absolute distinctness of all dream-images, due to implicit faith in their substantial reality, recalls the conditions in which earlier mankind were placed, for whom hallucinations had extraordinary vividness, entire communities and even entire nations laboring simultaneously under them. Therefore: in sleep and in dream we make the pilgrimage of early mankind over again.

13. Logic of the Dream.—During sleep the nervous system, through various inner provocatives, is in constant agitation. Almost all the organs act independently and vigorously. The blood circulates rapidly. The posture of the sleeper compresses some portions of the body. The coverlets influence the sensations in different ways. The stomach carries on the digestive process and acts upon other organs thereby. The intestines are in motion. The position of the head induces unaccustomed action. The feet, shoeless, no longer pressing the ground, are the occasion of other sensations of novelty, as is, indeed, the changed garb of the entire body. All these things, following the bustle and change of the day, result, through their novelty, in a movement throughout the entire system that extends even to the brain functions. Thus there are a hundred circumstances to induce perplexity in the mind, a questioning as to the cause of this excitation. Now, the dream is a seeking and presenting of reasons for these excitations of feeling, of the supposed reasons, that is to say. Thus, for example, whoever has his feet bound with two threads will probably dream that a pair of serpents are coiled about his feet. This is at first a hypothesis, then a belief with an accompanying imaginative picture and the argument: "these snakes must be the causa of those sensations which I, the sleeper, now have." So reasons the mind of the sleeper. The conditions precedent, as thus conjectured, become, owing to the excitation of the fancy, present realities. Everyone knows from experience how a dreamer will transform one piercing sound, for example, that of a bell, into another of quite a different nature, say, the report of cannon. In his dream he becomes aware first of the effects, which he explains by a subsequent hypothesis and becomes persuaded of the purely conjectural nature of the sound. But how comes it that the mind of the dreamer goes so far astray when the same mind, awake, is habitually cautious, careful, and so conservative in its dealings with hypotheses? why does the first plausible hypothesis of the cause of a sensation gain credit in the dreaming state? (For in a dream we look upon that dream as reality, that is, we accept our hypotheses as fully established). I have no doubt that as men argue in their dreams to-day, mankind argued, even in their waking moments, for thousands of years: the first causa, that occurred to the mind with reference to anything that stood in need of explanation, was accepted as the true explanation and served as such. (Savages show the same tendency in operation, as the reports

of travelers agree). In the dream this atavistic relic of humanity manifests its existence within us, for it is the foundation upon which the higher rational faculty developed itself and still develops itself in every individual. Dreams carry us back to the earlier stages of human culture and afford us a means of understanding it more clearly. Dream thought comes so easily to us now because we are so thoroughly trained to it through the interminable stages of evolution during which this fanciful and facile form of theorising has prevailed. To a certain extent the dream is a restorative for the brain, which, during the day, is called upon to meet the many demands for trained thought made upon it by the conditions of a higher civilization.—We may, if we please, become sensible, even in our waking moments, of a condition that is as a door and vestibule to dreaming. If we close our eyes the brain immediately conjures up a medley of impressions of light and color, apparently a sort of imitation and echo of the impressions forced in upon the brain during its waking moments. And now the mind, in co-operation with the imagination, transforms this formless play of light and color into definite figures, moving groups, landscapes. What really takes place is a sort of reasoning from effect back to cause. As the brain inquires: whence these impressions of light and color? it posits as the inducing causes of such lights and colors, those shapes and figures. They serve the brain as the occasions of those lights and colors because the brain, when the eyes are open and the senses awake, is accustomed to perceiving the cause of every impression of light and color made upon it. Here again the imagination is continually interposing its images inasmuch as it participates in the production of the impressions made through the senses day by day: and the dream-fancy does exactly the same thing—that is, the presumed cause is determined from the effect and after the effect: all this, too, with extraordinary rapidity, so that in this matter, as in a matter of jugglery or sleight-of-hand, a confusion of the mind is produced and an after effect is made to appear a simultaneous action, an inverted succession of events, even.—From these considerations we can see how late strict, logical thought, the true notion of cause and effect must have been in developing, since our intellectual and rational faculties to this very day revert to these primitive processes of deduction, while practically half our lifetime is spent in the super-inducing conditions.—Even the poet, the artist, ascribes to his sentimental and emotional states causes which are not the true ones. To that extent he is a reminder of early mankind and can aid us in its comprehension.

14. Association.[9]—All strong feelings are associated with a variety of allied sentiments and emotions. They stir up the memory at the same time. When we are under their influence we are reminded of similar states and we feel a renewal of them within us. Thus are formed habitual successions of feelings and notions,

which, at last, when they follow one another with lightning rapidity are no longer felt as complexities but as unities. In this sense we hear of moral feelings, of religious feelings, as if they were absolute unities. In reality they are streams with a hundred sources and tributaries. Here again, the unity of the word speaks nothing for the unity of the thing.

15. No Within and Without in the World.[10]—As Democritus transferred the notions above and below to limitless space, where they are destitute of meaning, so the philosophers do generally with the idea "within and without," as regards the form and substance (Wesen und Erscheinung) of the world. What they claim is that through the medium of profound feelings one can penetrate deep into the soul of things (Innre), draw close to the heart of nature. But these feelings are deep only in so far as with them are simultaneously aroused, although almost imperceptibly, certain complicated groups of thoughts (Gedankengruppen) which we call deep: a feeling is deep because we deem the thoughts accompanying it deep. But deep thought can nevertheless be very widely sundered from truth, as for instance every metaphysical thought. Take from deep feeling the element of thought blended with it and all that remains is strength of feeling which is no voucher for the validity of knowledge, as intense faith is evidence only of its own intensity and not of the truth of that in which the faith is felt.

16. Phenomenon and Thing-in-Itself.—The philosophers are in the habit of placing themselves in front of life and experience—that which they call the world of phenomena—as if they were standing before a picture that is unrolled before them in its final completeness. This panorama, they think, must be studied in every detail in order to reach some conclusion regarding the object represented by the picture. From effect, accordingly is deduced cause and from cause is deduced the unconditioned. This process is generally looked upon as affording the all sufficient explanation of the world of phenomena. On the other hand one must, (while putting the conception of the metaphysical distinctly forward as that of the unconditioned, and consequently of the unconditioning) absolutely deny any connection between the unconditioned (of the metaphysical world) and the world known to us: so that throughout phenomena there is no manifestation of the thing-in-itself, and getting from one to the other is out of the question. Thus is left quite ignored the circumstance that the picture—that which we now call life and experience—is a gradual evolution, is, indeed, still in process of evolution and for that reason should not be regarded as an enduring whole from which any conclusion as to its author (the all-sufficient reason) could be arrived at, or even pronounced out of the question. It is because we have for thousands of years looked into the world with moral, aesthetic, religious predispositions, with blind prejudice, passion or fear, and surfeited ourselves with indulgence in the follies

of illogical thought, that the world has gradually become so wondrously motley, frightful, significant, soulful: it has taken on tints, but we have been the colorists: the human intellect, upon the foundation of human needs, of human passions, has reared all these "phenomena" and injected its own erroneous fundamental conceptions into things. Late, very late, the human intellect checks itself: and now the world of experience and the thing-in-itself seem to it so severed and so antithetical that it denies the possibility of one's hinging upon the other—or else summons us to surrender our intellect, our personal will, to the secret and the awe-inspiring in order that thereby we may attain certainty of certainty hereafter. Again, there are those who have combined all the characteristic features of our world of phenomena—that is, the conception of the world which has been formed and inherited through a series of intellectual vagaries—and instead of holding the intellect responsible for it all, have pronounced the very nature of things accountable for the present very sinister aspect of the world, and preached annihilation of existence. Through all these views and opinions the toilsome, steady process of science (which now for the first time begins to celebrate its greatest triumph in the genesis of thought) will definitely work itself out, the result, being, perhaps, to the following effect: That which we now call the world is the result of a crowd of errors and fancies which gradually developed in the general evolution of organic nature, have grown together and been transmitted to us as the accumulated treasure of all the past—as the treasure, for whatever is worth anything in our humanity rests upon it. From this world of conception it is in the power of science to release us only to a slight extent—and this is all that could be wished—inasmuch as it cannot eradicate the influence of hereditary habits of feeling, but it can light up by degrees the stages of the development of that world of conception, and lift us, at least for a time, above the whole spectacle. Perhaps we may then perceive that the thing-in-itself is a meet subject for Homeric laughter: that it seemed so much, everything, indeed, and is really a void—void, that is to say, of meaning.

17. Metaphysical Explanation.—Man, when he is young, prizes metaphysical explanations, because they make him see matters of the highest import in things he found disagreeable or contemptible: and if he is not satisfied with himself, this feeling of dissatisfaction is soothed when he sees the most hidden world-problem or world-pain in that which he finds so displeasing in himself. To feel himself more unresponsible and at the same time to find things (Dinge) more interesting—that is to him the double benefit he owes to metaphysics. Later, indeed, he acquires distrust of the whole metaphysical method of explaining things: he then perceives, perhaps, that those effects could have been attained just as well and more scientifically by another method: that physical and historical

explanations would, at least, have given that feeling of freedom from personal responsibility just as well, while interest in life and its problems would be stimulated, perhaps, even more.

18. The Fundamental Problems of Metaphysics.—If a history of the development of thought is ever written, the following proposition, advanced by a distinguished logician, will be illuminated with a new light: "The universal, primordial law of the apprehending subject consists in the inner necessity of cognizing every object by itself, as in its essence a thing unto itself, therefore as self-existing and unchanging, in short, as a substance." Even this law, which is here called "primordial," is an evolution: it has yet to be shown how gradually this evolution takes place in lower organizations: how the dim, mole eyes of such organizations see, at first, nothing but a blank sameness: how later, when the various excitations of desire and aversion manifest themselves, various substances are gradually distinguished, but each with an attribute, that is, a special relationship to such an organization. The first step towards the logical is judgment, the essence of which, according to the best logicians, is belief. At the foundation of all beliefs lie sensations of pleasure or pain in relation to the apprehending subject. A third feeling, as the result of two prior, single, separate feelings, is judgment in its crudest form. We organic beings are primordially interested by nothing whatever in any thing (Ding) except its relation to ourselves with reference to pleasure and pain. Between the moments in which we are conscious of this relation, (the states of feeling) lie the moments of rest, of not-feeling: then the world and every thing (Ding) have no interest for us: we observe no change in them (as at present a person absorbed in something does not notice anyone passing by). To plants all things are, as a rule, at rest, eternal, every object like itself. From the period of lower organisms has been handed down to man the belief that there are like things (gleiche Dinge): only the trained experience attained through the most advanced science contradicts this postulate. The primordial belief of all organisms is, perhaps, that all the rest of the world is one thing and motionless.—Furthest away from this first step towards the logical is the notion of causation: even to-day we think that all our feelings and doings are, at bottom, acts of the free will; when the sentient individual contemplates himself he deems every feeling, every change, a something isolated, disconnected, that is to say, unqualified by any thing; it comes suddenly to the surface, independent of anything that went before or came after. We are hungry, but originally we do not know that the organism must be nourished: on the contrary that feeling seems to manifest itself without reason or purpose; it stands out by itself and seems quite independent. Therefore: the belief in the freedom of the will is a primordial error of everything organic as old as the very earliest inward

prompting of the logical faculty; belief in unconditioned substances and in like things (gleiche Dinge) is also a primordial and equally ancient error of everything organic. Inasmuch as all metaphysic has concerned itself particularly with substance and with freedom of the will, it should be designated as the science that deals with the fundamental errors of mankind as if they were fundamental truths.

19. Number.—The invention of the laws of number has as its basis the primordial and prior-prevailing delusion that many like things exist (although in point of fact there is no such thing is a duplicate), or that, at least, there are things (but there is no "thing"). The assumption of plurality always presupposes that something exists which manifests itself repeatedly, but just here is where the delusion prevails; in this very matter we feign realities, unities, that have no existence. Our feelings, notions, of space and time are false for they lead, when duly tested, to logical contradictions. In all scientific demonstrations we always unavoidably base our calculation upon some false standards [of duration or measurement] but as these standards are at least constant, as, for example, our notions of time and space, the results arrived at by science possess absolute accuracy and certainty in their relationship to one another: one can keep on building upon them—until is reached that final limit at which the erroneous fundamental conceptions, (the invariable breakdown) come into conflict with the results established—as, for example, in the case of the atomic theory. Here we always find ourselves obliged to give credence to a "thing" or material "substratum" that is set in motion, although, at the same time, the whole scientific programme has had as its aim the resolving of everything material into motions [themselves]: here again we distinguish with our feeling [that which does the] moving and [that which is] moved,[11] and we never get out of this circle, because the belief in things[12] has been from time immemorial rooted in our nature.—When Kant says "the intellect does not derive its laws from nature, but dictates them to her" he states the full truth as regards the idea of nature which we form (nature = world, as notion, that is, as error) but which is merely the synthesis of a host of errors of the intellect. To a world not [the outcome of] our conception, the laws of number are wholly inapplicable: such laws are valid only in the world of mankind.

20. Some Backward Steps.—One very forward step in education is taken when man emerges from his superstitious and religious ideas and fears and, for instance, no longer believes in the dear little angels or in original sin, and has stopped talking about the salvation of the soul: when he has taken this step to freedom he has, nevertheless, through the utmost exertion of his mental power, to overcome metaphysics. Then a backward movement is necessary: he must

appreciate the historical justification, and to an equal extent the psychological considerations, in such a movement. He must understand that the greatest advances made by mankind have resulted from such a course and that without this very backward movement the highest achievements of man hitherto would have been impossible.—With regard to philosophical metaphysics I see ever more and more who have arrived at the negative goal (that all positive metaphysic is a delusion) but as yet very few who go a few steps backward: one should look out over the last rungs of the ladder, but not try to stand on them, that is to say. The most advanced as yet go only far enough to free themselves from metaphysic and look back at it with an air of superiority: whereas here, no less than in the hippodrome, it is necessary to turn around in order to reach the end of the course.

21. Presumable [Nature of the] Victory of Doubt.—Let us assume for a moment the validity of the skeptical standpoint: granted that there is no metaphysical world, and that all the metaphysical explanations of the only world we know are useless to us, how would we then contemplate men and things? [Menschen und Dinge]. This can be thought out and it is worth while doing so, even if the question whether anything metaphysical has ever been demonstrated by or through Kant and Schopenhauer, be put altogether aside. For it is, to all appearances, highly probable that men, on this point, will be, in the mass, skeptical. The question thus becomes: what sort of a notion will human society, under the influence of such a state of mind, form of itself? Perhaps the scientific demonstration of any metaphysical world is now so difficult that mankind will never be free from a distrust of it. And when there is formed a feeling of distrust of metaphysics, the results are, in the mass, the same as if metaphysics were refuted altogether and could no longer be believed. In both cases the historical question, with regard to an unmetaphysical disposition in mankind, remains the same.

22. Disbelief in the "monumentum aere perennius".[13]—A decided disadvantage, attending the termination of metaphysical modes of thought, is that the individual fixes his mind too attentively upon his own brief lifetime and feels no strong inducement to aid in the foundation of institutions capable of enduring for centuries: he wishes himself to gather the fruit from the tree that he plants and consequently he no longer plants those trees which require centuries of constant cultivation and are destined to afford shade to generation after generation in the future. For metaphysical views inspire the belief that in them is afforded the final sure foundation upon which henceforth the whole future of mankind may rest and be built up: the individual promotes his own salvation; when, for example, he builds a church or a monastery he is of opinion that he is

doing something for the salvation of his immortal soul:—Can science, as well, inspire such faith in the efficacy of her results? In actual fact, science requires doubt and distrust as her surest auxiliaries; nevertheless, the sum of the irresistible (that is all the onslaughts of skepticism, all the disintegrating effects of surviving truths) can easily become so great (as, for instance, in the case of hygienic science) as to inspire the determination to build "eternal" works upon it. At present the contrast between our excited ephemeral existence and the tranquil repose of metaphysical epochs is too great because both are as yet in too close juxtaposition. The individual man himself now goes through too many stages of inner and outer evolution for him to venture to make a plan even for his life time alone. A perfectly modern man, indeed, who wants to build himself a house feels as if he were walling himself up alive in a mausoleum.

23. Age of Comparison.—The less men are bound by tradition, the greater is the inner activity of motives, the greater, correspondingly, the outer restlessness, the promiscuous flow of humanity, the polyphony of strivings. Who now feels any great impulse to establish himself and his posterity in a particular place? For whom, moreover, does there exist, at present, any strong tie? As all the methods of the arts were copied from one another, so were all the methods and advancements of moral codes, of manners, of civilizations.—Such an age derives its significance from the fact that in it the various ideas, codes, manners and civilizations can be compared and experienced side by side; which was impossible at an earlier period in view of the localised nature of the rule of every civilization, corresponding to the limitation of all artistic effects by time and place. To-day the growth of the aesthetic feeling is decided, owing to the great number of [artistic] forms which offer themselves for comparison. The majority—those that are condemned by the method of comparison—will be allowed to die out. In the same way there is to-day taking place a selection of the forms and customs of the higher morality which can result only in the extinction of the vulgar moralities. This is the age of comparison! That is its glory—but also its pain. Let us not, however shrink from this pain. Rather would we comprehend the nature of the task imposed upon us by our age as adequately as we can: posterity will bless us for doing so—a posterity that knows itself to be [developed] through and above the narrow, early race-civilizations as well as the culture-civilization of comparison, but yet looks gratefully back upon both as venerable monuments of antiquity.

24. Possibility of Progress.—When a master of the old civilization (den alten Cultur) vows to hold no more discussion with men who believe in progress, he is quite right. For the old civilization[14] has its greatness and its advantages behind it, and historic training forces one to acknowledge that it can never again acquire vigor: only intolerable stupidity or equally intolerable fanaticism could fail to

perceive this fact. But men may consciously determine to evolve to a new civilization where formerly they evolved unconsciously and accidentally. They can now devise better conditions for the advancement of mankind, for their nourishment, training and education, they can administer the earth as an economic power, and, particularly, compare the capacities of men and select them accordingly. This new, conscious civilization is killing the other which, on the whole, has led but an unreflective animal and plant life: it is also destroying the doubt of progress itself—progress is possible. I mean: it is hasty and almost unreflective to assume that progress must necessarily take place: but how can it be doubted that progress is possible? On the other hand, progress in the sense and along the lines of the old civilization is not even conceivable. If romantic fantasy employs the word progress in connection with certain aims and ends identical with those of the circumscribed primitive national civilizations, the picture presented of progress is always borrowed from the past. The idea and the image of progress thus formed are quite without originality.

25. Private Ethics and World Ethics.—Since the extinction of the belief that a god guides the general destiny of the world and, notwithstanding all the contortions and windings of the path of mankind, leads it gloriously forward, men must shape oecumenical, world-embracing ends for themselves. The older ethics, namely Kant's, required of the individual such a course of conduct as he wishes all men to follow. This evinces much simplicity—as if any individual could determine off hand what course of conduct would conduce to the welfare of humanity, and what course of conduct is preëminently desirable! This is a theory like that of freedom of competition, which takes it for granted that the general harmony [of things] must prevail of itself in accordance with some inherent law of betterment or amelioration. It may be that a later contemplation of the needs of mankind will reveal that it is by no means desirable that all men should regulate their conduct according to the same principle; it may be best, from the standpoint of certain ends yet to be attained, that men, during long periods should regulate their conduct with reference to special, and even, in certain circumstances, evil, objects. At any rate, if mankind is not to be led astray by such a universal rule of conduct, it behooves it to attain a knowledge of the condition of culture that will serve as a scientific standard of comparison in connection with cosmical ends. Herein is comprised the tremendous mission of the great spirits of the next century.

26. Reaction as Progress.—Occasionally harsh, powerful, impetuous, yet nevertheless backward spirits, appear, who try to conjure back some past era in the history of mankind: they serve as evidence that the new tendencies which they oppose, are not yet potent enough, that there is something lacking in them:

otherwise they [the tendencies] would better withstand the effects of this conjuring back process. Thus Luther's reformation shows that in his century all the impulses to freedom of the spirit were still uncertain, lacking in vigor, and immature. Science could not yet rear her head. Indeed the whole Renaissance appears but as an early spring smothered in snow. But even in the present century Schopenhauer's metaphysic shows that the scientific spirit is not yet powerful enough: for the whole mediaeval Christian world-standpoint (Weltbetrachtung) and conception of man (Mensch-Empfindung)[15] once again, notwithstanding the slowly wrought destruction of all Christian dogma, celebrated a resurrection in Schopenhauer's doctrine. There is much science in his teaching although the science does not dominate, but, instead of it, the old, trite "metaphysical necessity." It is one of the greatest and most priceless advantages of Schopenhauer's teaching that by it our feelings are temporarily forced back to those old human and cosmical standpoints to which no other path could conduct us so easily. The gain for history and justice is very great. I believe that without Schopenhauer's aid it would be no easy matter for anyone now to do justice to Christianity and its Asiatic relatives—a thing impossible as regards the christianity that still survives. After according this great triumph to justice, after we have corrected in so essential a respect the historical point of view which the age of learning brought with it, we may begin to bear still farther onward the banner of enlightenment—a banner bearing the three names: Petrarch, Erasmus, Voltaire. We have taken a forward step out of reaction.

27. A Substitute for Religion.—It is supposed to be a recommendation for philosophy to say of it that it provides the people with a substitute for religion. And in fact, the training of the intellect does necessitate the convenient laying out of the track of thought, since the transition from religion by way of science entails a powerful, perilous leap,—something that should be advised against. With this qualification, the recommendation referred to is a just one. At the same time, it should be further explained that the needs which religion satisfies and which science must now satisfy, are not immutable. Even they can be diminished and uprooted. Think, for instance, of the christian soul-need, the sighs over one's inner corruption, the anxiety regarding salvation—all notions that arise simply out of errors of the reason and require no satisfaction at all, but annihilation. A philosophy can either so affect these needs as to appease them or else put them aside altogether, for they are acquired, circumscribed needs, based upon hypotheses which those of science explode. Here, for the purpose of affording the means of transition, for the sake of lightening the spirit overburdened with feeling, art can be employed to far better purpose, as these hypotheses receive far

less support from art than from a metaphysical philosophy. Then from art it is easier to go over to a really emancipating philosophical science.

28. Discredited Words.—Away with the disgustingly over-used words optimism and pessimism! For the occasion for using them grows daily less; only drivelers now find them indispensably necessary. What earthly reason could anyone have for being an optimist unless he had a god to defend who must have created the best of all possible worlds, since he is himself all goodness and perfection?—but what thinking man has now any need for the hypothesis that there is a god?—There is also no occasion whatever for a pessimistic confession of faith, unless one has a personal interest in denouncing the advocate of god, the theologian or the theological philosopher, and maintaining the counter proposition that evil reigns, that wretchedness is more potent than joy, that the world is a piece of botch work, that phenomenon (Erscheinung) is but the manifestation of some evil spirit. But who bothers his head about the theologians any more—except the theologians themselves? Apart from all theology and its antagonism, it is manifest that the world is neither good nor bad, (to say nothing about its being the best or the worst) and that these ideas of "good" and "bad" have significance only in relation to men, indeed, are without significance at all, in view of the sense in which they are usually employed. The contemptuous and the eulogistic point of view must, in every case, be repudiated.

29. Intoxicated by the Perfume of Flowers.—The ship of humanity, it is thought, acquires an ever deeper draught the more it is laden. It is believed that the more profoundly man thinks, the more exquisitely he feels, the higher the standard he sets for himself, the greater his distance from the other animals—the more he appears as a genius (Genie) among animals—the nearer he gets to the true nature of the world and to comprehension thereof: this, indeed, he really does through science, but he thinks he does it far more adequately through his religions and arts. These are, certainly, a blossoming of the world, but not, therefore, nearer the roots of the world than is the stalk. One cannot learn best from it the nature of the world, although nearly everyone thinks so. Error has made men so deep, sensitive and imaginative in order to bring forth such flowers as religions and arts. Pure apprehension would be unable to do that. Whoever should disclose to us the essence of the world would be undeceiving us most cruelly. Not the world as thing-in-itself but the world as idea[16] (as error) is rich in portent, deep, wonderful, carrying happiness and unhappiness in its womb. This result leads to a philosophy of world negation: which, at any rate, can be as well combined with a practical world affirmation as with its opposite.

30. Evil Habits in Reaching Conclusions.—The most usual erroneous conclusions of men are these: a thing[17] exists, therefore it is right: Here from

capacity to live is deduced fitness, from fitness, is deduced justification. So also: an opinion gives happiness, therefore it is the true one, its effect is good, therefore it is itself good and true. Here is predicated of the effect that it gives happiness, that it is good in the sense of utility, and there is likewise predicated of the cause that it is good, but good in the sense of logical validity. Conversely, the proposition would run: a thing[17] cannot attain success, cannot maintain itself, therefore it is evil: a belief troubles [the believer], occasions pain, therefore it is false. The free spirit, who is sensible of the defect in this method of reaching conclusions and has had to suffer its consequences, often succumbs to the temptation to come to the very opposite conclusions (which, in general, are, of course, equally erroneous): a thing cannot maintain itself: therefore it is good; a belief is troublesome, therefore it is true.

31. The Illogical is Necessary.—Among the things which can bring a thinker to distraction is the knowledge that the illogical is necessary to mankind and that from the illogical springs much that is good. The illogical is so imbedded in the passions, in language, in art, in religion and, above all, in everything that imparts value to life that it cannot be taken away without irreparably injuring those beautiful things. Only men of the utmost simplicity can believe that the nature man knows can be changed into a purely logical nature. Yet were there steps affording approach to this goal, how utterly everything would be lost on the way! Even the most rational man needs nature again, from time to time, that is, his illogical fundamental relation (Grundstellung) to all things.

32. Being Unjust is Essential.—All judgments of the value of life are illogically developed and therefore unjust. The vice of the judgment consists, first, in the way in which the subject matter comes under observation, that is, very incompletely; secondly in the way in which the total is summed up; and, thirdly, in the fact that each single item in the totality of the subject matter is itself the result of defective perception, and this from absolute necessity. No practical knowledge of a man, for example, stood he never so near to us, can be complete—so that we could have a logical right to form a total estimate of him; all estimates are summary and must be so. Then the standard by which we measure, (our being) is not an immutable quantity; we have moods and variations, and yet we should know ourselves as an invariable standard before we undertake to establish the nature of the relation of any thing (Sache) to ourselves. Perhaps it will follow from all this that one should form no judgments whatever; if one could but merely live without having to form estimates, without aversion and without partiality!—for everything most abhorred is closely connected with an estimate, as well as every strongest partiality. An inclination towards a thing, or from a thing, without an accompanying feeling that the beneficial is desired and

the pernicious contemned, an inclination without a sort of experiential estimation of the desirability of an end, does not exist in man. We are primordially illogical and hence unjust beings and can recognise this fact: this is one of the greatest and most baffling discords of existence.

33. Error Respecting Living for the Sake of Living Essential.—Every belief in the value and worthiness of life rests upon defective thinking; it is for this reason alone possible that sympathy with the general life and suffering of mankind is so imperfectly developed in the individual. Even exceptional men, who can think beyond their own personalities, do not have this general life in view, but isolated portions of it. If one is capable of fixing his observation upon exceptional cases, I mean upon highly endowed individuals and pure souled beings, if their development is taken as the true end of world-evolution and if joy be felt in their existence, then it is possible to believe in the value of life, because in that case the rest of humanity is overlooked: hence we have here defective thinking. So, too, it is even if all mankind be taken into consideration, and one species only of impulses (the less egoistic) brought under review and those, in consideration of the other impulses, exalted: then something could still be hoped of mankind in the mass and to that extent there could exist belief in the value of life: here, again, as a result of defective thinking. Whatever attitude, thus, one may assume, one is, as a result of this attitude, an exception among mankind. Now, the great majority of mankind endure life without any great protest, and believe, to this extent, in the value of existence, but that is because each individual decides and determines alone, and never comes out of his own personality like these exceptions: everything outside of the personal has no existence for them or at the utmost is observed as but a faint shadow. Consequently the value of life for the generality of mankind consists simply in the fact that the individual attaches more importance to himself than he does to the world. The great lack of imagination from which he suffers is responsible for his inability to enter into the feelings of beings other than himself, and hence his sympathy with their fate and suffering is of the slightest possible description. On the other hand, whosoever really could sympathise, necessarily doubts the value of life; were it possible for him to sum up and to feel in himself the total consciousness of mankind, he would collapse with a malediction against existence,—for mankind is, in the mass, without a goal, and hence man cannot find, in the contemplation of his whole course, anything to serve him as a mainstay and a comfort, but rather a reason to despair. If he looks beyond the things that immediately engage him to the final aimlessness of humanity, his own conduct assumes in his eyes the character of a frittering away. To feel oneself, however, as humanity (not alone as an individual) frittered away exactly as we see the stray leaves frittered away by nature, is a feeling

transcending all feeling. But who is capable of it? Only a poet, certainly: and poets always know how to console themselves.

34. For Tranquility.—But will not our philosophy become thus a tragedy? Will not truth prove the enemy of life, of betterment? A question seems to weigh upon our tongue and yet will not put itself into words: whether one can knowingly remain in the domain of the untruthful? or, if one must, whether, then, death would not be preferable? For there is no longer any ought (Sollen), morality; so far as it is involved "ought," is, through our point of view, as utterly annihilated as religion. Our knowledge can permit only pleasure and pain, benefit and injury, to subsist as motives. But how can these motives be distinguished from the desire for truth? Even they rest upon error (in so far, as already stated, partiality and dislike and their very inaccurate estimates palpably modify our pleasure and our pain). The whole of human life is deeply involved in untruth. The individual cannot extricate it from this pit without thereby fundamentally clashing with his whole past, without finding his present motives of conduct, (as that of honor) illegitimate, and without opposing scorn and contempt to the ambitions which prompt one to have regard for the future and for one's happiness in the future. Is it true, does there, then, remain but one way of thinking, which, as a personal consequence brings in its train despair, and as a theoretical [consequence brings in its train] a philosophy of decay, disintegration, self annihilation? I believe the deciding influence, as regards the after-effect of knowledge, will be the temperament of a man; I can, in addition to this after-effect just mentioned, suppose another, by means of which a much simpler life, and one freer from disturbances than the present, could be lived; so that at first the old motives of vehement passion might still have strength, owing to hereditary habit, but they would gradually grow weaker under the influence of purifying knowledge. A man would live, at last, both among men and unto himself, as in the natural state, without praise, reproach, competition, feasting one's eyes, as if it were a play, upon much that formerly inspired dread. One would be rid of the strenuous element, and would no longer feel the goad of the reflection that man is not even [as much as] nature, nor more than nature. To be sure, this requires, as already stated, a good temperament, a fortified, gentle and naturally cheerful soul, a disposition that has no need to be on its guard against its own eccentricities and sudden outbreaks and that in its utterances manifests neither sullenness nor a snarling tone—those familiar, disagreeable characteristics of old dogs and old men that have been a long time chained up. Rather must a man, from whom the ordinary bondages of life have fallen away to so great an extent, so do that he only lives on in order to grow continually in knowledge, and to learn to resign, without envy and without disappointment, much, yes nearly everything, that has

value in the eyes of men. He must be content with such a free, fearless soaring above men, manners, laws and traditional estimates of things, as the most desirable of all situations. He will freely share the joy of being in such a situation, and he has, perhaps, nothing else to share—in which renunciation and self-denial really most consist. But if more is asked of him, he will, with a benevolent shake of the head, refer to his brother, the free man of fact, and will, perhaps, not dissemble a little contempt: for, as regards his "freedom," thereby hangs a tale.[18]

History of the Moral Feelings.

35. Advantages of Psychological Observation.—That reflection regarding the human, all-too-human—or as the learned jargon is: psychological observation—is among the means whereby the burden of life can be made lighter, that practice in this art affords presence of mind in difficult situations and entertainment amid a wearisome environment, aye, that maxims may be culled in the thorniest and least pleasing paths of life and invigoration thereby obtained: this much was believed, was known—in former centuries. Why was this forgotten in our own century, during which, at least in Germany, yes in Europe, poverty as regards psychological observation would have been manifest in many ways had there been anyone to whom this poverty could have manifested itself. Not only in the novel, in the romance, in philosophical standpoints—these are the works of exceptional men; still more in the state of opinion regarding public events and personages; above all in general society, which says much about men but nothing whatever about man, there is totally lacking the art of psychological analysis and synthesis. But why is the richest and most harmless source of entertainment thus allowed to run to waste? Why is the greatest master of the psychological maxim no longer read?—for, with no exaggeration whatever be it said: the educated person in Europe who has read La Rochefoucauld and his intellectual and artistic affinities is very hard to find; still harder, the person who knows them and does not disparage them. Apparently, too, this unusual reader takes far less pleasure in them than the form adopted by these artists should afford him: for the subtlest mind cannot adequately appreciate the art of maxim-making unless it has had training in it, unless it has competed in it. Without such practical acquaintance, one is apt to look upon this making and forming as a much easier thing than it really is; one is not keenly enough alive to the felicity and the charm of success. Hence present day readers of maxims have but a moderate, tempered pleasure in them, scarcely, indeed, a true perception of their merit, so that their experiences are about the same as those of the average beholder of cameos: people who praise because they cannot appreciate, and are very ready to admire and still readier to turn away.

36. Objection.—Or is there a counter-proposition to the dictum that psychological observation is one of the means of consoling, lightening, charming existence? Have enough of the unpleasant effects of this art been experienced to justify the person striving for culture in turning his regard away from it? In all truth, a certain blind faith in the goodness of human nature, an implanted distaste for any disparagement of human concerns, a sort of shamefacedness at the nakedness of the soul, may be far more desirable things in the general happiness of a man, than this only occasionally advantageous quality of psychological sharpsightedness; and perhaps belief in the good, in virtuous men and actions, in a plenitude of disinterested benevolence has been more productive of good in the world of men in so far as it has made men less distrustful. If Plutarch's heroes are enthusiastically imitated and a reluctance is experienced to looking too critically into the motives of their actions, not the knowledge but the welfare of human society is promoted thereby: psychological error and above all obtuseness in regard to it, help human nature forward, whereas knowledge of the truth is more promoted by means of the stimulating strength of a hypothesis; as La Rochefoucauld in the first edition of his "Sentences and Moral Maxims" has expressed it: "What the world calls virtue is ordinarily but a phantom created by the passions, and to which we give a good name in order to do whatever we please with impunity." La Rochefoucauld and those other French masters of soul-searching (to the number of whom has lately been added a German, the author of "Psychological Observations") are like expert marksmen who again and again hit the black spot—but it is the black spot in human nature. Their art inspires amazement, but finally some spectator, inspired, not by the scientific spirit but by a humanitarian feeling, execrates an art that seems to implant in the soul a taste for belittling and impeaching mankind.

37. Nevertheless.—The matter therefore, as regards pro and con, stands thus: in the present state of philosophy an awakening of the moral observation is essential. The repulsive aspect of psychological dissection, with the knife and tweezers entailed by the process, can no longer be spared humanity. Such is the imperative duty of any science that investigates the origin and history of the so-called moral feelings and which, in its progress, is called upon to posit and to solve advanced social problems:—The older philosophy does not recognize the newer at all and, through paltry evasions, has always gone astray in the investigation of the origin and history of human estimates (Werthschätzungen). With what results may now be very clearly perceived, since it has been shown by many examples, how the errors of the greatest philosophers have their origin in a false explanation of certain human actions and feelings; how upon the

foundation of an erroneous analysis (for example, of the so called disinterested actions), a false ethic is reared, to support which religion and like mythological monstrosities are called in, until finally the shades of these troubled spirits collapse in physics and in the comprehensive world point of view. But if it be established that superficiality of psychological observation has heretofore set the most dangerous snares for human judgment and deduction, and will continue to do so, all the greater need is there of that steady continuance of labor that never wearies putting stone upon stone, little stone upon little stone; all the greater need is there of a courage that is not ashamed of such humble labor and that will oppose persistence, to all contempt. It is, finally, also true that countless single observations concerning the human, all-too-human, have been first made and uttered in circles accustomed, not to furnish matter for scientific knowledge, but for intellectual pleasure-seeking; and the original home atmosphere—a very seductive atmosphere—of the moral maxim has almost inextricably interpenetrated the entire species, so that the scientific man involuntarily manifests a sort of mistrust of this species and of its seriousness. But it is sufficient to point to the consequences: for already it is becoming evident that events of the most portentous nature are developing in the domain of psychological observation. What is the leading conclusion arrived at by one of the subtlest and calmest of thinkers, the author of the work "Concerning the Origin of the Moral Feelings", as a result of his thorough and incisive analysis of human conduct? "The moral man," he says, "stands no nearer the knowable (metaphysical) world than the physical man."[19] This dictum, grown hard and cutting beneath the hammer-blow of historical knowledge, can some day, perhaps, in some future or other, serve as the axe that will be laid to the root of the "metaphysical necessities" of men—whether more to the blessing than to the banning of universal well being who can say?—but in any event a dictum fraught with the most momentous consequences, fruitful and fearful at once, and confronting the world in the two faced way characteristic of all great facts.

38. To What Extent Useful.—Therefore, whether psychological observation is more an advantage than a disadvantage to mankind may always remain undetermined: but there is no doubt that it is necessary, because science can no longer dispense with it. Science, however, recognizes no considerations of ultimate goals or ends any more than nature does; but as the latter duly matures things of the highest fitness for certain ends without any intention of doing it, so will true science, doing with ideas what nature does with matter,[20] promote the purposes and the welfare of humanity, (as occasion may afford, and in many ways) and attain fitness [to ends]—but likewise without having intended it. He to whom the atmospheric conditions of such a prospect are too wintry, has too little

fire in him: let him look about him, and he will become sensible of maladies requiring an icy air, and of people who are so "kneaded together" out of ardor and intellect that they can scarcely find anywhere an atmosphere too cold and cutting for them. Moreover: as too serious individuals and nations stand in need of trivial relaxations; as others, too volatile and excitable require onerous, weighty ordeals to render them entirely healthy: should not we, the more intellectual men of this age, which is swept more and more by conflagrations, catch up every cooling and extinguishing appliance we can find that we may always remain as self contained, steady and calm as we are now, and thereby perhaps serve this age as its mirror and self reflector, when the occasion arises?

39. The Fable of Discretionary Freedom.—The history of the feelings, on the basis of which we make everyone responsible, hence, the so-called moral feelings, is traceable in the following leading phases. At first single actions are termed good or bad without any reference to their motive, but solely because of the utilitarian or prejudicial consequences they have for the community. In time, however, the origin of these designations is forgotten [but] it is imagined that action in itself, without reference to its consequences, contains the property "good" or "bad": with the same error according to which language designates the stone itself as hard[ness] the tree itself as green[ness]—for the reason, therefore, that what is a consequence is comprehended as a cause. Accordingly, the good[ness] or bad[ness] is incorporated into the motive and [any] deed by itself is regarded as morally ambiguous. A step further is taken, and the predication good or bad is no longer made of the particular motives but of the entire nature of a man, out of which motive grows as grow the plants out of the soil. Thus man is successively made responsible for his [particular] acts, then for his [course of] conduct, then for his motives and finally for his nature. Now, at last, is it discovered that this nature, even, cannot be responsible, inasmuch as it is only and wholly a necessary consequence and is synthesised out of the elements and influence of past and present things: therefore, that man is to be made responsible for nothing, neither for his nature, nor his motives, nor his [course of] conduct nor his [particular] acts. By this [process] is gained the knowledge that the history of moral estimates is the history of error, of the error of responsibility: as is whatever rests upon the error of the freedom of the will. Schopenhauer concluded just the other way, thus: since certain actions bring depression ("consciousness of guilt") in their train, there must, then, exist responsibility, for there would be no basis for this depression at hand if all man's affairs did not follow their course of necessity—as they do, indeed, according to the opinion of this philosopher, follow their course—but man himself, subject to the same necessity, would be just the man that he is—which Schopenhauer denies. From the fact of such depression

Schopenhauer believes himself able to prove a freedom which man in some way must have had, not indeed in regard to his actions but in regard to his nature: freedom, therefore, to be thus and so, not to act thus and so. Out of the esse, the sphere of freedom and responsibility, follows, according to his opinion, the operari, the spheres of invariable causation, necessity and irresponsibility. This depression, indeed, is due apparently to the operari—in so far as it be delusive—but in truth to whatever esse be the deed of a free will, the basic cause of the existence of an individual: [in order to] let man become whatever he wills to become, his [to] will (Wollen) must precede his existence.—Here, apart from the absurdity of the statement just made, there is drawn the wrong inference that the fact of the depression explains its character, the rational admissibility of it: from such a wrong inference does Schopenhauer first come to his fantastic consequent of the so called discretionary freedom (intelligibeln Freiheit). (For the origin of this fabulous entity Plato and Kant are equally responsible). But depression after the act does not need to be rational: indeed, it is certainly not so at all, for it rests upon the erroneous assumption that the act need not necessarily have come to pass. Therefore: only because man deems himself free, but not because he is free, does he experience remorse and the stings of conscience.—Moreover, this depression is something that can be grown out of; in many men it is not present at all as a consequence of acts which inspire it in many other men. It is a very varying thing and one closely connected with the development of custom and civilization, and perhaps manifest only during a relatively brief period of the world's history.—No one is responsible for his acts, no one for his nature; to judge is tantamount to being unjust. This applies as well when the individual judges himself. The proposition is as clear as sunlight, and yet here everyone prefers to go back to darkness and untruth: for fear of the consequences.

40. Above Animal.—The beast in us must be wheedled: ethic is necessary, that we may not be torn to pieces. Without the errors involved in the assumptions of ethics, man would have remained an animal. Thus has he taken himself as something higher and imposed rigid laws upon himself. He feels hatred, consequently, for states approximating the animal: whence the former contempt for the slave as a not-yet-man, as a thing, is to be explained.

41. Unalterable Character.—That character is unalterable is not, in the strict sense, true; rather is this favorite proposition valid only to the extent that during the brief life period of a man the potent new motives can not, usually, press down hard enough to obliterate the lines imprinted by ages. Could we conceive of a man eighty thousand years old, we should have in him an absolutely alterable character; so that the maturities of successive, varying individuals would develop

in him. The shortness of human life leads to many erroneous assertions concerning the qualities of man.

42. Classification of Enjoyments and Ethic.—The once accepted comparative classification of enjoyments, according to which an inferior, higher, highest egoism may crave one or another enjoyment, now decides as to ethical status or unethical status. A lower enjoyment (for example, sensual pleasure) preferred to a more highly esteemed one (for example, health) rates as unethical, as does welfare preferred to freedom. The comparative classification of enjoyments is not, however, alike or the same at all periods; when anyone demands satisfaction of the law, he is, from the point of view of an earlier civilization, moral, from that of the present, non-moral. "Unethical" indicates, therefore, that a man is not sufficiently sensible to the higher, finer impulses which the present civilization has brought with it, or is not sensible to them at all; it indicates backwardness, but only from the point of view of the contemporary degree of distinction.—The comparative classification of enjoyments itself is not determined according to absolute ethics; but after each new ethical adjustment, it is then decided whether conduct be ethical or the reverse.

43. Inhuman Men as Survivals.—Men who are now inhuman must serve us as surviving specimens of earlier civilizations. The mountain height of humanity here reveals its lower formations, which might otherwise remain hidden from view. There are surviving specimens of humanity whose brains through the vicissitudes of heredity, have escaped proper development. They show us what we all were and thus appal us; but they are as little responsible on this account as is a piece of granite for being granite. In our own brains there must be courses and windings corresponding to such characters, just as in the forms of some human organs there survive traces of fishhood. But these courses and windings are no longer the bed in which flows the stream of our feeling.

44. Gratitude and Revenge.—The reason the powerful man is grateful is this. His benefactor has, through his benefaction, invaded the domain of the powerful man and established himself on an equal footing: the powerful man in turn invades the domain of the benefactor and gets satisfaction through the act of gratitude. It is a mild form of revenge. By not obtaining the satisfaction of gratitude the powerful would have shown himself powerless and have ranked as such thenceforward. Hence every society of the good, that is to say, of the powerful originally, places gratitude among the first of duties.—Swift has added the dictum that man is grateful in the same degree that he is revengeful.

45. Two-fold Historical Origin of Good and Evil.—The notion of good and bad has a two-fold historical origin: namely, first, in the spirit of ruling races and castes. Whoever has power to requite good with good and evil with evil and

actually brings requital, (that is, is grateful and revengeful) acquires the name of being good; whoever is powerless and cannot requite is called bad. A man belongs, as a good individual, to the "good" of a community, who have a feeling in common, because all the individuals are allied with one another through the requiting sentiment. A man belongs, as a bad individual, to the "bad," to a mass of subjugated, powerless men who have no feeling in common. The good are a caste, the bad are a quantity, like dust. Good and bad is, for a considerable period, tantamount to noble and servile, master and slave. On the other hand an enemy is not looked upon as bad: he can requite. The Trojan and the Greek are in Homer both good. Not he, who does no harm, but he who is despised, is deemed bad. In the community of the good individuals [the quality of] good[ness] is inherited; it is impossible for a bad individual to grow from such a rich soil. If, notwithstanding, one of the good individuals does something unworthy of his goodness, recourse is had to exorcism; thus the guilt is ascribed to a deity, the while it is declared that this deity bewitched the good man into madness and blindness.—Second, in the spirit of the subjugated, the powerless. Here every other man is, to the individual, hostile, inconsiderate, greedy, inhuman, avaricious, be he noble or servile; bad is the characteristic term for man, for every living being, indeed, that is recognized at all, even for a god: human, divine, these notions are tantamount to devilish, bad. Manifestations of goodness, sympathy, helpfulness, are regarded with anxiety as trickiness, preludes to an evil end, deception, subtlety, in short, as refined badness. With such a predisposition in individuals, a feeling in common can scarcely arise at all, at most only the rudest form of it: so that everywhere that this conception of good and evil prevails, the destruction of the individuals, their race and nation, is imminent.—Our existing morality has developed upon the foundation laid by ruling races and castes.

46. Sympathy Greater than Suffering.—There are circumstances in which sympathy is stronger than the suffering itself. We feel more pain, for instance, when one of our friends becomes guilty of a reprehensible action than if we had done the deed ourselves. We once, that is, had more faith in the purity of his character than he had himself. Hence our love for him, (apparently because of this very faith) is stronger than is his own love for himself. If, indeed, his egoism really suffers more, as a result, than our egoism, inasmuch as he must take the consequences of his fault to a greater extent than ourselves, nevertheless, the unegoistic—this word is not to be taken too strictly, but simply as a modified form of expression—in us is more affected by his guilt than the unegoistic in him.

47. Hypochondria.—There are people who, from sympathy and anxiety for others become hypochondriacal. The resulting form of compassion is nothing else than sickness. So, also, is there a Christian hypochondria, from which those

singular, religiously agitated people suffer who place always before their eyes the suffering and death of Christ.

48. Economy of Blessings.—The advantageous and the pleasing, as the healthiest growths and powers in the intercourse of men, are such precious treasures that it is much to be wished the use made of these balsamic means were as economical as possible: but this is impossible. Economy in the use of blessings is the dream of the craziest of Utopians.

49. Well-Wishing.—Among the small, but infinitely plentiful and therefore very potent things to which science must pay more attention than to the great, uncommon things, well-wishing[21] must be reckoned; I mean those manifestations of friendly disposition in intercourse, that laughter of the eye, every hand pressure, every courtesy from which, in general, every human act gets its quality. Every teacher, every functionary adds this element as a gratuity to whatever he does as a duty; it is the perpetual well spring of humanity, like the waves of light in which everything grows; thus, in the narrowest circles, within the family, life blooms and flowers only through this kind feeling. The cheerfulness, friendliness and kindness of a heart are unfailing sources of unegoistic impulse and have made far more for civilization than those other more noised manifestations of it that are styled sympathy, benevolence and sacrifice. But it is customary to depreciate these little tokens of kindly feeling, and, indeed, there is not much of the unegoistic in them. The sum of these little doses is very great, nevertheless; their combined strength is of the greatest of strengths.—Thus, too, much more happiness is to be found in the world than gloomy eyes discover: that is, if the calculation be just, and all these pleasing moments in which every day, even the meanest human life, is rich, be not forgotten.

50. The Desire to Inspire Compassion.—La Rochefoucauld, in the most notable part of his self portraiture (first printed 1658) reaches the vital spot of truth when he warns all those endowed with reason to be on their guard against compassion, when he advises that this sentiment be left to men of the masses who stand in need of the promptings of the emotions (since they are not guided by reason) to induce them to give aid to the suffering and to be of service in misfortune: whereas compassion, in his (and Plato's) view, deprives the heart of strength. To be sure, sympathy should be manifested but men should take care not to feel it; for the unfortunate are rendered so dull that the manifestation of sympathy affords them the greatest happiness in the world.—Perhaps a more effectual warning against this compassion can be given if this need of the unfortunate be considered not simply as stupidity and intellectual weakness, not as a sort of distraction of the spirit entailed by misfortune itself (and thus, indeed, does La Rochefoucauld seem to view it) but as something quite different and more

momentous. Let note be taken of children who cry and scream in order to be compassionated and who, therefore, await the moment when their condition will be observed; come into contact with the sick and the oppressed in spirit and try to ascertain if the wailing and sighing, the posturing and posing of misfortune do not have as end and aim the causing of pain to the beholder: the sympathy which each beholder manifests is a consolation to the weak and suffering only in as much as they are made to perceive that at least they have the power, notwithstanding all their weakness, to inflict pain. The unfortunate experiences a species of joy in the sense of superiority which the manifestation of sympathy entails; his imagination is exalted; he is always strong enough, then, to cause the world pain. Thus is the thirst for sympathy a thirst for self enjoyment and at the expense of one's fellow creatures: it shows man in the whole ruthlessness of his own dear self: not in his mere "dullness" as La Rochefoucauld thinks.—In social conversation three fourths of all the questions are asked, and three fourths of all the replies are made in order to inflict some little pain; that is why so many people crave social intercourse: it gives them a sense of their power. In these countless but very small doses in which the quality of badness is administered it proves a potent stimulant of life: to the same extent that well wishing—(Wohl-wollen) distributed through the world in like manner, is one of the ever ready restoratives.—But will many honorable people be found to admit that there is any pleasure in administering pain? that entertainment—and rare entertainment—is not seldom found in causing others, at least in thought, some pain, and in raking them with the small shot of wickedness? The majority are too ignoble and a few are too good to know anything of this pudendum: the latter may, consequently, be prompt to deny that Prosper Mérimée is right when he says: "Know, also, that nothing is more common than to do wrong for the pleasure of doing it."

51. How Appearance Becomes Reality.—The actor cannot, at last, refrain, even in moments of the deepest pain, from thinking of the effect produced by his deportment and by his surroundings—for example, even at the funeral of his own child: he will weep at his own sorrow and its manifestations as though he were his own audience. The hypocrite who always plays one and the same part, finally ceases to be a hypocrite; as in the case of priests who, when young men, are always, either consciously or unconsciously, hypocrites, and finally become naturally and then really, without affectation, mere priests: or if the father does not carry it to this extent, the son, who inherits his father's calling and gets the advantage of the paternal progress, does. When anyone, during a long period, and persistently, wishes to appear something, it will at last prove difficult for him to be anything else. The calling of almost every man, even of the artist, begins

with hypocrisy, with an imitation of deportment, with a copying of the effective in manner. He who always wears the mask of a friendly man must at last gain a power over friendliness of disposition, without which the expression itself of friendliness is not to be gained—and finally friendliness of disposition gains the ascendancy over him—he is benevolent.

52. The Point of Honor in Deception.—In all great deceivers one characteristic is prominent, to which they owe their power. In the very act of deception, amid all the accompaniments, the agitation in the voice, the expression, the bearing, in the crisis of the scene, there comes over them a belief in themselves; this it is that acts so effectively and irresistibly upon the beholders. Founders of religions differ from such great deceivers in that they never come out of this state of self deception, or else they have, very rarely, a few moments of enlightenment in which they are overcome by doubt; generally, however, they soothe themselves by ascribing such moments of enlightenment to the evil adversary. Self deception must exist that both classes of deceivers may attain far reaching results. For men believe in the truth of all that is manifestly believed with due implicitness by others.

53. Presumed Degrees of Truth.—One of the most usual errors of deduction is: because someone truly and openly is against us, therefore he speaks the truth. Hence the child has faith in the judgments of its elders, the Christian in the assertions of the founder of the church. So, too, it will not be admitted that all for which men sacrificed life and happiness in former centuries was nothing but delusion: perhaps it is alleged these things were degrees of truth. But what is really meant is that, if a person sincerely believes a thing and has fought and died for his faith, it would be too unjust if only delusion had inspired him. Such a state of affairs seems to contradict eternal justice. For that reason the heart of a sensitive man pronounces against his head the judgment: between moral conduct and intellectual insight there must always exist an inherent connection. It is, unfortunately, otherwise: for there is no eternal justice.

54. Falsehood.—Why do men, as a rule, speak the truth in the ordinary affairs of life? Certainly not for the reason that a god has forbidden lying. But because first: it is more convenient, as falsehood entails invention, make-believe and recollection (wherefore Swift says that whoever invents a lie seldom realises the heavy burden he takes up: he must, namely, for every lie that he tells, insert twenty more). Therefore, because in plain ordinary relations of life it is expedient to say without circumlocution: I want this, I have done this, and the like; therefore, because the way of freedom and certainty is surer than that of ruse.—But if it happens that a child is brought up in sinister domestic circumstances, it will then indulge in falsehood as matter of course, and

involuntarily say anything its own interests may prompt: an inclination for truth, an aversion to falsehood, is quite foreign and uncongenial to it, and hence it lies in all innocence.

55. Ethic Discredited for Faith's Sake.—No power can sustain itself when it is represented by mere humbugs: the Catholic Church may possess ever so many "worldly" sources of strength, but its true might is comprised in those still numberless priestly natures who make their lives stern and strenuous and whose looks and emaciated bodies are eloquent of night vigils, fasts, ardent prayer, perhaps even of whip lashes: these things make men tremble and cause them anxiety: what, if it be really imperative to live thus? This is the dreadful question which their aspect occasions. As they spread this doubt, they lay anew the prop of their power: even the free thinkers dare not oppose such disinterestedness with severe truth and cry: "Thou deceived one, deceive not!"—Only the difference of standpoint separates them from him: no difference in goodness or badness. But things we cannot accomplish ourselves, we are apt to criticise unfairly. Thus we are told of the cunning and perverted acts of the Jesuits, but we overlook the self mastery that each Jesuit imposes upon himself and also the fact that the easy life which the Jesuit manuals advocate is for the benefit, not of the Jesuits but the laity. Indeed, it may be questioned whether we enlightened ones would become equally competent workers as the result of similar tactics and organization, and equally worthy of admiration as the result of self mastery, indefatigable industry and devotion.

56. Victory of Knowledge over Radical Evil.—It proves a material gain to him who would attain knowledge to have had during a considerable period the idea that mankind is a radically bad and perverted thing: it is a false idea, as is its opposite, but it long held sway and its roots have reached down even to ourselves and our present world. In order to understand ourselves we must understand it; but in order to attain a loftier height we must step above it. We then perceive that there is no such thing as sin in the metaphysical sense: but also, in the same sense, no such thing as virtue; that this whole domain of ethical notions is one of constant variation; that there are higher and deeper conceptions of good and evil, moral and immoral. Whoever desires no more of things than knowledge of them attains speedily to peace of mind and will at most err through lack of knowledge, but scarcely through eagerness for knowledge (or through sin, as the world calls it). He will not ask that eagerness for knowledge be interdicted and rooted out; but his single, all powerful ambition to know as thoroughly and as fully as possible, will soothe him and moderate all that is strenuous in his circumstances. Moreover, he is now rid of a number of disturbing notions; he is

no longer beguiled by such words as hell-pain, sinfulness, unworthiness: he sees in them merely the flitting shadow pictures of false views of life and of the world.

57. Ethic as Man's Self-Analysis.—A good author, whose heart is really in his work, wishes that someone would arise and wholly refute him if only thereby his subject be wholly clarified and made plain. The maid in love wishes that she could attest the fidelity of her own passion through the faithlessness of her beloved. The soldier wishes to sacrifice his life on the field of his fatherland's victory: for in the victory of his fatherland his highest end is attained. The mother gives her child what she deprives herself of—sleep, the best nourishment and, in certain circumstances, her health, her self.—But are all these acts unegoistic? Are these moral deeds miracles because they are, in Schopenhauer's phrase "impossible and yet accomplished"? Is it not evident that in all four cases man loves one part of himself, (a thought, a longing, an experience) more than he loves another part of himself? that he thus analyses his being and sacrifices one part of it to another part? Is this essentially different from the behavior of the obstinate man who says "I would rather be shot than go a step out of my way for this fellow"?—Preference for something (wish, impulse, longing) is present in all four instances: to yield to it, with all its consequences, is not "unegoistic."—In the domain of the ethical man conducts himself not as individuum but as dividuum.

58. What Can be Promised.—Actions can be promised, but not feelings, for these are involuntary. Whoever promises somebody to love him always, or to hate him always, or to be ever true to him, promises something that it is out of his power to bestow. But he really can promise such courses of conduct as are the ordinary accompaniments of love, of hate, of fidelity, but which may also have their source in motives quite different: for various ways and motives lead to the same conduct. The promise to love someone always, means, consequently: as long as I love you, I will manifest the deportment of love; but if I cease to love you my deportment, although from some other motive, will be just the same, so that to the people about us it will seem as if my love remained unchanged.—Hence it is the continuance of the deportment of love that is promised in every instance in which eternal love (provided no element of self deception be involved) is sworn.

59. Intellect and Ethic.—One must have a good memory to be able to keep the promises one makes. One must have a strong imagination in order to feel sympathy. So closely is ethics connected with intellectual capacity.

60. Desire for Vengeance and Vengeance Itself.—To meditate revenge and attain it is tantamount to an attack of fever, that passes away: but to meditate revenge without possessing the strength or courage to attain it is tantamount to suffering from a chronic malady, or poisoning of body and soul. Ethics, which takes only the motive into account, rates both cases alike: people generally

estimate the first case as the worst (because of the consequences which the deed of vengeance may entail). Both views are short sighted.

61. Ability to Wait.—Ability to wait is so hard to acquire that great poets have not disdained to make inability to wait the central motive of their poems. So Shakespeare in Othello, Sophocles in Ajax, whose suicide would not have seemed to him so imperative had he only been able to cool his ardor for a day, as the oracle foreboded: apparently he would then have repulsed somewhat the fearful whispers of distracted thought and have said to himself: Who has not already, in my situation, mistaken a sheep for a hero? is it so extraordinary a thing? On the contrary it is something universally human: Ajax should thus have soothed himself. Passion will not wait: the tragic element in the lives of great men does not generally consist in their conflict with time and the inferiority of their fellowmen but in their inability to put off their work a year or two: they cannot wait.—In all duels, the friends who advise have but to ascertain if the principals can wait: if this be not possible, a duel is rational inasmuch as each of the combatants may say: "either I continue to live and the other dies instantly, or vice versa." To wait in such circumstances would be equivalent to the frightful martyrdom of enduring dishonor in the presence of him responsible for the dishonor: and this can easily cost more anguish than life is worth.

62. Glutting Revenge.—Coarse men, who feel a sense of injury, are in the habit of rating the extent of their injury as high as possible and of stating the occasion of it in greatly exaggerated language, in order to be able to feast themselves on the sentiments of hatred and revenge thus aroused.

63. Value of Disparagement.—Not a few, perhaps the majority of men, find it necessary, in order to retain their self esteem and a certain uprightness in conduct, to mentally disparage and belittle all the people they know. But as the inferior natures are in the majority and as a great deal depends upon whether they retain or lose this uprightness, so—

64. The Man in a Rage.—We should be on our guard against the man who is enraged against us, as against one who has attempted our life, for the fact that we still live consists solely in the inability to kill: were looks sufficient, it would have been all up with us long since. To reduce anyone to silence by physical manifestations of savagery or by a terrorizing process is a relic of under civilization. So, too, that cold look which great personages cast upon their servitors is a remnant of the caste distinction between man and man; a specimen of rude antiquity: women, the conservers of the old, have maintained this survival, too, more perfectly than men.

65. Whither Honesty May Lead.—Someone once had the bad habit of expressing himself upon occasion, and with perfect honesty, on the subject of the

motives of his conduct, which were as good or as bad as the motives of all men. He aroused first disfavor, then suspicion, became gradually of ill repute and was pronounced a person of whom society should beware, until at last the law took note of such a perverted being for reasons which usually have no weight with it or to which it closes its eyes. Lack of taciturnity concerning what is universally held secret, and an irresponsible predisposition to see what no one wants to see—oneself—brought him to prison and to early death.

66. Punishable, not Punished.—Our crime against criminals consists in the fact that we treat them as rascals.

67. Sancta simplicitas of Virtue.—Every virtue has its privilege: for example, that of contributing its own little bundle of wood to the funeral pyre of one condemned.

68. Morality and Consequence.—Not alone the beholders of an act generally estimate the ethical or unethical element in it by the result: no, the one who performed the act does the same. For the motives and the intentions are seldom sufficiently apparent, and amid them the memory itself seems to become clouded by the results of the act, so that a man often ascribes the wrong motives to his acts or regards the remote motives as the direct ones. Success often imparts to an action all the brilliance and honor of good intention, while failure throws the shadow of conscience over the most estimable deeds. Hence arises the familiar maxim of the politician: "Give me only success: with it I can win all the noble souls over to my side—and make myself noble even in my own eyes."—In like manner will success prove an excellent substitute for a better argument. To this very day many well educated men think the triumph of Christianity over Greek philosophy is a proof of the superior truth of the former—although in this case it was simply the coarser and more powerful that triumphed over the more delicate and intellectual. As regards superiority of truth, it is evident that because of it the reviving sciences have connected themselves, point for point, with the philosophy of Epicurus, while Christianity has, point for point, recoiled from it.

69. Love and Justice.—Why is love so highly prized at the expense of justice and why are such beautiful things spoken of the former as if it were a far higher entity than the latter? Is the former not palpably a far more stupid thing than the latter?—Certainly, and on that very account so much the more agreeable to everybody: it is blind and has a rich horn of plenty out of which it distributes its gifts to everyone, even when they are unmerited, even when no thanks are returned. It is impartial like the rain, which according to the bible and experience, wets not alone the unjust but, in certain circumstances, the just as well, and to their skins at that.

70. Execution.—How comes it that every execution causes us more pain than a murder? It is the coolness of the executioner, the painful preparation, the perception that here a man is being used as an instrument for the intimidation of others. For the guilt is not punished even if there be any: this is ascribable to the teachers, the parents, the environment, in ourselves, not in the murderer—I mean the predisposing circumstances.

71. Hope.—Pandora brought the box containing evils and opened it. It was the gift of the gods to men, a gift of most enticing appearance externally and called the "box of happiness." Thereupon all the evils, (living, moving things) flew out: from that time to the present they fly about and do ill to men by day and night. One evil only did not fly out of the box: Pandora shut the lid at the behest of Zeus and it remained inside. Now man has this box of happiness perpetually in the house and congratulates himself upon the treasure inside of it; it is at his service: he grasps it whenever he is so disposed, for he knows not that the box which Pandora brought was a box of evils. Hence he looks upon the one evil still remaining as the greatest source of happiness—it is hope.—Zeus intended that man, notwithstanding the evils oppressing him, should continue to live and not rid himself of life, but keep on making himself miserable. For this purpose he bestowed hope upon man: it is, in truth, the greatest of evils for it lengthens the ordeal of man.

72. Degree of Moral Susceptibility Unknown.—The fact that one has or has not had certain profoundly moving impressions and insights into things—for example, an unjustly executed, slain or martyred father, a faithless wife, a shattering, serious accident,—is the factor upon which the excitation of our passions to white heat principally depends, as well as the course of our whole lives. No one knows to what lengths circumstances (sympathy, emotion) may lead him. He does not know the full extent of his own susceptibility. Wretched environment makes him wretched. It is as a rule not the quality of our experience but its quantity upon which depends the development of our superiority or inferiority, from the point of view of good and evil.

73. The Martyr Against His Will.—In a certain movement there was a man who was too cowardly and vacillating ever to contradict his comrades. He was made use of in each emergency, every sacrifice was demanded of him because he feared the disfavor of his comrades more than he feared death: he was a petty, abject spirit. They perceived this and upon the foundation of the qualities just mentioned they elevated him to the altitude of a hero, and finally even of a martyr. Although the cowardly creature always inwardly said No, he always said Yes with his lips, even upon the scaffold, where he died for the tenets of his party: for beside him stood one of his old associates who so domineered him with look

and word that he actually went to his death with the utmost fortitude and has ever since been celebrated as a martyr and exalted character.

74. General Standard.—One will rarely err if extreme actions be ascribed to vanity, ordinary actions to habit and mean actions to fear.

75. Misunderstanding of Virtue.—Whoever has obtained his experience of vice in connection with pleasure as in the case of one with a youth of wild oats behind him, comes to the conclusion that virtue must be connected with self denial. Whoever, on the other hand, has been very much plagued by his passions and vices, longs to find in virtue the rest and peace of the soul. That is why it is possible for two virtuous people to misunderstand one another wholly.

76. The Ascetic.—The ascetic makes out of virtue a slavery.

77. Honor Transferred from Persons to Things.—Actions prompted by love or by the spirit of self sacrifice for others are universally honored wherever they are manifest. Hence is magnified the value set upon whatever things may be loved or whatever things conduce to self sacrifice: although in themselves they may be worth nothing much. A valiant army is evidence of the value of the thing it fights for.

78. Ambition a Substitute for Moral Feeling.—Moral feeling should never become extinct in natures that are destitute of ambition. The ambitious can get along without moral feeling just as well as with it.—Hence the sons of retired, ambitionless families, generally become by a series of rapid gradations, when they lose moral feeling, the most absolute lunkheads.

79. Vanity Enriches.—How poor the human mind would be without vanity! As it is, it resembles a well stacked and ever renewed ware-emporium that attracts buyers of every class: they can find almost everything, have almost everything, provided they bring with them the right kind of money—admiration.

80. Senility and Death.—Apart from the demands made by religion, it may well be asked why it is more honorable in an aged man, who feels the decline of his powers, to await slow extinction than to fix a term to his existence himself? Suicide in such a case is a quite natural and due proceeding that ought to command respect as a triumph of reason: and did in fact command respect during the times of the masters of Greek philosophy and the bravest Roman patriots, who usually died by their own hand. Eagerness, on the other hand, to keep alive from day to day with the anxious counsel of physicians, without capacity to attain any nearer to one's ideal of life, is far less worthy of respect.—Religions are very rich in refuges from the mandate of suicide: hence they ingratiate themselves with those who cling to life.

81. Delusions Regarding Victim and Regarding Evil Doer.—When the rich man takes a possession away from the poor man (for example, a prince who

deprives a plebeian of his beloved) there arises in the mind of the poor man a delusion: he thinks the rich man must be wholly perverted to take from him the little that he has. But the rich man appreciates the value of a single possession much less because he is accustomed to many possessions, so that he cannot put himself in the place of the poor man and does not act by any means as ill as the latter supposes. Both have a totally false idea of each other. The iniquities of the mighty which bulk most largely in history are not nearly so monstrous as they seem. The hereditary consciousness of being a superior being with superior environment renders one very callous and lulls the conscience to rest. We all feel, when the difference between ourselves and some other being is exceedingly great, that no element of injustice can be involved, and we kill a fly with no qualms of conscience whatever. So, too, it is no indication of wickedness in Xerxes (whom even the Greeks represent as exceptionally noble) that he deprived a father of his son and had him drawn and quartered because the latter had manifested a troublesome, ominous distrust of an entire expedition: the individual was in this case brushed aside as a pestiferous insect. He was too low and mean to justify continued sentiments of compunction in the ruler of the world. Indeed no cruel man is ever as cruel, in the main, as his victim thinks. The idea of pain is never the same as the sensation. The rule is precisely analogous in the case of the unjust judge, and of the journalist who by means of devious rhetorical methods, leads public opinion astray. Cause and effect are in all these instances entwined with totally different series of feeling and thoughts, whereas it is unconsciously assumed that principal and victim feel and think exactly alike, and because of this assumption the guilt of the one is based upon the pain of the other.

82. The Soul's Skin.—As the bones, flesh, entrails and blood vessels are enclosed by a skin that renders the aspect of men endurable, so the impulses and passions of the soul are enclosed by vanity: it is the skin of the soul.

83. Sleep of Virtue.—If virtue goes to sleep, it will be more vigorous when it awakes.

84. Subtlety of Shame.—Men are not ashamed of obscene thoughts, but they are ashamed when they suspect that obscene thoughts are attributed to them.

85. Naughtiness Is Rare.—Most people are too much absorbed in themselves to be bad.

86. The Mite in the Balance.—We are praised or blamed, as the one or the other may be expedient, for displaying to advantage our power of discernment.

87. Luke 18:14 Improved.—He that humbleth himself wisheth to be exalted.

88. Prevention of Suicide.—There is a justice according to which we may deprive a man of life, but none that permits us to deprive him of death: this is merely cruelty.

89. Vanity.—We set store by the good opinion of men, first because it is of use to us and next because we wish to give them pleasure (children their parents, pupils their teacher, and well disposed persons all others generally). Only when the good opinion of men is important to somebody, apart from personal advantage or the desire to give pleasure, do we speak of vanity. In this last case, a man wants to give himself pleasure, but at the expense of his fellow creatures, inasmuch as he inspires them with a false opinion of himself or else inspires "good opinion" in such a way that it is a source of pain to others (by arousing envy). The individual generally seeks, through the opinion of others, to attest and fortify the opinion he has of himself; but the potent influence of authority—an influence as old as man himself—leads many, also, to strengthen their own opinion of themselves by means of authority, that is, to borrow from others the expedient of relying more upon the judgment of their fellow men than upon their own.—Interest in oneself, the wish to please oneself attains, with the vain man, such proportions that he first misleads others into a false, unduly exalted estimate of himself and then relies upon the authority of others for his self estimate; he thus creates the delusion that he pins his faith to.—It must, however, be admitted that the vain man does not desire to please others so much as himself and he will often go so far, on this account, as to overlook his own interests: for he often inspires his fellow creatures with malicious envy and renders them ill disposed in order that he may thus increase his own delight in himself.

90. Limits of the Love of Mankind.—Every man who has declared that some other man is an ass or a scoundrel, gets angry when the other man conclusively shows that the assertion was erroneous.

91. Weeping Morality.—How much delight morality occasions! Think of the ocean of pleasing tears that has flowed from the narration of noble, great-hearted deeds!—This charm of life would disappear if the belief in complete irresponsibility gained the upper hand.

92. Origin of Justice.—Justice (reasonableness) has its origin among approximate equals in power, as Thucydides (in the dreadful conferences of the Athenian and Melian envoys) has rightly conceived. Thus, where there exists no demonstrable supremacy and a struggle leads but to mutual, useless damage, the reflection arises that an understanding would best be arrived at and some compromise entered into. The reciprocal nature is hence the first nature of justice. Each party makes the other content inasmuch as each receives what it prizes more highly than the other. Each surrenders to the other what the other wants and receives in return its own desire. Justice is therefore reprisal and exchange upon the basis of an approximate equality of power. Thus revenge

pertains originally to the domain of justice as it is a sort of reciprocity. Equally so, gratitude.—Justice reverts naturally to the standpoint of self preservation, therefore to the egoism of this consideration: "why should I injure myself to no purpose and perhaps never attain my end?"—So much for the origin of justice. Only because men, through mental habits, have forgotten the original motive of so called just and rational acts, and also because for thousands of years children have been brought to admire and imitate such acts, have they gradually assumed the appearance of being unegotistical. Upon this appearance is founded the high estimate of them, which, moreover, like all estimates, is continually developing, for whatever is highly esteemed is striven for, imitated, made the object of self sacrifice, while the merit of the pain and emulation thus expended is, by each individual, ascribed to the thing esteemed.—How slightly moral would the world appear without forgetfulness! A poet could say that God had posted forgetfulness as a sentinel at the portal of the temple of human merit!

93. Concerning the Law of the Weaker.—Whenever any party, for instance, a besieged city, yields to a stronger party, under stipulated conditions, the counter stipulation is that there be a reduction to insignificance, a burning and destruction of the city and thus a great damage inflicted upon the stronger party. Thus arises a sort of equalization principle upon the basis of which a law can be established. The enemy has an advantage to gain by its maintenance.—To this extent there is also a law between slaves and masters, limited only by the extent to which the slave may be useful to his master. The law goes originally only so far as the one party may appear to the other potent, invincible, stable, and the like. To such an extent, then, the weaker has rights, but very limited ones. Hence the famous dictum that each has as much law on his side as his power extends (or more accurately, as his power is believed to extend).

94. The Three Phases of Morality Hitherto.—It is the first evidence that the animal has become human when his conduct ceases to be based upon the immediately expedient, but upon the permanently useful; when he has, therefore, grown utilitarian, capable of purpose. Thus is manifested the first rule of reason. A still higher stage is attained when he regulates his conduct upon the basis of honor, by means of which he gains mastery of himself and surrenders his desires to principles; this lifts him far above the phase in which he was actuated only by considerations of personal advantage as he understood it. He respects and wishes to be respected. This means that he comprehends utility as a thing dependent upon what his opinion of others is and their opinion of him. Finally he regulates his conduct (the highest phase of morality hitherto attained) by his own standard of men and things. He himself decides, for himself and for others, what is honorable and what is useful. He has become a law giver to opinion, upon the

basis of his ever higher developing conception of the utilitarian and the honorable. Knowledge makes him capable of placing the highest utility, (that is, the universal, enduring utility) before merely personal utility,—of placing ennobling recognition of the enduring and universal before the merely temporary: he lives and acts as a collective individuality.

95. Ethic of the Developed Individual.—Hitherto the altruistic has been looked upon as the distinctive characteristic of moral conduct, and it is manifest that it was the consideration of universal utility that prompted praise and recognition of altruistic conduct. Must not a radical departure from this point of view be imminent, now that it is being ever more clearly perceived that in the most personal considerations the most general welfare is attained: so that conduct inspired by the most personal considerations of advantage is just the sort which has its origin in the present conception of morality (as a universal utilitarianism)? To contemplate oneself as a complete personality and bear the welfare of that personality in mind in all that one does—this is productive of better results than any sympathetic susceptibility and conduct in behalf of others. Indeed we all suffer from such disparagement of our own personalities, which are at present made to deteriorate from neglect. Capacity is, in fact, divorced from our personality in most cases, and sacrificed to the state, to science, to the needy, as if it were the bad which deserved to be made a sacrifice. Now, we are willing to labor for our fellowmen but only to the extent that we find our own highest advantage in so doing, no more, no less. The whole matter depends upon what may be understood as one's advantage: the crude, undeveloped, rough individualities will be the very ones to estimate it most inadequately.

96. Usage and Ethic.—To be moral, virtuous, praiseworthy means to yield obedience to ancient law and hereditary usage. Whether this obedience be rendered readily or with difficulty is long immaterial. Enough that it be rendered. "Good" finally comes to mean him who acts in the traditional manner, as a result of heredity or natural disposition, that is to say does what is customary with scarcely an effort, whatever that may be (for example revenges injuries when revenge, as with the ancient Greeks, was part of good morals). He is called good because he is good "to some purpose," and as benevolence, sympathy, considerateness, moderation and the like come, in the general course of conduct, to be finally recognized as "good to some purpose" (as utilitarian) the benevolent man, the helpful man, is duly styled "good". (At first other and more important kinds of utilitarian qualities stand in the foreground.) Bad is "not habitual" (unusual), to do things not in accordance with usage, to oppose the traditional, however rational or the reverse the traditional may be. To do injury to one's social group or community (and to one's neighbor as thus understood) is looked

upon, through all the variations of moral laws, in different ages, as the peculiarly "immoral" act, so that to-day we associate the word "bad" with deliberate injury to one's neighbor or community. "Egoistic" and "non-egoistic" do not constitute the fundamental opposites that have brought mankind to make a distinction between moral and immoral, good and bad; but adherence to traditional custom, and emancipation from it. How the traditional had its origin is quite immaterial; in any event it had no reference to good and bad or any categorical imperative but to the all important end of maintaining and sustaining the community, the race, the confederation, the nation. Every superstitious custom that originated in a misinterpreted event or casualty entailed some tradition, to adhere to which is moral. To break loose from it is dangerous, more prejudicial to the community than to the individual (because divinity visits the consequences of impiety and sacrilege upon the community rather than upon the individual). Now every tradition grows ever more venerable—the more remote is its origin, the more confused that origin is. The reverence due to it increases from generation to generation. The tradition finally becomes holy and inspires awe. Thus it is that the precept of piety is a far loftier morality than that inculcated by altruistic conduct.

97. Delight in the Moral.—A potent species of joy (and thereby the source of morality) is custom. The customary is done more easily, better, therefore preferably. A pleasure is felt in it and experience thus shows that since this practice has held its own it must be good. A manner or moral that lives and lets live is thus demonstrated advantageous, necessary, in contradistinction to all new and not yet adopted practices. The custom is therefore the blending of the agreeable and the useful. Moreover it does not require deliberation. As soon as man can exercise compulsion, he exercises it to enforce and establish his customs, for they are to him attested lifewisdom. So, too, a community of individuals constrains each one of their number to adopt the same moral or custom. The error herein is this: Because a certain custom has been agreeable to the feelings or at least because it proves a means of maintenance, this custom must be imperative, for it is regarded as the only thing that can possibly be consistent with well being. The well being of life seems to spring from it alone. This conception of the customary as a condition of existence is carried into the slightest detail of morality. Inasmuch as insight into true causation is quite restricted in all inferior peoples, a superstitious anxiety is felt that everything be done in due routine. Even when a custom is exceedingly burdensome it is preserved because of its supposed vital utility. It is not known that the same degree of satisfaction can be experienced through some other custom and even higher degrees of satisfaction, too. But it is fully appreciated that all customs do become more agreeable with

the lapse of time, no matter how difficult they may have been found in the beginning, and that even the severest way of life may be rendered a matter of habit and therefore a pleasure.

98. Pleasure and Social Instinct.—Through his relations with other men, man derives a new species of delight in those pleasurable emotions which his own personality affords him; whereby the domain of pleasurable emotions is made infinitely more comprehensive. No doubt he has inherited many of these feelings from the brutes, which palpably feel delight when they sport with one another, as mothers with their young. So, too, the sexual relations must be taken into account: they make every young woman interesting to every young man from the standpoint of pleasure, and conversely. The feeling of pleasure originating in human relationships makes men in general better. The delight in common, the pleasures enjoyed together heighten one another. The individual feels a sense of security. He becomes better natured. Distrust and malice dissolve. For the man feels the sense of benefit and observes the same feeling in others. Mutual manifestations of pleasure inspire mutual sympathy, the sentiment of homogeneity. The same effect is felt also at mutual sufferings, in a common danger, in stormy weather. Upon such a foundation are built the earliest alliances: the object of which is the mutual protection and safety from threatening misfortunes, and the welfare of each individual. And thus the social instinct develops from pleasure.

99. The Guiltless Nature of So-Called Bad Acts.—All "bad" acts are inspired by the impulse to self preservation or, more accurately, by the desire for pleasure and for the avoidance of pain in the individual. Thus are they occasioned, but they are not, therefore, bad. "Pain self prepared" does not exist, except in the brains of the philosophers, any more than "pleasure self prepared" (sympathy in the Schopenhauer sense). In the condition anterior to the state we kill the creature, be it man or ape, that attempts to pluck the fruit of a tree before we pluck it ourselves should we happen to be hungry at the time and making for that tree: as we would do to-day, so far as the brute is concerned, if we were wandering in savage regions.—The bad acts which most disturb us at present do so because of the erroneous supposition that the one who is guilty of them towards us has a free will in the matter and that it was within his discretion not to have done these evil things. This belief in discretionary power inspires hate, thirst for revenge, malice, the entire perversion of the mental processes, whereas we would feel in no way incensed against the brute, as we hold it irresponsible. To inflict pain not from the instinct of self preservation but in requital—this is the consequence of false judgment and is equally a guiltless course of conduct. The individual can, in that condition which is anterior to the state, act with fierceness and violence

for the intimidation of another creature, in order to render his own power more secure as a result of such acts of intimidation. Thus acts the powerful, the superior, the original state founder, who subjugates the weaker. He has the right to do so, as the state nowadays assumes the same right, or, to be more accurate, there is no right that can conflict with this. A foundation for all morality can first be laid only when a stronger individuality or a collective individuality, for example society, the state, subjects the single personalities, hence builds upon their unification and establishes a bond of union. Morality results from compulsion, it is indeed itself one long compulsion to which obedience is rendered in order that pain may be avoided. At first it is but custom, later free obedience and finally almost instinct. At last it is (like everything habitual and natural) associated with pleasure—and is then called virtue.

100. Shame.—Shame exists wherever a "mystery" exists: but this is a religious notion which in the earlier period of human civilization had great vogue. Everywhere there were circumscribed spots to which access was denied on account of some divine law, except in special circumstances. At first these spots were quite extensive, inasmuch as stipulated areas could not be trod by the uninitiated, who, when near them, felt tremors and anxieties. This sentiment was frequently transferred to other relationships, for example to sexual relations, which, as the privilege and gateway of mature age, must be withdrawn from the contemplation of youth for its own advantage: relations which many divinities were busy in preserving and sanctifying, images of which divinities were duly placed in marital chambers as guardians. (In Turkish such an apartment is termed a harem or holy thing, the same word also designating the vestibule of a mosque). So, too, Kingship is regarded as a centre from which power and brilliance stream forth, as a mystery to the subjects, impregnated with secrecy and shame, sentiments still quite operative among peoples who in other respects are without any shame at all. So, too, is the whole world of inward states, the so-called "soul," even now, for all non-philosophical persons, a "mystery," and during countless ages it was looked upon as a something of divine origin, in direct communion with deity. It is, therefore, an adytum and occasions shame.

101. Judge Not.—Care must be taken, in the contemplation of earlier ages, that there be no falling into unjust scornfulness. The injustice in slavery, the cruelty in the subjugation of persons and peoples must not be estimated by our standard. For in that period the instinct of justice was not so highly developed. Who dare reproach the Genoese Calvin for burning the physician Servetus at the stake? It was a proceeding growing out of his convictions. And the Inquisition, too, had its justification. The only thing is that the prevailing views were false and led to those proceedings which seem so cruel to us, simply because such views have

become foreign to us. Besides, what is the burning alive of one individual compared with eternal hell pains for everybody else? And yet this idea then had hold of all the world without in the least vitiating, with its frightfulness, the other idea of a god. Even we nowadays are hard and merciless to political revolutionists, but that is because we are in the habit of believing the state a necessity, and hence the cruelty of the proceeding is not so much understood as in the other cases where the points of view are repudiated. The cruelty to animals shown by children and Italians is due to the same misunderstanding. The animal, owing to the exigencies of the church catechism, is placed too far below the level of mankind.—Much, too, that is frightful and inhuman in history, and which is almost incredible, is rendered less atrocious by the reflection that the one who commands and the one who executes are different persons. The former does not witness the performance and hence it makes no strong impression on him. The latter obeys a superior and hence feels no responsibility. Most princes and military chieftains appear, through lack of true perception, cruel and hard without really being so.—Egoism is not bad because the idea of the "neighbor"—the word is of Christian origin and does not correspond to truth—is very weak in us, and we feel ourselves, in regard to him, as free from responsibility as if plants and stones were involved. That another is in suffering must be learned and it can never be wholly learned.

102. "Man Always Does Right."—We do not blame nature when she sends a thunder storm and makes us wet: why then do we term the man who inflicts injury immoral? Because in the latter case we assume a voluntary, ruling, free will, and in the former necessity. But this distinction is a delusion. Moreover, even the intentional infliction of injury is not, in all circumstances termed immoral. Thus, we kill a fly intentionally without thinking very much about it, simply because its buzzing about is disagreeable; and we punish a criminal and inflict pain upon him in order to protect ourselves and society. In the first case it is the individual who, for the sake of preserving himself or in order to spare himself pain, does injury with design: in the second case, it is the state. All ethic deems intentional infliction of injury justified by necessity; that is when it is a matter of self preservation. But these two points of view are sufficient to explain all bad acts done by man to men. It is desired to obtain pleasure or avoid pain. In any sense, it is a question, always, of self preservation. Socrates and Plato are right: whatever man does he always does right: that is, does what seems to him good (advantageous) according to the degree of advancement his intellect has attained, which is always the measure of his rational capacity.

103. The Inoffensive in Badness.—Badness has not for its object the infliction of pain upon others but simply our own satisfaction as, for instance, in the case

of thirst for vengeance or of nerve excitation. Every act of teasing shows what pleasure is caused by the display of our power over others and what feelings of delight are experienced in the sense of domination. Is there, then, anything immoral in feeling pleasure in the pain of others? Is malicious joy devilish, as Schopenhauer says? In the realm of nature we feel joy in breaking boughs, shattering rocks, fighting with wild beasts, simply to attest our strength thereby. Should not the knowledge that another suffers on our account here, in this case, make the same kind of act, (which, by the way, arouses no qualms of conscience in us) immoral also? But if we had not this knowledge there would be no pleasure in one's own superiority or power, for this pleasure is experienced only in the suffering of another, as in the case of teasing. All pleasure is, in itself, neither good nor bad. Whence comes the conviction that one should not cause pain in others in order to feel pleasure oneself? Simply from the standpoint of utility, that is, in consideration of the consequences, of ultimate pain, since the injured party or state will demand satisfaction and revenge. This consideration alone can have led to the determination to renounce such pleasure.—Sympathy has the satisfaction of others in view no more than, as already stated, badness has the pain of others in view. For there are at least two (perhaps many more) elementary ingredients in personal gratification which enter largely into our self satisfaction: one of them being the pleasure of the emotion, of which species is sympathy with tragedy, and another, when the impulse is to action, being the pleasure of exercising one's power. Should a sufferer be very dear to us, we divest ourselves of pain by the performance of acts of sympathy.—With the exception of some few philosophers, men have placed sympathy very low in the rank of moral feelings: and rightly.

104. Self Defence.—If self defence is in general held a valid justification, then nearly every manifestation of so called immoral egoism must be justified, too. Pain is inflicted, robbery or killing done in order to maintain life or to protect oneself and ward off harm. A man lies when cunning and delusion are valid means of self preservation. To injure intentionally when our safety and our existence are involved, or the continuance of our well being, is conceded to be moral. The state itself injures from this motive when it hangs criminals. In unintentional injury the immoral, of course, can not be present, as accident alone is involved. But is there any sort of intentional injury in which our existence and the maintenance of our well being be not involved? Is there such a thing as injuring from absolute badness, for example, in the case of cruelty? If a man does not know what pain an act occasions, that act is not one of wickedness. Thus the child is not bad to the animal, not evil. It disturbs and rends it as if it were one of its playthings. Does a man ever fully know how much pain an act may cause

another? As far as our nervous system extends, we shield ourselves from pain. If it extended further, that is, to our fellow men, we would never cause anyone else any pain (except in such cases as we cause it to ourselves, when we cut ourselves, surgically, to heal our ills, or strive and trouble ourselves to gain health). We conclude from analogy that something pains somebody and can in consequence, through recollection and the power of imagination, feel pain also. But what a difference there always is between the tooth ache and the pain (sympathy) that the spectacle of tooth ache occasions! Therefore when injury is inflicted from so called badness the degree of pain thereby experienced is always unknown to us: in so far, however, as pleasure is felt in the act (a sense of one's own power, of one's own excitation) the act is committed to maintain the well being of the individual and hence comes under the purview of self defence and lying for self preservation. Without pleasure, there is no life; the struggle for pleasure is the struggle for life. Whether the individual shall carry on this struggle in such a way that he be called good or in such a way that he be called bad is something that the standard and the capacity of his own intellect must determine for him.

105. Justice that Rewards.—Whoever has fully understood the doctrine of absolute irresponsibility can no longer include the so called rewarding and punishing justice in the idea of justice, if the latter be taken to mean that to each be given his due. For he who is punished does not deserve the punishment. He is used simply as a means to intimidate others from certain acts. Equally, he who is rewarded does not merit the reward. He could not act any differently than he did act. Hence the reward has only the significance of an encouragement to him and others as a motive for subsequent acts. The praise is called out only to him who is running in the race and not to him who has arrived at the goal. Something that comes to someone as his own is neither a punishment nor a reward. It is given to him from utiliarian considerations, without his having any claim to it in justice. Hence one must say "the wise man praises not because a good act has been done" precisely as was once said: "the wise man punishes not because a bad act has been done but in order that a bad act may not be done." If punishment and reward ceased, there would cease with them the most powerful incentives to certain acts and away from other acts. The purposes of men demand their continuance [of punishment and reward] and inasmuch as punishment and reward, blame and praise operate most potently upon vanity, these same purposes of men imperatively require the continuance of vanity.

106. The Water Fall.—At the sight of a water fall we may opine that in the countless curves, spirations and dashes of the waves we behold freedom of the will and of the impulses. But everything is compulsory, everything can be mathematically calculated. Thus it is, too, with human acts. We would be able to

calculate in advance every single action if we were all knowing, as well as every advance in knowledge, every delusion, every bad deed. The acting individual himself is held fast in the illusion of volition. If, on a sudden, the entire movement of the world stopped short, and an all knowing and reasoning intelligence were there to take advantage of this pause, he could foretell the future of every being to the remotest ages and indicate the path that would be taken in the world's further course. The deception of the acting individual as regards himself, the assumption of the freedom of the will, is a part of this computable mechanism.

107. Non-Responsibility and Non-Guilt.—The absolute irresponsibility of man for his acts and his nature is the bitterest drop in the cup of him who has knowledge, if he be accustomed to behold in responsibility and duty the patent of nobility of his human nature. All his estimates, preferences, dislikes are thus made worthless and false. His deepest sentiment, with which he honored the sufferer, the hero, sprang from an error. He may no longer praise, no longer blame, for it is irrational to blame and praise nature and necessity. Just as he cherishes the beautiful work of art, but does not praise it (as it is incapable of doing anything for itself), just as he stands in the presence of plants, he must stand in the presence of human conduct, his own included. He may admire strength, beauty, capacity, therein, but he can discern no merit. The chemical process and the conflict of the elements, the ordeal of the invalid who strives for convalescence, are no more merits than the soul-struggles and extremities in which one is torn this way and that by contending motives until one finally decides in favor of the strongest—as the phrase has it, although, in fact, it is the strongest motive that decides for us. All these motives, however, whatever fine names we may give them, have grown from the same roots in which we believe the baneful poisons lurk. Between good and bad actions there is no difference in kind but, at most, in degree. Good acts are sublimated evil. Bad acts are degraded, imbruted good. The very longing of the individual for self gratification (together with the fear of being deprived of it) obtains satisfaction in all circumstances, let the individual act as he may, that is, as he must: be it in deeds of vanity, revenge, pleasure, utility, badness, cunning, be it in deeds of self sacrifice, sympathy or knowledge. The degrees of rational capacity determine the direction in which this longing impels: every society, every individual has constantly present a comparative classification of benefits in accordance with which conduct is determined and others are judged. But this standard perpetually changes. Many acts are called bad that are only stupid, because the degree of intelligence that decided for them was low. Indeed, in a certain sense, all acts now are stupid, for the highest degree of human intelligence that has yet been attained

will in time most certainly be surpassed and then, in retrospection, all our present conduct and opinion will appear as narrow and petty as we now deem the conduct and opinion of savage peoples and ages.—To perceive all these things may occasion profound pain but there is, nevertheless, a consolation. Such pains are birth pains. The butterfly insists upon breaking through the cocoon, he presses through it, tears it to pieces, only to be blinded and confused by the strange light, by the realm of liberty. By such men as are capable of this sadness—how few there are!—will the first attempt be made to see if humanity may convert itself from a thing of morality to a thing of wisdom. The sun of a new gospel sheds its first ray upon the loftiest height in the souls of those few: but the clouds are massed there, too, thicker than ever, and not far apart are the brightest sunlight and the deepest gloom. Everything is necessity—so says the new knowledge: and this knowledge is itself necessity. All is guiltlessness, and knowledge is the way to insight into this guiltlessness. If pleasure, egoism, vanity be necessary to attest the moral phenomena and their richest blooms, the instinct for truth and accuracy of knowledge; if delusion and confusion of the imagination were the only means whereby mankind could gradually lift itself up to this degree of self enlightenment and self emancipation—who would venture to disparage the means? Who would have the right to feel sad if made aware of the goal to which those paths lead? Everything in the domain of ethic is evolved, changeable, tottering; all things flow, it is true—but all things are also in the stream: to their goal. Though within us the hereditary habit of erroneous judgment, love, hate, may be ever dominant, yet under the influence of awaking knowledge it will ever become weaker: a new habit, that of understanding, not-loving, not-hating, looking from above, grows up within us gradually and in the same soil, and may, perhaps, in thousands of years be powerful enough to endow mankind with capacity to develop the wise, guiltless man (conscious of guiltlessness) as unfailingly as it now developes the unwise, irrational, guilt-conscious man—that is to say, the necessary higher step, not the opposite of it.

The Religious Life.

108. The Double Contest Against Evil.—If an evil afflicts us we can either so deal with it as to remove its cause or else so deal with it that its effect upon our feeling is changed: hence look upon the evil as a benefit of which the uses will perhaps first become evident in some subsequent period. Religion and art (and also the metaphysical philosophy) strive to effect an alteration of the feeling, partly by an alteration of our judgment respecting the experience (for example, with the aid of the dictum "whom God loves, he chastizes") partly by the

awakening of a joy in pain, in emotion especially (whence the art of tragedy had its origin). The more one is disposed to interpret away and justify, the less likely he is to look directly at the causes of evil and eliminate them. An instant alleviation and narcotizing of pain, as is usual in the case of tooth ache, is sufficient for him even in the severest suffering. The more the domination of religions and of all narcotic arts declines, the more searchingly do men look to the elimination of evil itself, which is a rather bad thing for the tragic poets—for there is ever less and less material for tragedy, since the domain of unsparing, immutable destiny grows constantly more circumscribed—and a still worse thing for the priests, for these last have lived heretofore upon the narcoticizing of human ill.

109. Sorrow is Knowledge.—How willingly would not one exchange the false assertions of the homines religiosi that there is a god who commands us to be good, who is the sentinel and witness of every act, every moment, every thought, who loves us, who plans our welfare in every misfortune—how willingly would not one exchange these for truths as healing, beneficial and grateful as those delusions! But there are no such truths. Philosophy can at most set up in opposition to them other metaphysical plausibilities (fundamental untruths as well). The tragedy of it all is that, although one cannot believe these dogmas of religion and metaphysics if one adopts in heart and head the potent methods of truth, one has yet become, through human evolution, so tender, susceptible, sensitive, as to stand in need of the most effective means of rest and consolation. From this state of things arises the danger that, through the perception of truth or, more accurately, seeing through delusion, one may bleed to death. Byron has put this into deathless verse:

"Sorrow is knowledge: they who know the most
Must mourn the deepest o'er the fatal truth,
The tree of knowledge is not that of life."

Against such cares there is no better protective than the light fancy of Horace, (at any rate during the darkest hours and sun eclipses of the soul) expressed in the words

"quid aeternis minorem
consiliis animum fatigas?
cur non sub alta vel platano vel hac
pinu jacentes."[22]

At any rate, light fancy or heavy heartedness of any degree must be better than a romantic retrogression and desertion of one's flag, an approach to Christianity in any form: for with it, in the present state of knowledge, one can have nothing to do without hopelessly defiling one's intellectual integrity and surrendering it unconditionally. These woes may be painful enough, but without pain one cannot become a leader and guide of humanity: and woe to him who would be such and lacks this pure integrity of the intellect!

110. The Truth in Religion.—In the ages of enlightenment justice was not done to the importance of religion, of this there can be no doubt. It is also equally certain that in the ensuing reaction of enlightenment, the demands of justice were far exceeded inasmuch as religion was treated with love, even with infatuation and proclaimed as a profound, indeed the most profound knowledge of the world, which science had but to divest of its dogmatic garb in order to possess "truth" in its unmythical form. Religions must therefore—this was the contention of all foes of enlightenment—sensu allegorico, with regard for the comprehension of the masses, give expression to that ancient truth which is wisdom in itself, inasmuch as all science of modern times has led up to it instead of away from it. So that between the most ancient wisdom of man and all later wisdom there prevails harmony, even similarity of viewpoint; and the advancement of knowledge—if one be disposed to concede such a thing—has to do not with its nature but with its propagation. This whole conception of religion and science is through and through erroneous, and none would to-day be hardy enough to countenance it had not Schopenhauer's rhetoric taken it under protection, this high sounding rhetoric which now gains auditors after the lapse of a generation. Much as may be gained from Schopenhauer's religio-ethical human and cosmical oracle as regards the comprehension of Christianity and other religions, it is nevertheless certain that he erred regarding the value of religion to knowledge. He himself was in this but a servile pupil of the scientific teachers of his time who had all taken romanticism under their protection and renounced the spirit of enlightenment. Had he been born in our own time it would have been impossible for him to have spoken of the sensus allegoricus of religion. He would instead have done truth the justice to say: never has a religion, directly or indirectly, either as dogma or as allegory, contained a truth. For all religions grew out of dread or necessity, and came into existence through an error of the reason. They have, perhaps, in times of danger from science, incorporated some philosophical doctrine or other into their systems in order to make it possible to continue one's existence within them. But this is but a theological work of art dating from the time in which a religion began to doubt of itself. These theological feats of art, which are most common in Christianity as the religion of a learned age, impregnated with philosophy, have led to this superstition of the sensus allegoricus, as has, even more, the habit of the philosophers (namely those half-natures, the poetical philosophers and the philosophising artists) of dealing with their own feelings as if they constituted the

fundamental nature of humanity and hence of giving their own religious feelings a predominant influence over the structure of their systems. As the philosophers mostly philosophised under the influence of hereditary religious habits, or at least under the traditional influence of this "metaphysical necessity," they naturally arrived at conclusions closely resembling the Judaic or Christian or Indian religious tenets—resembling, in the way that children are apt to look like their mothers: only in this case the fathers were not certain as to the maternity, as easily happens—but in the innocence of their admiration, they fabled regarding the family likeness of all religion and science. In reality, there exists between religion and true science neither relationship nor friendship, not even enmity: they dwell in different spheres. Every philosophy that lets the religious comet gleam through the darkness of its last outposts renders everything within it that purports to be science, suspicious. It is all probably religion, although it may assume the guise of science.—Moreover, though all the peoples agree concerning certain religious things, for example, the existence of a god (which, by the way, as regards this point, is not the case) this fact would constitute an argument against the thing agreed upon, for example the very existence of a god. The consensus gentium and especially hominum can probably amount only to an absurdity. Against it there is no consensus omnium sapientium whatever, on any point, with the exception of which Goethe's verse speaks:

"All greatest sages to all latest ages
Will smile, wink and slily agree
'Tis folly to wait till a fool's empty pate
Has learned to be knowing and free.
So children of wisdom must look upon fools
As creatures who're never the better for schools."

Stated without rhyme or metre and adapted to our case: the consensus sapientium is to the effect that the consensus gentium amounts to an absurdity.

111. Origin of Religious Worship.—Let us transport ourselves back to the times in which religious life flourished most vigorously and we will find a fundamental conviction prevalent which we no longer share and which has resulted in the closing of the door to religious life once for all so far as we are concerned: this conviction has to do with nature and intercourse with her. In those times nothing is yet known of nature's laws. Neither for earth nor for heaven is there a must. A season, sunshine, rain can come or stay away as it pleases. There is wanting, in particular, all idea of natural causation. If a man rows, it is not the oar that moves the boat, but rowing is a magical ceremony whereby a demon is constrained to move the boat. All illness, death itself, is a consequence of magical influences. In sickness and death nothing natural is conceived. The whole idea

of "natural course" is wanting. The idea dawns first upon the ancient Greeks, that is to say in a very late period of humanity, in the conception of a Moira [fate] ruling over the gods. If any person shoots off a bow, there is always an irrational strength and agency in the act. If the wells suddenly run dry, the first thought is of subterranean demons and their pranks. It must have been the dart of a god beneath whose invisible influence a human being suddenly collapses. In India, the carpenter (according to Lubbock) is in the habit of making devout offerings to his hammer and hatchet. A Brahmin treats the plume with which he writes, a soldier the weapon that he takes into the field, a mason his trowel, a laborer his plow, in the same way. All nature is, in the opinion of religious people, a sum total of the doings of conscious and willing beings, an immense mass of complex volitions. In regard to all that takes place outside of us no conclusion is permissible that anything will result thus and so, must result thus and so, that we are comparatively calculable and certain in our experiences, that man is the rule, nature the ruleless. This view forms the fundamental conviction that dominates crude, religion-producing, early civilizations. We contemporary men feel exactly the opposite: the richer man now feels himself inwardly, the more polyphone the music and the sounding of his soul, the more powerfully does the uniformity of nature impress him. We all, with Goethe, recognize in nature the great means of repose for the soul. We listen to the pendulum stroke of this great clock with longing for rest, for absolute calm and quiescence, as if we could drink in the uniformity of nature and thereby arrive first at an enjoyment of oneself. Formerly it was the reverse: if we carry ourselves back to the periods of crude civilization, or if we contemplate contemporary savages, we will find them most strongly influenced by rule, by tradition. The individual is almost automatically bound to rule and tradition and moves with the uniformity of a pendulum. To him nature—the uncomprehended, fearful, mysterious nature—must seem the domain of freedom, of volition, of higher power, indeed as an ultra-human degree of destiny, as god. Every individual in such periods and circumstances feels that his existence, his happiness, the existence and happiness of the family, the state, the success or failure of every undertaking, must depend upon these dispositions of nature. Certain natural events must occur at the proper time and certain others must not occur. How can influence be exercised over this fearful unknown, how can this domain of freedom be brought under subjection? thus he asks himself, thus he worries: Is there no means to render these powers of nature as subject to rule and tradition as you are yourself?—The cogitation of the superstitious and magic-deluded man is upon the theme of imposing a law upon nature: and to put it briefly, religious worship is the result of such cogitation. The problem which is present to every man is closely connected with this one: how can the weaker party dictate laws to the stronger, control its acts in reference to the weaker? At first the most harmless form of influence is recollected, that influence which is acquired when the partiality of anyone has been won. Through beseeching and prayer, through abject humiliation, through obligations to regular gifts and propitiations, through flattering homages, it is possible, therefore, to impose some guidance upon the forces of nature, to the extent that their partiality be won: love binds and is bound. Then agreements can be entered into by means of which certain courses of conduct are mutually concluded, vows are made and authorities prescribed. But far more potent is that species of power exercised by means of magic and incantation. As a man is able to injure a powerful enemy by means of the magician and render him helpless with fear, as the love potion operates at a distance, so can the mighty forces of nature, in the opinion of weaker mankind, be controlled by similar means. The principal means of effecting incantations is to acquire control of something belonging to the party to be influenced, hair, finger nails, food from his table, even his picture or his name. With such apparatus it is possible to act by means of magic, for the basic principle is that to everything spiritual corresponds something corporeal. With the aid of this corporeal element the spirit may be bound, injured or destroyed. The corporeal affords the handle by which the spiritual can be laid hold of. In the same way that man influences mankind does he influences some spirit of nature, for this latter has also its corporeal element that can be grasped. The tree, and on the same basis, the seed from which it grew: this puzzling sequence seems to demonstrate that in both forms the same spirit is embodied, now large, now small. A stone that suddenly rolls, is the body in which the spirit works. Does a huge boulder lie in a lonely moor? It is impossible to think of mortal power having placed it there. The stone must have moved itself there. That is to say some spirit must dominate it. Everything that has a body is subject to magic, including, therefore, the spirits of nature. If a god is directly connected with his portrait, a direct influence (by refraining from devout offerings, by whippings, chainings and the like) can be brought to bear upon him. The lower classes in China tie cords around the picture of their god in order to defy his departing favor, when he has left them in the lurch, and tear the picture to pieces, drag it through the streets into dung heaps and gutters, crying: "You dog of a spirit, we housed you in a beautiful temple, we gilded you prettily, we fed you well, we brought you offerings, and yet how ungrateful you are!" Similar displays of resentment have been made against pictures of the mother of god and pictures of saints in Catholic countries during the present century when such pictures would not do their duty during times of pestilence and drought. Through all these magical relationships to nature countless ceremonies are occasioned, and finally, when their complexity and confusion grow too great, pains are taken to systematize them, to arrange them so that the favorable course of nature's progress, namely the great yearly circle of the seasons, may be brought about by a corresponding course of the ceremonial progress. The aim of religious worship is to influence nature to human advantage, and hence to instil a subjection to law into her that originally she has not, whereas at present man desires to find out the subjection to law of nature in order to guide himself thereby. In brief, the system of religious worship rests upon the idea of magic between man and man, and the magician is older than the priest. But it rests equally upon other and higher ideas. It brings into prominence the sympathetic relation of man to man, the existence of benevolence, gratitude, prayer, of truces between enemies, of loans upon security, of arrangements for the protection of property. Man, even in very inferior degrees of civilization, does not stand in the presence of nature as a helpless slave, he is not willy-nilly the absolute servant of nature. In the Greek development of religion, especially in the relationship to the Olympian gods, it becomes possible to entertain the idea of an existence side by side of two castes, a higher, more powerful, and a lower, less powerful: but both are bound together in some way, on account of their origin and are one species. They need not be ashamed of one another. This is the element of distinction in Greek religion.

112. At the Contemplation of Certain Ancient Sacrificial Proceedings.—How many sentiments are lost to us is manifest in the union of the farcical, even of the obscene, with the religious feeling. The feeling that this mixture is possible is becoming extinct. We realize the mixture only historically, in the mysteries of Demeter and Dionysos and in the Christian Easter festivals and religious mysteries. But we still perceive the sublime in connection with the ridiculous, and the like, the emotional with the absurd. Perhaps a later age will be unable to understand even these combinations.

113. Christianity as Antiquity.—When on a Sunday morning we hear the old bells ringing, we ask ourselves: Is it possible? All this for a Jew crucified two thousand years ago who said he was God's son? The proof of such an assertion is lacking.—Certainly, the Christian religion constitutes in our time a protruding bit of antiquity from very remote ages and that its assertions are still generally believed—although men have become so keen in the scrutiny of claims—constitutes the oldest relic of this inheritance. A god who begets children by a mortal woman; a sage who demands that no more work be done, that no more justice be administered but that the signs of the approaching end of the world be heeded; a system of justice that accepts an innocent as a vicarious sacrifice in the place of the guilty; a person who bids his disciples drink his blood; prayers for miracles; sins against a god expiated upon a god; fear of a hereafter to

which death is the portal; the figure of the cross as a symbol in an age that no longer knows the purpose and the ignominy of the cross—how ghostly all these things flit before us out of the grave of their primitive antiquity! Is one to believe that such things can still be believed?

114. The Un-Greek in Christianity.—The Greeks did not look upon the Homeric gods above them as lords nor upon themselves beneath as servants, after the fashion of the Jews. They saw but the counterpart as in a mirror of the most perfect specimens of their own caste, hence an ideal, but no contradiction of their own nature. There was a feeling of mutual relationship, resulting in a mutual interest, a sort of alliance. Man thinks well of himself when he gives himself such gods and places himself in a relationship akin to that of the lower nobility with the higher; whereas the Italian races have a decidedly vulgar religion, involving perpetual anxiety because of bad and mischievous powers and soul disturbers. Wherever the Olympian gods receded into the background, there even Greek life became gloomier and more perturbed.—Christianity, on the other hand, oppressed and degraded humanity completely and sank it into deepest mire: into the feeling of utter abasement it suddenly flashed the gleam of divine compassion, so that the amazed and grace-dazzled stupefied one gave a cry of delight and for a moment believed that the whole of heaven was within him. Upon this unhealthy excess of feeling, upon the accompanying corruption of heart and head, Christianity attains all its psychological effects. It wants to annihilate, debase, stupefy, amaze, bedazzle. There is but one thing that it does not want: measure, standard (das Maas) and therefore is it in the worst sense barbarous, asiatic, vulgar, un-Greek.

115. Being Religious to Some Purpose.—There are certain insipid, traffic-virtuous people to whom religion is pinned like the hem of some garb of a higher humanity. These people do well to remain religious: it adorns them. All who are not versed in some professional weapon—including tongue and pen as weapons—are servile: to all such the Christian religion is very useful, for then their servility assumes the aspect of Christian virtue and is amazingly adorned.—People whose daily lives are empty and colorless are readily religious. This is comprehensible and pardonable, but they have no right to demand that others, whose daily lives are not empty and colorless, should be religious also.

116. The Everyday Christian.—If Christianity, with its allegations of an avenging God, universal sinfulness, choice of grace, and the danger of eternal damnation, were true, it would be an indication of weakness of mind and character not to be a priest or an apostle or a hermit, and toil for one's own salvation. It would be irrational to lose sight of one's eternal well being in comparison with temporary advantage: Assuming these dogmas to be generally

believed, the every day Christian is a pitiable figure, a man who really cannot count as far as three, and who, for the rest, just because of his intellectual incapacity, does not deserve to be as hard punished as Christianity promises he shall be.

117. Concerning the Cleverness of Christianity.—It is a master stroke of Christianity to so emphasize the unworthiness, sinfulness and degradation of men in general that contempt of one's fellow creatures becomes impossible. "He may sin as much as he pleases, he is not by nature different from me. It is I who in every way am unworthy and contemptible." So says the Christian to himself. But even this feeling has lost its keenest sting for the Christian does not believe in his individual degradation. He is bad in his general human capacity and he soothes himself a little with the assertion that we are all alike.

118. Personal Change.—As soon as a religion rules, it has for its opponents those who were its first disciples.

119. Fate of Christianity.—Christianity arose to lighten the heart, but now it must first make the heart heavy in order to be able to lighten it afterwards. Christianity will consequently go down.

120. The Testimony of Pleasure.—The agreeable opinion is accepted as true. This is the testimony of pleasure (or as the church says, the evidence of strength) of which all religions are so proud, although they should all be ashamed of it. If a belief did not make blessed it would not be believed. How little it would be worth, then!

121. Dangerous Play.—Whoever gives religious feeling room, must then also let it grow. He can do nothing else. Then his being gradually changes. The religious element brings with it affinities and kinships. The whole circle of his judgment and feeling is clouded and draped in religious shadows. Feeling cannot stand still. One should be on one's guard.

122. The Blind Pupil.—As long as one knows very well the strength and the weakness of one's dogma, one's art, one's religion, its strength is still low. The pupil and apostle who has no eye for the weaknesses of a dogma, a religion and so on, dazzled by the aspect of the master and by his own reverence for him, has, on that very account, generally more power than the master. Without blind pupils the influence of a man and his work has never become great. To give victory to knowledge, often amounts to no more than so allying it with stupidity that the brute force of the latter forces triumph for the former.

123. The Breaking off of Churches.—There is not sufficient religion in the world merely to put an end to the number of religions.

124. Sinlessness of Men.—If one have understood how "Sin came into the world," namely through errors of the reason, through which men in their

intercourse with one another and even individual men looked upon themselves as much blacker and wickeder than was really the case, one's whole feeling is much lightened and man and the world appear together in such a halo of harmlessness that a sentiment of well being is instilled into one's whole nature. Man in the midst of nature is as a child left to its own devices. This child indeed dreams a heavy, anxious dream. But when it opens its eyes it finds itself always in paradise.

125. Irreligiousness of Artists.—Homer is so much at home among his gods and is as a poet so good natured to them that he must have been profoundly irreligious. That which was brought to him by the popular faith—a mean, crude and partially repulsive superstition—he dealt with as freely as the Sculptor with his clay, therefore with the same freedom that Æschylus and Aristophanes evinced and with which in later times the great artists of the renaissance, and also Shakespeare and Goethe, drew their pictures.

126. Art and Strength of False Interpretation.—All the visions, fears, exhaustions and delights of the saint are well known symptoms of sickness, which in him, owing to deep rooted religious and psychological delusions, are explained quite differently, that is not as symptoms of sickness.—So, too, perhaps, the demon of Socrates was nothing but a malady of the ear that he explained, in view of his predominant moral theory, in a manner different from what would be thought rational to-day. Nor is the case different with the frenzy and the frenzied speeches of the prophets and of the priests of the oracles. It is always the degree of wisdom, imagination, capacity and morality in the heart and mind of the interpreters that got so much out of them. It is among the greatest feats of the men who are called geniuses and saints that they made interpreters for themselves who, fortunately for mankind, did not understand them.

127. Reverence for Madness.—Because it was perceived that an excitement of some kind often made the head clearer and occasioned fortunate inspirations, it was concluded that the utmost excitement would occasion the most fortunate inspirations. Hence the frenzied being was revered as a sage and an oracle giver. A false conclusion lies at the bottom of all this.

128. Promises of Wisdom.—Modern science has as its object as little pain as possible, as long a life as possible—hence a sort of eternal blessedness, but of a very limited kind in comparison with the promises of religion.

129. Forbidden Generosity.—There is not enough of love and goodness in the world to throw any of it away on conceited people.

130. Survival of Religious Training in the Disposition.—The Catholic Church, and before it all ancient education, controlled the whole domain of means through which man was put into certain unordinary moods and withdrawn from

the cold calculation of personal advantage and from calm, rational reflection. A church vibrating with deep tones; gloomy, regular, restraining exhortations from a priestly band, who involuntarily communicate their own tension to their congregation and lead them to listen almost with anxiety as if some miracle were in course of preparation; the awesome pile of architecture which, as the house of a god, rears itself vastly into the vague and in all its shadowy nooks inspires fear of its nerve-exciting power—who would care to reduce men to the level of these things if the ideas upon which they rest became extinct? But the results of all these things are nevertheless not thrown away: the inner world of exalted, emotional, prophetic, profoundly repentant, hope-blessed moods has become inborn in man largely through cultivation. What still exists in his soul was formerly, as he germinated, grew and bloomed, thoroughly disciplined.

131. Religious After-Pains.—Though one believe oneself absolutely weaned away from religion, the process has yet not been so thorough as to make impossible a feeling of joy at the presence of religious feelings and dispositions without intelligible content, as, for example, in music; and if a philosophy alleges to us the validity of metaphysical hopes, through the peace of soul therein attainable, and also speaks of "the whole true gospel in the look of Raphael's Madonna," we greet such declarations and innuendoes with a welcome smile. The philosopher has here a matter easy of demonstration. He responds with that which he is glad to give, namely a heart that is glad to accept. Hence it is observable how the less reflective free spirits collide only with dogmas but yield readily to the magic of religious feelings; it is a source of pain to them to let the latter go simply on account of the former.—Scientific philosophy must be very much on its guard lest on account of this necessity—an evolved and hence, also, a transitory necessity—delusions are smuggled in. Even logicians speak of "presentiments" of truth in ethics and in art (for example of the presentiment that the essence of things is unity) a thing which, nevertheless, ought to be prohibited. Between carefully deduced truths and such "foreboded" things there lies the abysmal distinction that the former are products of the intellect and the latter of the necessity. Hunger is no evidence that there is food at hand to appease it. I hunger merely craves food. "Presentiment" does not denote that the existence of a thing is known in any way whatever. It denotes merely that it is deemed possible to the extent that it is desired or feared. The "presentiment" is not one step forward in the domain of certainty.—It is involuntarily believed that the religious tinted sections of a philosophy are better attested than the others, but the case is at bottom just the opposite: there is simply the inner wish that it may be so, that the thing which beautifies may also be true. This wish leads us to accept bad grounds as good.

132. Of the Christian Need of Salvation.—Careful consideration must render it possible to propound some explanation of that process in the soul of a Christian which is termed need of salvation, and to propound an explanation, too, free from mythology: hence one purely psychological. Heretofore psychological explanations of religious conditions and processes have really been in disrepute, inasmuch as a theology calling itself free gave vent to its unprofitable nature in this domain; for its principal aim, so far as may be judged from the spirit of its creator, Schleier-macher, was the preservation of the Christian religion and the maintenance of the Christian theology. It appeared that in the psychological analysis of religious "facts" a new anchorage and above all a new calling were to be gained. Undisturbed by such predecessors, we venture the following exposition of the phenomena alluded to. Man is conscious of certain acts which are very firmly implanted in the general course of conduct: indeed he discovers in himself a predisposition to such acts that seems to him to be as unalterable as his very being. How gladly he would essay some other kind of acts which in the general estimate of conduct are rated the best and highest, how gladly he would welcome the consciousness of well doing which ought to follow unselfish motive! Unfortunately, however, it goes no further than this longing: the discontent consequent upon being unable to satisfy it is added to all other kinds of discontent which result from his life destiny in particular or which may be due to so called bad acts; so that a deep depression ensues accompanied by a desire for some physician to remove it and all its causes.—This condition would not be found so bitter if the individual but compared himself freely with other men: for then he would have no reason to be discontented with himself in particular as he is merely bearing his share of the general burden of human discontent and incompleteness. But he compares himself with a being who alone must be capable of the conduct that is called unegoistic and of an enduring consciousness of unselfish motive, with God. It is because he gazes into this clear mirror, that his own self seems so extraordinarily distracted and so troubled. Thereupon the thought of that being, in so far as it flits before his fancy as retributive justice, occasions him anxiety. In every conceivable small and great experience he believes he sees the anger of the being, his threats, the very implements and manacles of his judge and prison. What succors him in this danger, which, in the prospect of an eternal duration of punishment, transcends in hideousness all the horrors that can be presented to the imagination?

133. Before we consider this condition in its further effects, we would admit to ourselves that man is betrayed into this condition not through his "fault" and "sin" but through a series of delusions of the reason; that it was the fault of the mirror if his own self appeared to him in the highest degree dark and hateful, and

that that mirror was his own work, the very imperfect work of human imagination and judgment. In the first place a being capable of absolutely unegoistic conduct is as fabulous as the phoenix. Such a being is not even thinkable for the very reason that the whole notion of "unegoistic conduct," when closely examined, vanishes into air. Never yet has a man done anything solely for others and entirely without reference to a personal motive; indeed how could he possibly do anything that had no reference to himself, that is without inward compulsion (which must always have its basis in a personal need)? How could the ego act without ego?—A god, who, on the other hand, is all love, as he is usually represented, would not be capable of a solitary unegoistic act: whence one is reminded of a reflection of Lichtenberg's which is, in truth, taken from a lower sphere: "We cannot possibly feel for others, as the expression goes; we feel only for ourselves. The assertion sounds hard, but it is not, if rightly understood. A man loves neither his father nor his mother nor his wife nor his child, but simply the feelings which they inspire." Or, as La Rochefoucauld says: "If you think you love your mistress for the mere love of her, you are very much mistaken." Why acts of love are more highly prized than others, namely not on account of their nature, but on account of their utility, has already been explained in the section on the origin of moral feelings. But if a man should wish to be all love like the god aforesaid, and want to do all things for others and nothing for himself, the procedure would be fundamentally impossible because he must do a great deal for himself before there would be any possibility of doing anything for the love of others. It is also essential that others be sufficiently egoistic to accept always and at all times this self sacrifice and living for others, so that the men of love and self sacrifice have an interest in the survival of unloving and selfish egoists, while the highest morality, in order to maintain itself must formally enforce the existence of immorality (wherein it would be really destroying itself.)—Further: the idea of a god perturbs and discourages as long as it is accepted but as to how it originated can no longer, in the present state of comparative ethnological science, be a matter of doubt, and with the insight into the origin of this belief all faith collapses. What happens to the Christian who compares his nature with that of God is exactly what happened to Don Quixote, who depreciated his own prowess because his head was filled with the wondrous deeds of the heroes of chivalrous romance. The standard of measurement which both employ belongs to the domain of fable.—But if the idea of God collapses, so too, does the feeling of "sin" as a violation of divine rescript, as a stain upon a god-like creation. There still apparently remains that discouragement which is closely allied with fear of the punishment of worldly justice or of the contempt of one's fellow men. The keenest thorn in the sentiment of sin is dulled when it is perceived that one's acts have contravened human tradition, human rules and human laws without having thereby endangered the "eternal salvation of the soul" and its relations with deity. If finally men attain to the conviction of the absolute necessity of all acts and of their utter irresponsibility and then absorb it into their flesh and blood, every relic of conscience pangs will disappear.

134. If now, as stated, the Christian, through certain delusive feelings, is betrayed into self contempt, that is by a false and unscientific view of his acts and feelings, he must, nevertheless, perceive with the utmost amazement that this state of self contempt, of conscience pangs, of despair in particular, does not last, that there are hours during which all these things are wafted away from the soul and he feels himself once more free and courageous. The truth is that joy in his own being, the fulness of his own powers in connection with the inevitable decline of his profound excitation with the lapse of time, bore off the palm of victory. The man loves himself once more, he feels it—but this very new love, this new self esteem seems to him incredible. He can see in it only the wholly unmerited stream of the light of grace shed down upon him. If he formerly saw in every event merely warnings, threats, punishments and every kind of indication of divine anger, he now reads into his experiences the grace of god. The latter circumstance seems to him full of love, the former as a helpful pointing of the way, and his entirely joyful frame of mind now seems to him to be an absolute proof of the goodness of God. As formerly in his states of discouragement he interpreted his conduct falsely so now he does the same with his experiences. His state of consolation is now regarded as the effect produced by some external power. The love with which, at bottom, he loves himself, seems to be the divine love. That which he calls grace and the preliminary of salvation is in reality self-grace, self-salvation.

135. Therefore a certain false psychology, a certain kind of imaginativeness in the interpretation of motives and experiences is the essential preliminary to being a Christian and to experiencing the need of salvation. Upon gaining an insight into this wandering of the reason and the imagination, one ceases to be a Christian.

136. Of Christian Asceticism and Sanctity.—Much as some thinkers have exerted themselves to impart an air of the miraculous to those singular phenomena known as asceticism and sanctity, to question which or to account for which upon a rational basis would be wickedness and sacrilege, the temptation to this wickedness is none the less great. A powerful impulse of nature has in every age led to protest against such phenomena. At any rate science, inasmuch as it is the imitation of nature, permits the casting of doubts upon the inexplicable character and the supernal degree of such phenomena. It is true that

heretofore science has not succeeded in its attempts at explanation. The phenomena remain unexplained still, to the great satisfaction of those who revere moral miracles. For, speaking generally, the unexplained must rank as the inexplicable, the inexplicable as the non-natural, supernatural, miraculous—so runs the demand in the souls of all the religious and all the metaphysicians (even the artists if they happen to be thinkers), whereas the scientific man sees in this demand the "evil principle."—The universal, first, apparent truth that is encountered in the contemplation of sanctity and asceticism is that their nature is complicated; for nearly always, within the physical world as well as in the moral, the apparently miraculous may be traced successfully to the complex, the obscure, the multi-conditioned. Let us venture then to isolate a few impulses in the soul of the saint and the ascetic, to consider them separately and then view them as a synthetic development.

137. There is an obstinacy against oneself, certain sublimated forms of which are included in asceticism. Certain kinds of men are under such a strong necessity of exercising their power and dominating impulses that, if other objects are lacking or if they have not succeeded with other objects they will actually tyrannize over some portions of their own nature or over sections and stages of their own personality. Thus do many thinkers bring themselves to views which are far from likely to increase or improve their fame. Many deliberately bring down the contempt of others upon themselves although they could easily have retained consideration by silence. Others contradict earlier opinions and do not shrink from the ordeal of being deemed inconsistent. On the contrary they strive for this and act like eager riders who enjoy horseback exercise most when the horse is skittish. Thus will men in dangerous paths ascend to the highest steeps in order to laugh to scorn their own fear and their own trembling limbs. Thus will the philosopher embrace the dogmas of asceticism, humility, sanctity, in the light of which his own image appears in its most hideous aspect. This crushing of self, this mockery of one's own nature, this *spernere se sperni* out of which religions have made so much is in reality but a very high development of vanity. The whole ethic of the sermon on the mount belongs in this category: man has a true delight in mastering himself through exaggerated pretensions or excessive expedients and later deifying this tyrannically exacting something within him. In every scheme of ascetic ethics, man prays to one part of himself as if it were god and hence it is necessary for him to treat the rest of himself as devil.

138. Man is Not at All Hours Equally Moral; this is established. If one's morality be judged according to one's capacity for great, self sacrificing resolutions and abnegations (which when continual, and made a habit are known as sanctity) one is, in affection, or disposition, the most moral: while higher excitement

supplies wholly new impulses which, were one calm and cool as ordinarily, one would not deem oneself even capable of. How comes this? Apparently from the propinquity of all great and lofty emotional states. If a man is brought to an extraordinary pitch of feeling he can resolve upon a fearful revenge or upon a fearful renunciation of his thirst for vengeance indifferently. He craves, under the influences of powerful emotion, the great, the powerful, the immense, and if he chances to perceive that the sacrifice of himself will afford him as much satisfaction as the sacrifice of another, or will afford him more, he will choose self sacrifice. What concerns him particularly is simply the unloading of his emotion. Hence he readily, to relieve his tension, grasps the darts of the enemy and buries them in his own breast. That in self abnegation and not in revenge the element of greatness consisted must have been brought home to mankind only after long habituation. A god who sacrifices himself would be the most powerful and most effective symbol of this sort of greatness. As the conquest of the most hardly conquered enemy, the sudden mastering of a passion—thus does such abnegation appear: hence it passes for the summit of morality. In reality all that is involved is the exchange of one idea for another whilst the temperament remained at a like altitude, a like tidal state. Men when coming out of the spell, or resting from such passionate excitation, no longer understand the morality of such instants, but the admiration of all who participated in the occasion sustains them. Pride is their support if the passion and the comprehension of their act weaken. Therefore, at bottom even such acts of self-abnegation are not moral inasmuch as they are not done with a strict regard for others. Rather do others afford the high strung temperament an opportunity to lighten itself through such abnegation.

139. Even the Ascetic Seeks to Make Life Easier, and generally by means of absolute subjection to another will or to an all inclusive rule and ritual, pretty much as the Brahmin leaves absolutely nothing to his own volition but is guided in every moment of his life by some holy injunction or other. This subjection is a potent means of acquiring dominion over oneself. One is occupied, hence time does not hang heavy and there is no incitement of the personal will and of the individual passion. The deed once done there is no feeling of responsibility nor the sting of regret. One has given up one's own will once for all and this is easier than to give it up occasionally, as it is also easier wholly to renounce a desire than to yield to it in measured degree. When we consider the present relation of man to the state we perceive unconditional obedience is easier than conditional. The holy person also makes his lot easier through the complete surrender of his life personality and it is all delusion to admire such a phenomenon as the loftiest heroism of morality. It is always more difficult to assert one's personality without

shrinking and without hesitation than to give it up altogether in the manner indicated, and it requires moreover more intellect and thought.

140. After having discovered in many of the less comprehensible actions mere manifestations of pleasure in emotion for its own sake, I fancy I can detect in the self contempt which characterises holy persons, and also in their acts of self torture (through hunger and scourgings, distortions and chaining of the limbs, acts of madness) simply a means whereby such natures may resist the general exhaustion of their will to live (their nerves). They employ the most painful expedients to escape if only for a time from the heaviness and weariness in which they are steeped by their great mental indolence and their subjection to a will other than their own.

141. The Most Usual Means by which the ascetic and the sanctified individual seeks to make life more endurable comprises certain combats of an inner nature involving alternations of victory and prostration. For this purpose an enemy is necessary and he is found in the so called "inner enemy." That is, the holy individual makes use of his tendency to vanity, domineering and pride, and of his mental longings in order to contemplate his life as a sort of continuous battle and himself as a battlefield, in which good and evil spirits wage war with varying fortune. It is an established fact that the imagination is restrained through the regularity and adequacy of sexual intercourse while on the other hand abstention from or great irregularity in sexual intercourse will cause the imagination to run riot. The imaginations of many of the Christian saints were obscene to a degree; and because of the theory that sexual desires were in reality demons that raged within them, the saints did not feel wholly responsible for them. It is to this conviction that we are indebted for the highly instructive sincerity of their evidence against themselves. It was to their interest that this contest should always be kept up in some fashion because by means of this contest, as already stated, their empty lives gained distraction. In order that the contest might seem sufficiently great to inspire sympathy and admiration in the unsanctified, it was essential that sexual capacity be ever more and more damned and denounced. Indeed the danger of eternal damnation was so closely allied to this capacity that for whole generations Christians showed their children with actual conscience pangs. What evil may not have been done to humanity through this! And yet here the truth is just upside down: an exceedingly unseemly attitude for the truth. Christianity, it is true, had said that every man is conceived and born in sin, and in the intolerable and excessive Christianity of Calderon this thought is again perverted and entangled into the most distorted paradox extant in the well known lines

The greatest sin of man

Is the sin of being born.

In all pessimistic religions the act of procreation is looked upon as evil in itself. This is far from being the general human opinion. It is not even the opinion of all pessimists. Empedocles, for example, knows nothing of anything shameful, devilish and sinful in it. He sees rather in the great field of bliss of unholiness simply a healthful and hopeful phenomenon, Aphrodite. She is to him an evidence that strife does not always rage but that some time a gentle demon is to wield the sceptre. The Christian pessimists of practice, had, as stated, a direct interest in the prevalence of an opposite belief. They needed in the loneliness and the spiritual wilderness of their lives an ever living enemy, and a universally known enemy through whose conquest they might appear to the unsanctified as utterly incomprehensible and half unnatural beings. When this enemy at last, as a result of their mode of life and their shattered health, took flight forever, they were able immediately to people their inner selves with new demons. The rise and fall of the balance of cheerfulness and despair maintained their addled brains in a totally new fluctuation of longing and peace of soul. And in that period psychology served not only to cast suspicion on everything human but to wound and scourge it, to crucify it. Man wanted to find himself as base and evil as possible. Man sought to become anxious about the state of his soul, he wished to be doubtful of his own capacity. Everything natural with which man connects the idea of badness and sinfulness (as, for instance, is still customary in regard to the erotic) injures and degrades the imagination, occasions a shamed aspect, leads man to war upon himself and makes him uncertain, distrustful of himself. Even his dreams acquire a tincture of the unclean conscience. And yet this suffering because of the natural element in certain things is wholly superfluous. It is simply the result of opinions regarding the things. It is easy to understand why men become worse than they are if they are brought to look upon the unavoidably natural as bad and later to feel it as of evil origin. It is the master stroke of religions and metaphysics that wish to make man out bad and sinful by nature, to render nature suspicious in his eyes and to so make himself evil, for he learns to feel himself evil when he cannot divest himself of nature. He gradually comes to look upon himself, after a long life lived naturally, so oppressed by a weight of sin that supernatural powers become necessary to relieve him of the burden; and with this notion comes the so called need of salvation, which is the result not of a real but of an imaginary sinfulness. Go through the separate moral expositions in the vouchers of christianity and it will always be found that the demands are excessive in order that it may be impossible for man to satisfy them. The object is not that he may become moral but that he may feel as sinful as possible. If this feeling had not been rendered agreeable to man—why should he have improvised such an ideal and clung to it so long? As in the ancient world an incalculable strength of intellect and capacity for feeling was squandered in order to increase the joy of living through feastful systems of worship, so in the era of christianity an equally incalculable quantity of intellectual capacity has been sacrificed in another endeavor: that man should in every way feel himself sinful and thereby be moved, inspired, inspirited. To move, to inspire, to inspirit at any cost—is not this the freedom cry of an exhausted, over-ripe, over cultivated age? The circle of all the natural sensations had been gone through a hundred times: the soul had grown weary. Then the saints and the ascetics found a new order of ecstacies. They set themselves before the eyes of all not alone as models for imitation to many, but as fearful and yet delightful spectacles on the boundary line between this world and the next world, where in that period everyone thought he saw at one time rays of heavenly light, at another fearful, threatening tongues of flame. The eye of the saint, directed upon the fearful significance of the shortness of earthly life, upon the imminence of the last judgment, upon eternal life hereafter; this glowering eye in an emaciated body caused men, in the old time world, to tremble to the depths of their being. To look, to look away and shudder, to feel anew the fascination of the spectacle, to yield to it, sate oneself upon it until the soul trembled with ardor and fever—that was the last pleasure left to classical antiquity when its sensibilities had been blunted by the arena and the gladiatorial show.

142. To Sum Up All That Has Been Said: that condition of soul at which the saint or expectant saint is rejoiced is a combination of elements which we are all familiar with, except that under other influences than those of mere religious ideation they customarily arouse the censure of men in the same way that when combined with religion itself and regarded as the supreme attainment of sanctity, they are object of admiration and even of prayer—at least in more simple times. Very soon the saint turns upon himself that severity that is so closely allied to the instinct of domination at any price and which inspire even in the most solitary individual the sense of power. Soon his swollen sensitiveness of feeling breaks forth from the longing to restrain his passions within it and is transformed into a longing to master them as if they were wild steeds, the master impulse being ever that of a proud spirit; next he craves a complete cessation of all perturbing, fascinating feelings, a waking sleep, an enduring repose in the lap of a dull, animal, plant-like indolence. Next he seeks the battle and extinguishes it within himself because weariness and boredom confront him. He binds his self-deification with self-contempt. He delights in the wild tumult of his desires and the sharp pain of sin, in the very idea of being lost. He is able to play his very passions, for instance the desire to domineer, a trick so that he goes to the other

extreme of abject humiliation and subjection, so that his overwrought soul is without any restraint through this antithesis. And, finally, when indulgence in visions, in talks with the dead or with divine beings overcomes him, this is really but a form of gratification that he craves, perhaps a form of gratification in which all other gratifications are blended. Novalis, one of the authorities in matters of sanctity, because of his experience and instinct, betrays the whole secret with the utmost simplicity when he says: "It is remarkable that the close connection of gratification, religion and cruelty has not long ago made men aware of their inner relationship and common tendency."

143. Not What the Saint is but what he was in the eyes of the non-sanctified gives him his historical importance. Because there existed a delusion respecting the saint, his soul states being falsely viewed and his personality being sundered as much as possible from humanity as a something incomparable and supernatural, because of these things he attained the extraordinary with which he swayed the imaginations of whole nations and whole ages. Even he knew himself not for even he regarded his dispositions, passions and actions in accordance with a system of interpretation as artificial and exaggerated as the pneumatic interpretation of the bible. The distorted and diseased in his own nature with its blending of spiritual poverty, defective knowledge, ruined health, overwrought nerves, remained as hidden from his view as from the view of his beholders. He was neither a particularly good man nor a particularly bad man but he stood for something that was far above the human standard in wisdom and goodness. Faith in him sustained faith in the divine and miraculous, in a religious significance of all existence, in an impending day of judgment. In the last rays of the setting sun of the ancient world, which fell upon the christian peoples, the shadowy form of the saint attained enormous proportions—to such enormous proportions, indeed, that down even to our own age, which no longer believes in god, there are thinkers who believe in the saints.

144. It stands to reason that this sketch of the saint, made upon the model of the whole species, can be confronted with many opposing sketches that would create a more agreeable impression. There are certain exceptions among the species who distinguish themselves either by especial gentleness or especial humanity, and perhaps by the strength of their own personality. Others are in the highest degree fascinating because certain of their delusions shed a particular glow over their whole being, as is the case with the founder of christianity who took himself for the only begotten son of God and hence felt himself sinless; so that through his imagination—that should not be too harshly judged since the whole of antiquity swarmed with sons of god—he attained the same goal, the sense of complete sinlessness, complete irresponsibility, that can now be attained

by every individual through science.—In the same manner I have viewed the saints of India who occupy an intermediate station between the christian saints and the Greek philosophers and hence are not to be regarded as a pure type. Knowledge and science—as far as they existed—and superiority to the rest of mankind by logical discipline and training of the intellectual powers were insisted upon by the Buddhists as essential to sanctity, just as they were denounced by the christian world as the indications of sinfulness.

Footnotes:

[1] Ungerechtigkeit, literally wrongfulness, injustice, unrighteousness.

[2] Rangordnung: the meaning is "the problem of grasping the relative importance of things."

[3] Uebereinander: one over another.

[4] geworden.

[5] Pneumatic is here used in the sense of spiritual. Pneuma being the Greek word in the New Testament for the Holy Spirit.—Ed.

[6] Anderssein.

[7] "Wesen der Welt an sich."

[8] Glaube an die gefundene Wahrheit, as distinguished from faith in what is taken on trust as truth.

[9] Miterklingen: to sound simultaneously with.

[10] Kein Innen und Aussen in der Welt: the above translation may seem too literal but some dispute has arisen concerning the precise idea the author means to convey.

[11] Wir scheiden auch hier noch mit unserer Empfindung Bewegendes und Bewegtes.

[12] Glaube an Dinge.

[13] Monument more enduring than brass: Horace, Odes III:XXX.

[14] Cultur, culture, civilisation etc., but there is no exact English equivalent.

[15] Literally man-feeling or human outlook.

[16] Vorstellung: this word sometimes corresponds to the English word "idea", at others to "conception" or "notion."

[17] Sache, thing but not in the sense of Ding. Sache is of very indefinite application (res).

[18] den mit dessen "Freiheit" hat es eine eigene Bewandtniss.

[19] "Der moralische Mensch, sagt er, steht der intelligiblen (metaphysischen) Welt nicht näher, als der physische Mensch."

[20] als die Nachahmung der Natur in Begriffen, literally: "as the counterfeit of nature in (regard to) ideas."

[21] Wohl-wollen, kind feeling. It stands here for benevolence but not benevolence in the restricted sense of the word now prevailing.

[22]Then wherefore should you, who are mortal, outwear
Your soul with a profitless burden of care
Say, why should we not, flung at ease neath this pine,
Or a plane-tree's broad umbrage, quaff gaily our wine?
(Translation of Sir Theodore Martin.)

Part II

Translated By Paul V. Cohn

Translator's Introduction.

The publication of Human, all-too-Human extends over the period 1878-1880. Of the two divisions which constitute the Second Part, "Miscellaneous Maxims and Opinions" appeared in 1879, and "The Wanderer and his Shadow" in 1880, Nietzsche being then in his thirty-sixth year. The Preface was added in 1886. The whole book forms Nietzsche's first lengthy contribution to literature. His previous works comprise only the philological treatises, The Birth of Tragedy, and the essays on Strauss, Schopenhauer, and Wagner in Thoughts out of Season.

With the volumes of Human, all-too-Human Nietzsche appears for the first time in his true colours as philosopher. His purely scholarly publications, his essays in literary and musical criticism—especially the essay on Richard Wagner at Bayreuth—had, of course, foreshadowed his work as a thinker.

These efforts, however, had been mere fragments, from which hardly any one could observe that a new philosophical star had arisen on the horizon. But by 1878 the period of transition had definitely set in. Outwardly, the new departure is marked by Nietzsche's resignation in that year of his professorship at Bâle—a resignation due partly to ill-health, and partly to his conviction that his was a voice that should speak not merely to students of philology, but to all mankind.

Nietzsche himself characterises Human, all-too-Human as "the monument of a crisis." He might as fitly have called it the first-fruits of a new harvest. Now, for the first time, he practises the form which he was to make so peculiarly his own. We are told—and we may well believe—that the book came as a surprise even to his most intimate friends. Wagner had already seen how matters stood at the publication of the first part, and the gulf between the two probably widened on the appearance of the Second Part.

Several aphorisms are here, varying in length as in subject, and ranging over the whole human province—the emotions and aspirations, the religions and cultures and philosophies, the arts and literatures and politics of mankind. Equally varied is the range of style, the incisive epigram and the passage of pure poetry jostling each other on the same page. In this curious power of alternating between cynicism and lyricism, Nietzsche appears as the prose counterpart of Heine.

One or two of the aphorisms are of peculiar interest to English readers. The essay (as it may almost be called) on Sterne (p. 60, No. 113) does ample justice, if not more than justice, to that wayward genius. The allusion to Milton (p. 77, No. 150) will come as somewhat of a shock to English readers, especially to those who hold that in Milton Art triumphed over Puritanism. It should be remembered, however, that Nietzsche's view coincides with Goethe's. The dictum that Shakespeare's gold is to be valued for its quantity rather than its quality (p. 81, No. 162) also betrays a certain exclusiveness—a legacy from that eighteenth-century France which appealed so strongly to Nietzsche on its intellectual side. To Nietzsche, as to Voltaire, Shakespeare is after all "the great barbarian."

The title of the book may be explained from a phrase in Thus Spake Zarathustra: "Verily, even the greatest I found—all-too-human." The keynote of these volumes is indeed disillusion and destruction. Nor is this to be wondered at, for all men must sweep away the rubbish before they can build. Hence we find here little of the constructive philosophy of Nietzsche—so far as he had a constructive philosophy. The Superman appears but faintly, the doctrine of Eternal Recurrence not at all. For this very reason, Human, all-too-Human is perhaps the best starting-point for the study of Nietzsche. The difficulties in style and thought of the later work—difficulties that at times become well-nigh insuperable in Thus Spake Zarathustra—are here practically absent. The book may, in fact, almost be described as "popular," bearing the same relation to Nietzsche's later productions as Wagner's Tannhäuser and Lohengrin bear to the Ring.

The translator's thanks are due to Mr. Thomas Common for his careful revision of the manuscript and many valuable suggestions.

P. V. C.

Preface.

1. One should only speak where one cannot remain silent, and only speak of what one has conquered—the rest is all chatter, "literature," bad breeding. My writings speak only of my conquests, "I" am in them, with all that is hostile to me, ego ipsissimus, or, if a more haughty expression be permitted, ego ipsissimum. It may be guessed that I have many below me.... But first I always needed time, convalescence, distance, separation, before I felt the stirrings of a desire to flay, despoil, lay bare, "represent" (or whatever one likes to call it) for the additional knowledge of the world, something that I had lived through and outlived, something done or suffered. Hence all my writings,—with one exception, important, it is true,—must be ante-dated—they always tell of a "behind-me." Some even, like the first three Thoughts out of Season, must be thrown back before the period of creation and experience of a previously published book (The Birth of Tragedy in the case cited, as any one with subtle powers of observation and comparison could not fail to perceive). That wrathful outburst against the Germanism, smugness, and raggedness of speech of old David Strauss, the contents of the first Thought out of Season, gave a vent to feelings that had

inspired me long before, as a student, in the midst of German culture and cultured Philistinism (I claim the paternity of the now much used and misused phrase "cultured Philistinism"). What I said against the "historical disease" I said as one who had slowly and laboriously recovered from that disease, and who was not at all disposed to renounce "history" in the future because he had suffered from her in the past. When in the third Thought out of Season I gave expression to my reverence for my first and only teacher, the great Arthur Schopenhauer—I should now give it a far more personal and emphatic voice—I was for my part already in the throes of moral scepticism and dissolution, that is, as much concerned with the criticism as with the study of all pessimism down to the present day. I already did not believe in "a blessed thing," as the people say, not even in Schopenhauer. It was at this very period that an unpublished essay of mine, "On Truth and Falsehood in an Extra-Moral Sense," came into being. Even my ceremonial oration in honour of Richard Wagner, on the occasion of his triumphal celebration at Bayreuth in 1876—Bayreuth signifies the greatest triumph that an artist has ever won—a work that bears the strongest stamp of "individuality," was in the background an act of homage and gratitude to a bit of the past in me, to the fairest but most perilous calm of my sea-voyage ... and as a matter of fact a severance and a farewell. (Was Richard Wagner mistaken on this point? I do not think so. So long as we still love, we do not paint such pictures, we do not yet "examine," we do not place ourselves so far away as is essential for one who "examines." "Examining needs at least a secret antagonism, that of an opposite point of view," it is said on page 46 of the above-named work itself, with an insidious, melancholy application that was perhaps understood by few.) The composure that gave me the power to speak after many intervening years of solitude and abstinence, first came with the book, Human, All-too Human, to which this second preface and apologia[1] is dedicated. As a book for "free spirits" it shows some trace of that almost cheerful and inquisitive coldness of the psychologist, who has behind him many painful things that he keeps under him, and moreover establishes them for himself and fixes them firmly as with a needle-point. Is it to be wondered at that at such sharp, ticklish work blood flows now and again, that indeed the psychologist has blood on his fingers and not only on his fingers?

2. The Miscellaneous Maxims and Opinions were in the first place, like The Wanderer and His Shadow, published separately as continuations and appendices to the above-mentioned human, all-too human Book for Free Spirits: and at the same time, as a continuation and confirmation of an intellectual cure, consisting in a course of anti-romantic self-treatment, such as my instinct, which had always remained healthy, had itself discovered and prescribed against a

temporary attack of the most dangerous form of romantics. After a convalescence of six years I may well be permitted to collect these same writings and publish them as a second volume of Human, All-too Human. Perhaps, if surveyed together, they will more clearly and effectively teach their lesson—a lesson of health that may be recommended as a *disciplina voluntatis* to the more intellectual natures of the rising generation. Here speaks a pessimist who has often leaped out of his skin but has always returned into it, thus, a pessimist with goodwill towards pessimism—at all events a romanticist no longer. And has not a pessimist, who possesses this serpentine knack of changing his skin, the right to read a lecture to our pessimists of to-day, who are one and all still in the toils of romanticism? Or at least to show them how it is—done?

3. It was then, in fact, high time to bid farewell, and I soon received proof. Richard Wagner, who seemed all-conquering, but was in reality only a decayed and despairing romantic, suddenly collapsed, helpless and broken, before the Christian Cross.... Was there not a single German with eyes in his head and sympathy in his heart for this appalling spectacle? Was I the only one whom he caused—suffering? In any case, the unexpected event illumined for me in one lightning flash the place that I had abandoned, and also the horror that is felt by every one who is unconscious of a great danger until he has passed through it. As I went forward alone, I shuddered, and not long afterwards I was ill, or rather more than ill—weary: weary from my ceaseless disappointment about all that remained to make us modern men enthusiastic, at the thought of the power, work, hope, youth, love, flung to all the winds: weary from disgust at the effeminacy and undisciplined rhapsody of this romanticism, at the whole tissue of idealistic lies and softening of conscience, which here again had won the day over one of the bravest of men: last, and not least, weary from the bitterness of an inexorable suspicion—that after this disappointment I was doomed to mistrust more thoroughly, to despise more thoroughly, to be alone more thoroughly than ever before. My task—whither had it flown? Did it not look now as if my task were retreating from me and as if I should for a long future period have no more right to it? What was I to do to endure this most terrible privation?—I began by entirely forbidding myself all romantic music, that ambiguous, pompous, stifling art, which robs the mind of its sternness and its joyousness and provides a fertile soil for every kind of vague yearning and spongy sensuality. "Cave musicam" is even to-day my advice to all who are enough of men to cling to purity in matters of the intellect. Such music enervates, softens, feminises, its "eternal feminine" draws us—down![2] My first suspicion, my most immediate precaution, was directed against romantic music. If I hoped for anything at all from music, it was in the

expectation of the coming of a musician bold, subtle, malignant, southern, healthy enough to take an immortal revenge upon that other music.

4. Lonely now and miserably self-distrustful, I took sides, not without resentment, against myself and for everything that hurt me and was hard to me. Thus I once more found the way to that courageous pessimism that is the antithesis of all romantic fraud, and, as it seems to me to-day, the way to "myself," to my task. That hidden masterful Something, for which we long have no name until at last it shows itself as our task—that tyrant in us exacts a terrible price for every attempt that we make to escape him or give him the slip, for every premature act of self-constraint, for every reconciliation with those to whom we do not belong, for every activity, however reputable, which turns us aside from our main purpose, yes, even for every virtue that would fain protect us from the cruelty of our most individual responsibility. "Disease" is always the answer when we wish to have doubts of our rights to our own task, when we begin to make it easier for ourselves in any way. How strange and how terrible! It is our very alleviations for which we have to make the severest atonement! And if we want to return to health, we have no choice left—we must load ourselves more heavily than we were ever laden before.

5. It was then that I learnt the hermitical habit of speech acquired only by the most silent and suffering. I spoke without witnesses, or rather indifferent to the presence of witnesses, so as not to suffer from silence, I spoke of various things that did not concern me in a style that gave the impression that they did. Then, too, I learnt the art of showing myself cheerful, objective, inquisitive in the presence of all that is healthy and evil—is this, in an invalid, as it seems to me, his "good taste"? Nevertheless, a more subtle eye and sympathy will not miss what perhaps gives a charm to these writings—the fact that here speaks one who has suffered and abstained in such a way as if he had never suffered or abstained. Here equipoise, composure, even gratitude towards life shall be maintained, here rules a stern, proud, ever vigilant, ever susceptible will, which has undertaken the task of defending life against pain and snapping off all conclusions that are wont to grow like poisonous fungi from pain, disappointment, satiety, isolation and other morasses. Perhaps this gives our pessimists a hint to self-examination? For it was then that I hit upon the aphorism, "a sufferer has as yet no right to pessimism," and that I engaged in a tedious, patient campaign against the unscientific first principles of all romantic pessimism, which seeks to magnify and interpret individual, personal experiences into "general judgments," universal condemnations—it was then, in short, that I sighted a new world. Optimism for the sake of restitution, in order at some time to have the right to become a pessimist—do you understand that? Just as a physician transfers his patient to

totally strange surroundings, in order to displace him from his entire "past," his troubles, friends, letters, duties, stupid mistakes and painful memories, and teaches him to stretch out hands and senses towards new nourishment, a new sun, a new future: so I, as physician and invalid in one, forced myself into an utterly different and untried zone of the soul, and particularly into an absorbing journey to a strange land, a strange atmosphere, into a curiosity for all that was strange. A long process of roaming, seeking, changing followed, a distaste for fixity of any kind—a dislike for clumsy affirmation and negation: and at the same time a dietary and discipline which aimed at making it as easy as possible for the soul to fly high, and above all constantly to fly away. In fact a minimum of life, an unfettering from all coarser forms of sensuality, an independence in the midst of all marks of outward disfavour, together with the pride in being able to live in the midst of all this disfavour: a little cynicism perhaps, a little of the "tub of Diogenes," a good deal of whimsical happiness, whimsical gaiety, much calm, light, subtle folly, hidden enthusiasm—all this produced in the end a great spiritual strengthening, a growing joy and exuberance of health. Life itself rewards us for our tenacious will to life, for such a long war as I waged against the pessimistic weariness of life, even for every observant glance of our gratitude, glances that do not miss the smallest, most delicate, most fugitive gifts.... In the end we receive Life's great gifts, perhaps the greatest it can bestow—we regain our task.

6. Should my experience—the history of an illness and a convalescence, for it resulted in a convalescence—be only my personal experience? and merely just my "Human, All-too-human"? To-day I would fain believe the reverse, for I am becoming more and more confident that my books of travel were not penned for my sole benefit, as appeared for a time to be the case. May I, after six years of growing assurance, send them once more on a journey for an experiment?—May I commend them particularly to the ears and hearts of those who are afflicted with some sort of a "past," and have enough intellect left to suffer even intellectually from their past? But above all would I commend them to you whose burden is heaviest, you choice spirits, most encompassed with perils, most intellectual, most courageous, who must be the conscience of the modern soul and as such be versed in its science:[3] in whom is concentrated all of disease, poison or danger that can exist to-day: whose lot decrees that you must be more sick than any individual because you are not "mere individuals": whose consolation it is to know and, ah! to walk the path to a new health, a health of to-morrow and the day after: you men of destiny, triumphant, conquerors of time, the healthiest and the strongest, you good Europeans!

7. To express finally in a single formula my opposition to the romantic pessimism of the abstinent, the unfortunate, the conquered: there is a will to the tragic and to pessimism, which is a sign as much of the severity as of the strength of the intellect (taste, emotion, conscience). With this will in our hearts we do not fear, but we investigate ourselves the terrible and the problematical elements characteristic of all existence. Behind such a will stand courage and pride and the desire for a really great enemy. That was my pessimistic outlook from the first—a new outlook, methinks, an outlook that even at this day is new and strange? To this moment I hold to it firmly and (if it will be believed) not only for myself but occasionally against myself.... You would prefer to have that proved first? Well, what else does all this long preface—prove?

Sils-Maria, Upper Engadine,
September, 1886.

Part I. Miscellaneous Maxims And Opinions.

1. To the Disillusioned in Philosophy.—If you hitherto believed in the highest value of life and now find yourselves disillusioned, must you immediately get rid of life at the lowest possible price?

2. Overnice.—One can even become overnice as regards the clearness of concepts. How disgusted one is then at having truck with the half-clear, the hazy, the aspiring, the doubting! How ridiculous and yet not mirth-provoking is their eternal fluttering and straining without ever being able to fly or to grasp!

3. The Wooers of Reality.—He who realises at last how long and how thoroughly he has been befooled, embraces out of spite even the ugliest reality. So that in the long run of the world's history the best men have always been wooers of reality, for the best have always been longest and most thoroughly deceived.

4. Advance of Freethinking.—The difference between past and present freethinking cannot better be characterised than by that aphorism for the recognition and expression of which all the fearlessness of the eighteenth century was needed, and which even then, if measured by our modern view, sinks into an unconscious naïveté. I mean Voltaire's aphorism, "croyez-moi, mon ami, l'erreur aussi a son mérite."

5. A Hereditary Sin of Philosophers.—Philosophers have at all times appropriated and corrupted the maxims of censors of men (moralists), by taking them over without qualification and trying to prove as necessary what the moralists only meant as a rough indication or as a truth suited to their fellow-countrymen or fellow-townsmen for a single decade. Moreover, the philosophers thought that they were thereby raising themselves above the

moralists! Thus it will be found that the celebrated teachings of Schopenhauer as to the supremacy of the will over the intellect, of the immutability of character, the negativity of pleasure—all errors, in the sense in which he understands them—rest upon principles of popular wisdom enunciated by the moralists. Take the very word "will," which Schopenhauer twisted so as to become a common denotation of several human conditions and with which he filled a gap in the language (to his own great advantage, in so far as he was a moralist, for he became free to speak of the will as Pascal had spoken of it). In the hands of its creator, Schopenhauer's "will," through the philosophic craze for generalisation, already turned out to be a bane to knowledge. For this will was made into a poetic metaphor, when it was held that all things in nature possess will. Finally, that it might be applied to all kinds of disordered mysticism, the word was misused by a fraudulent convention. So now all our fashionable philosophers repeat it and seem to be perfectly certain that all things have a will and are in fact One Will. According to the description generally given of this All-One-Will, this is much as if one should positively try to have the stupid Devil for one's God.

6. Against Visionaries.—The visionary denies the truth to himself, the liar only to others.

7. Enmity to Light.—If we make it clear to any one that, strictly, he can never speak of truth, but only of probability and of its degrees, we generally discover, from the undisguised joy of our pupil, how greatly men prefer the uncertainty of their intellectual horizon, and how in their heart of hearts they hate truth because of its definiteness.—Is this due to a secret fear felt by all that the light of truth may at some time be turned too brightly upon themselves? To their wish to be of some consequence, and accordingly their concealment from the world of what they are? Or is it to be traced to their horror of the all-too brilliant light, to which their crepuscular, easily dazzled, bat-like souls are not accustomed, so that hate it they must?

8. Christian Scepticism.—Pilate, with his question, "What is Truth?" is now gleefully brought on the scene as an advocate of Christ, in order to cast suspicion on all that is known or knowable as being mere appearance, and to erect the Cross on the appalling background of the Impossibility of Knowledge.

9. "Natural Law," a Phrase of Superstition.—When you talk so delightedly of Nature acting according to law, you must either assume that all things in Nature follow their law from a voluntary obedience imposed by themselves—in which case you admire the morality of Nature: or you are enchanted with the idea of a creative mechanician, who has made a most cunning watch with human beings as accessory ornaments.—Necessity, through the expression, "conformity to law,"

then becomes more human and a coign of refuge in the last instance for mythological reveries.

10. Fallen Forfeit to History.—All misty philosophers and obscurers of the world, in other words all metaphysicians of coarse or refined texture are seized with eyeache, earache, and toothache when they begin to suspect that there is truth in the saying: "All philosophy has from now fallen forfeit to history." In view of their aches and pains we may pardon them for throwing stones and filth at him who talks like this, but this teaching may itself thereby become dirty and disreputable for a time and lose in effect.

11. The Pessimist of the Intellect.—He whose intellect is really free will think freely about the intellect itself, and will not shut his eyes to certain terrible aspects of its source and tendency. For this reason others will perhaps designate him the bitterest opponent of free thought and give him that dreadful, abusive name of "pessimist of the intellect": accustomed as they are to typify a man not by his strong point, his pre-eminent virtue, but by the quality that is most foreign to his nature.

12. The Metaphysicians' Knapsack.—To all who talk so boastfully of the scientific basis of their metaphysics it is best to make no reply. It is enough to tug at the bundle that they rather shyly keep hidden behind their backs. If one succeeds in lifting it, the results of that "scientific basis" come to light, to their great confusion: a dear little "God," a genteel immortality, perhaps a little spiritualism, and in any case a complicated mass of poor-sinners'-misery and pharisee-arrogance.

13. Occasional Harmfulness of Knowledge.—The utility involved in the unchecked investigation of knowledge is so constantly proved in a hundred different ways that one must remember to include in the bargain the subtler and rarer damage which individuals must suffer on that account. The chemist cannot avoid occasionally being poisoned or burnt at his experiments. What applies to the chemist, is true of the whole of our culture. This, it may be added, clearly shows that knowledge should provide itself with healing balsam against burns and should always have antidotes ready against poisons.

14. The Craving of the Philistine.—The Philistine thinks that his most urgent need is a purple patch or turban of metaphysics, nor will he let it slip. Yet he would look less ridiculous without this adornment.

15. Enthusiasts.—With all that enthusiasts say in favour of their gospel or their master they are defending themselves, however much they comport themselves as the judges and not the accused: because they are involuntarily reminded almost at every moment that they are exceptions and have to assert their legitimacy.

16. The Good Seduces to Life.—All good things, even all good books that are written against life, are strong means of attraction to life.

17. The Happiness of the Historian.—"When we hear the hair-splitting metaphysicians and prophets of the after-world speak, we others feel indeed that we are the 'poor in spirit,' but that ours is the heavenly kingdom of change, with spring and autumn, summer and winter, and theirs the after-world, with its grey, everlasting frosts and shadows." Thus soliloquised a man as he walked in the morning sunshine, a man who in his pursuit of history has constantly changed not only his mind but his heart. In contrast to the metaphysicians, he is happy to harbour in himself not an "immortal soul" but many mortal souls.

18. Three Varieties of Thinkers.—There are streaming, flowing, trickling mineral springs, and three corresponding varieties of thinkers. The layman values them by the volume of the water, the expert by the contents of the water—in other words, by the elements in them that are not water.

19. The Picture of Life.—The task of painting the picture of life, often as it has been attempted by poets and philosophers, is nevertheless irrational. Even in the hands of the greatest artist-thinkers, pictures and miniatures of one life only—their own—have come into being, and indeed no other result is possible. While in the process of developing, a thing that develops, cannot mirror itself as fixed and permanent, as a definite object.

20. Truth will have no Gods before it.—The belief in truth begins with the doubt of all truths in which one has previously believed.

21. Where Silence is Required.—If we speak of freethinking as of a highly dangerous journey over glaciers and frozen seas, we find that those who do not care to travel on this track are offended, as if they had been reproached with cowardice and weak knees. The difficult, which we find to be beyond our powers, must not even be mentioned in our presence.

22. Historia in Nuce.—The most serious parody I ever heard was this: "In the beginning was the nonsense, and the nonsense was with God, and the nonsense was God."[4]

23. Incurable.—The idealist is incorrigible: if he be thrown out of his Heaven, he makes himself a suitable ideal out of Hell. Disillusion him, and lo! he will embrace disillusionment with no less ardour than he recently embraced hope. In so far as his impulse belongs to the great incurable impulses of human nature, he can bring about tragic destinies and later become a subject for tragedy himself, for such tragedies as deal with the incurable, implacable, inevitable in the lot and character of man.

24. Applause Itself as the Continuation of the Play.—Sparkling eyes and an amiable smile are the tributes of applause paid to all the great comedy of world

and existence—but this applause is a comedy within a comedy, meant to tempt the other spectators to a plaudite amici.

25. Courage for Tedium.—He who has not the courage to allow himself and his work to be considered tedious, is certainly no intellect of the first rank, whether in the arts or in the sciences.—A scoffer, who happened for once in a way to be a thinker, might add, with a glance at the world and at history: "God did not possess this courage, for he wanted to make and he made all things so interesting."

022]

26. From the Most Intimate Experience of the Thinker.—Nothing is harder for a man than to conceive of an object impersonally, I mean to see in it an object and not a person. One may even ask whether it is possible for him to dispense for a single moment with the machinery of his instinct to create and construct a personality. After all, he associates with his thoughts, however abstract they may be, as with individuals, against whom he must fight or to whom he must attach himself, whom he must protect, support and nourish. Let us watch or listen to ourselves at the moment when we hear or discover a new idea. Perhaps it displeases us because it is so defiant and so autocratic, and we unconsciously ask ourselves whether we cannot place a contradiction of it by its side as an enemy, or fasten on to it a "perhaps" or a "sometimes": the mere little word "probably" gives us a feeling of satisfaction, for it shatters the oppressive tyranny of the unconditional. If, on the other hand, the new idea enters in gentle shape, sweetly patient and humble, and falling at once into the arms of contradiction, we put our autocracy to the test in another way. Can we not come to the aid of this weak creature, stroke it and feed it, give it strength and fulness, and truth and even unconditionality? Is it possible for us to show ourselves parental or chivalrous or compassionate towards our idea?—Then again, we see here a judgment and there a judgment, sundered from each other, never looking at or making any movement towards each other. So we are tickled by the thought, whether it be not here feasible to make a match, to draw a conclusion, with the anticipation that if a consequence follows this conclusion it is not only the two judgments united in wedlock but the matchmakers that will gain honour. If, however, we cannot acquire a hold upon that thought either on the path of defiance and ill-will or on that of good-will (if we hold it to be true)—then we submit to it and do homage to it as a leader and a prince, give it a chair of honour, and speak not of it without a flourish of trumpets: for we are bright in its brightness. Woe to him who tries to dim this brightness! Perhaps we ourselves one day grow suspicious of our idea. Then we, the indefatigable "king-makers" of the history of the intellect, cast it down from its throne and immediately exalt its adversary.

Surely if this be considered and thought out a little further, no one will speak of an "absolute impulse to knowledge"!

Why, then, does man prefer the true to the untrue, in this secret combat with thought-personalities, in this generally clandestine match-making of thoughts, constitution-founding of thoughts, child-rearing of thoughts, nursing and almsgiving of thoughts? For the same reason that he practises honesty in intercourse with real persons: now from habit, heredity, and training, originally because the true, like the fair and the just, is more expedient and more reputable than the untrue. For in the realm of thought it is difficult to assume a power and glory that are built on error or on falsehood. The feeling that such an edifice might at some time collapse is humiliating to the self-esteem of the architect—he is ashamed of the fragility of the material, and, as he considers himself more important than the rest of the world, he would fain construct nothing that is less durable than the rest of the world. In his longing for truth he embraces the belief in a personal immortality, the most arrogant and defiant idea that exists, closely allied as it is to the underlying thought, pereat mundus, dum ego salvus sim! His work has become his "ego," he transforms himself into the Imperishable with its universal challenge. It is his immeasurable pride that will only employ the best and hardest stones for the work—truths, or what he holds for such. Arrogance has always been justly called the "vice of the sage"; yet without this vice, fruitful in impulses, Truth and her status on earth would be in a parlous plight. In our propensity to fear our thoughts, concepts and words, and yet to honour ourselves in them, unconsciously to ascribe to them the power of rewarding, despising, praising, and blaming us, and so to associate with them as with free intellectual personalities, as with independent powers, as with our equals—herein lie the roots of the remarkable phenomenon which I have called "intellectual conscience." Thus something of the highest moral species has bloomed from a black root.

27. The Obscurantists.—The essential feature of the black art of obscurantism is not its intention of clouding the brain, but its attempt to darken the picture of the world and cloud our idea of existence. It often employs the method of thwarting all illumination of the intellect, but at times it uses the very opposite means, seeking by the highest refinement of the intellect to induce a satiety of the intellect's fruits. Hair-splitting metaphysicians, who pave the way for scepticism and by their excessive acumen provoke a distrust of acumen, are excellent instruments of the more subtle form of obscurantism.—Is it possible that even Kant may be applied to this purpose? Did he even intend something of the sort, for a time at least, to judge from his own notorious exposition: "to clear the way for belief by setting limitations to knowledge"?—Certainly he did not succeed, nor did his followers, on the wolf and fox tracks of this highly refined and dangerous

form of obscurantism—the most dangerous of all, for the black art here appears in the garb of light.

28. By what Kind of Philosophy Art is Corrupted.—When the mists of a metaphysical-mystical philosophy succeed in making all æsthetic phenomena opaque, it follows that these phenomena cannot be comparatively valued, inasmuch as each becomes individually inexplicable. But when once they cannot be compared for the sake of valuation, there arises an entire absence-of-criticism, a blind indulgence. From this source springs a continual diminution of the enjoyment of art (which is only distinguished from the crude satisfaction of a need by the highest refinement of taste and appreciation). The more taste diminishes, the more does the desire for art change and revert to a vulgar hunger, which the artist henceforth seeks to appease by ever coarser fare.

29. On Gethsemane.—The most painful thing a thinker can say to artists is: "Could ye not watch with me one hour?"

30. At the Loom.—There are many (artists and women, for instance) who work against the few that take a pleasure in untying the knot of things and unravelling their woof. The former always want to weave the woof together again and entangle it and so turn the conceived into the unconceived and if possible inconceivable. Whatever the result may be, the woof and knot always look rather untidy, because too many hands are working and tugging at them.

31. In the Desert of Science.—As the man of science proceeds on his modest and toilsome wanderings, which must often enough be journeys in the desert, he is confronted with those brilliant mirages known as "philosophic systems." With magic powers of deception they show him that the solution of all riddles and the most refreshing draught of true water of life are close at hand. His weary heart rejoices, and he well-nigh touches with his lips the goal of all scientific endurance and hardship, so that almost unconsciously he presses forward. Other natures stand still, as if spellbound by the beautiful illusion: the desert swallows them up, they become lost to science. Other natures, again, that have often experienced these subjective consolations, become very disheartened and curse the salty taste which these mirages leave behind in the mouth and from which springs a raging thirst—without one's having come one step nearer to any sort of a spring.

32. The So-called "Real Reality."—When the poet depicts the various callings—such as those of the warrior, the silk-weaver, the sailor—he feigns to know all these things thoroughly, to be an expert. Even in the exposition of human actions and destinies he behaves as if he had been present at the spinning of the whole web of existence. In so far he is an impostor. He practises his frauds on pure ignoramuses, and that is why he succeeds. They praise him for his deep, genuine knowledge, and lead him finally into the delusion that he really knows

as much as the individual experts and creators, yes, even as the great world-spinners themselves. In the end, the impostor becomes honest, and actually believes in his own sincerity. Emotional people say to his very face that he has the "higher" truth and sincerity—for they are weary of reality for the time being, and accept the poetic dream as a pleasant relaxation and a night's rest for head and heart. The visions of the dream now appear to them of more value, because, as has been said, they find them more beneficial, and mankind has always held that what is apparently of more value is more true, more real. All that is generally called reality, the poets, conscious of this power, proceed with intention to disparage and to distort into the uncertain, the illusory, the spurious, the impure, the sinful, sorrowful, and deceitful. They make use of all doubts about the limits of knowledge, of all sceptical excesses, in order to spread over everything the rumpled veil of uncertainty. For they desire that when this darkening process is complete their wizardry and soul-magic may be accepted without hesitation as the path to "true truth" and "real reality."

33. The Wish to be Just and the Wish to be a Judge.—Schopenhauer, whose profound understanding of what is human and all-too-human and original sense for facts was not a little impaired by the bright leopard-skin of his metaphysic (the skin must first be pulled off him if one wants to find the real moralist genius beneath)—Schopenhauer makes this admirable distinction, wherein he comes far nearer the mark than he would himself dare to admit: "Insight into the stern necessity of human actions is the boundary line that divides philosophic from other brains." He worked against that wonderful insight of which he was sometimes capable by the prejudice that he had in common with the moral man (not the moralist), a prejudice that he expresses quite guilelessly and devoutly as follows: "The ultimate and true explanation of the inner being of the entirety of things must of necessity be closely connected with that about the ethical significance of human actions." This connection is not "necessary" at all: such a connection must rather be rejected by that principle of the stern necessity of human actions, that is, the unconditioned non-freedom and non-responsibility of the will. Philosophic brains will accordingly be distinguished from others by their disbelief in the metaphysical significance of morality. This must create between the two kinds of brain a gulf of a depth and unbridgeableness of which the much-deplored gulf between "cultured" and "uncultured" scarcely gives a conception. It is true that many back doors, which the "philosophic brains," like Schopenhauer's own, have left for themselves, must be recognised as useless. None leads into the open, into the fresh air of the free will, but every door through which people had slipped hitherto showed behind it once more the gleaming brass wall of fate. For we are in a prison, and can only dream of

freedom, not make ourselves free. That the recognition of this fact cannot be resisted much longer is shown by the despairing and incredible postures and grimaces of those who still press against it and continue their wrestling-bout with it. Their attitude at present is something like this: "So no one is responsible for his actions? And all is full of guilt and the consciousness of guilt? But some one must be the sinner. If it is no longer possible or permissible to accuse and sentence the individual, the one poor wave in the inevitable rough-and-tumble of the waves of development—well, then, let this stormy sea, this development itself, be the sinner. Here is free will: this totality can be accused and sentenced, can atone and expiate. So let God be the sinner and man his redeemer. Let the world's history be guilt, expiation, and self-murder. Let the evil-doer be his own judge, the judge his own hangman." This Christianity strained to its limits—for what else is it?—is the last thrust in the fencing-match between the teaching of unconditioned morality and the teaching of unconditioned non-freedom. It would be quite horrible if it were anything more than a logical pose, a hideous grimace of the underlying thought, perhaps the death-convulsion of the heart that seeks a remedy in its despair, the heart to which delirium whispers: "Behold, thou art the lamb which taketh away the sin of God." This error lies not only in the feeling, "I am responsible," but just as much in the contradiction, "I am not responsible, but some one must be." That is simply not true. Hence the philosopher must say, like Christ, "Judge not," and the final distinction between the philosophic brains and the others would be that the former wish to be just and the latter wish to be judges.

34. Sacrifice.—You hold that sacrifice is the hallmark of moral action?—Just consider whether in every action that is done with deliberation, in the best as in the worst, there be not a sacrifice.

35. Against the "Triers of the Reins" of Morality.—One must know the best and the worst that a man is capable of in theory and in practice before one can judge how strong his moral nature is and can be. But this is an experiment that one can never carry out.

36. Serpent's Tooth.—Whether we have a serpent's tooth or not we cannot know before some one has set his heel upon our necks. A wife or a mother could say: until some one has put his heel upon the neck of our darling, our child.—Our character is determined more by the absence of certain experiences than by the experiences we have undergone.

37. Deception in Love.—We forget and purposely banish from our minds a good deal of our past. In other words, we wish our picture, that beams at us from the past, to belie us, to flatter our vanity—we are constantly engaged in this self-deception. And you who talk and boast so much of "self-oblivion in love," of

the "absorption of the ego in the other person"—you hold that this is something different? So you break the mirror, throw yourselves into another personality that you admire, and enjoy the new portrait of your ego, though calling it by the other person's name—and this whole proceeding is not to be thought self-deception, self-seeking, you marvellous beings?—It seems to me that those who hide something of themselves from themselves, or hide their whole selves from themselves, are alike committing a theft from the treasury of knowledge. It is clear, then, against what transgression the maxim "Know thyself" is a warning.

38. To the Denier of his Vanity.—He who denies his own vanity usually possesses it in so brutal a form that he instinctively shuts his eyes to avoid the necessity of despising himself.

39. Why the Stupid so often Become Malignant.—To those arguments of our adversary against which our head feels too weak our heart replies by throwing suspicion on the motives of his arguments.

40. The Art of Moral Exceptions.—An art that points out and glorifies the exceptional cases of morality—where the good becomes bad and the unjust just—should rarely be given a hearing: just as now and again we buy something from gipsies, with the fear that they are diverting to their own pockets much more than their mere profit from the purchase.

41. Enjoyment and Non-enjoyment of Poisons.—The only decisive argument that has always deterred men from drinking a poison is not that it is deadly, but that it has an unpleasant taste.

42. The World without Consciousness of Sin.—If men only committed such deeds as do not give rise to a bad conscience, the human world would still look bad and rascally enough, but not so sickly and pitiable as at present.—Enough wicked men without conscience have existed at all times, and many good honest folk lack the feeling of pleasure in a good conscience.

43. The Conscientious.—It is more convenient to follow one's conscience than one's intelligence, for at every failure conscience finds an excuse and an encouragement in itself. That is why there are so many conscientious and so few intelligent people.

44. Opposite Means of Avoiding Bitterness.—One temperament finds it useful to be able to give vent to its disgust in words, being made sweeter by speech. Another reaches its full bitterness only by speaking out: it is more advisable for it to have to gulp down something—the restraint that men of this stamp place upon themselves in the presence of enemies and superiors improves their character and prevents it from becoming too acrid and sour.

45. Not to be Too Dejected.—To get bed-sores is unpleasant, but no proof against the merits of the cure that prescribes that you should take to your bed.

Men who have long lived outside themselves, and have at last devoted themselves to the inward philosophic life, know that one can also get sores of character and intellect. This, again, is on the whole no argument against the chosen way of life, but necessitates a few small exceptions and apparent relapses.

46. The Human "Thing in Itself."—The most vulnerable and yet most unconquerable of things is human vanity: nay, through being wounded its strength increases and can grow to giant proportions.

47. The Farce of Many Industrious Persons.—By an excess of effort they win leisure for themselves, and then they can do nothing with it but count the hours until the tale is ended.

48. The Possession of Joy Abounding.—He that has joy abounding must be a good man, but perhaps he is not the cleverest of men, although he has reached the very goal towards which the cleverest man is striving with all his cleverness.

49. In the Mirror of Nature.—Is not a man fairly well described, when we are told that he likes to walk between tall fields of golden corn: that he prefers the forest and flower colours of sere and chilly autumn to all others, because they point to something more beautiful than Nature has ever attained: that he feels as much at home under big broad-leaved walnut trees as among his nearest kinsfolk: that in the mountains his greatest joy is to come across those tiny distant lakes from which the very eyes of solitude seem to peer at him: that he loves that grey calm of the misty twilight that steals along the windows on autumn and early winter evenings and shuts out all soulless sounds as with velvet curtains: that in unhewn stones he recognises the last remaining traces of the primeval age, eager for speech, and honours them from childhood upwards: that, lastly, the sea with its shifting serpent skin and wild-beast beauty is, and remains to him, unfamiliar?—Yes, something of the man is described herewith, but the mirror of Nature does not say that the same man, with (and not even "in spite of") all his idyllic sensibilities, might be disagreeable, stingy, and conceited. Horace, who was a good judge of such matters, in his famous beatus ille qui procul negotiis puts the tenderest feeling for country life into the mouth of a Roman money-lender.

50. Power without Victory.—The strongest cognition (that of the complete non-freedom of the human will) is yet the poorest in results, for it has always had the mightiest of opponents—human vanity.

51. Pleasure and Error.—A beneficial influence on friends is exerted by one man unconsciously, through his nature; by another consciously, through isolated actions. Although the former nature is held to be the higher, the latter alone is allied to good conscience and pleasure—the pleasure in justification by good works, which rests upon a belief in the volitional character of our good and evil doing—that is to say, upon a mistake.

52. The Folly of Committing Injustice.—The injustice we have inflicted ourselves is far harder to bear than the injustice inflicted upon us by others (not always from moral grounds, be it observed). After all, the doer is always the sufferer—that is, if he be capable of feeling the sting of conscience or of perceiving that by his action he has armed society against himself and cut himself off. For this reason we should beware still more of doing than of suffering injustice, for the sake of our own inward happiness—so as not to lose our feeling of well-being—quite apart from any consideration of the precepts of religion and morality. For in suffering injustice we have the consolation of a good conscience, of hope and of revenge, together with the sympathy and applause of the just, nay of the whole of society, which is afraid of the evil-doer. Not a few are skilled in the impure self-deception that enables them to transform every injustice of their own into an injustice inflicted upon them from without, and to reserve for their own acts the exceptional right to the plea of self-defence. Their object, of course, is to make their own burden lighter.

53. Envy with or without a Mouthpiece.—Ordinary envy is wont to cackle when the envied hen has laid an egg, thereby relieving itself and becoming milder. But there is a yet deeper envy that in such a case becomes dead silent, desiring that every mouth should be sealed and always more and more angry because this desire is not gratified. Silent envy grows in silence.

54. Anger as a Spy.—Anger exhausts the soul and brings its very dregs to light. Hence, if we know no other means of gaining certainty, we must understand how to arouse anger in our dependents and adversaries, in order to learn what is really done and thought to our detriment.

55. Defence Morally more Difficult than Attack.—The true heroic deed and masterpiece of the good man does not lie in attacking opinions and continuing to love their propounders, but in the far harder task of defending his own position without causing or intending to cause bitter heartburns to his opponent. The sword of attack is honest and broad, the sword of defence usually runs out to a needle point.

56. Honest towards Honesty.—One who is openly honest towards himself ends by being rather conceited about this honesty. He knows only too well why he is honest—for the same reason that another man prefers outward show and hypocrisy.

57. Coals of Fire.—The heaping of coals of fire on another's head is generally misunderstood and falls flat, because the other knows himself to be just as much in the right, and on his side too has thought of collecting coals.

58. Dangerous Books.—A man says: "Judging from my own case, I find that this book is harmful." Let him but wait, and perhaps one day he will confess that the

book did him a great service by thrusting forward and bringing to light the hidden disease of his soul.—Altered opinions alter not at all (or very little) the character of a man: but they illuminate individual facets of his personality, which hitherto, in another constellation of opinions, had remained dark and unrecognisable.

59. Simulated Pity.—We simulate pity when we wish to show ourselves superior to the feeling of animosity, but generally in vain. This point is not noticed without a considerable enhancement of that feeling of animosity.

60. Open Contradiction often Conciliatory.—At the moment when a man openly makes known his difference of opinion from a well-known party leader, the whole world thinks that he must be angry with the latter. Sometimes, however, he is just on the point of ceasing to be angry with him. He ventures to put himself on the same plane as his opponent, and is free from the tortures of suppressed envy.

61. Seeing our Light Shining.—In the darkest hour of depression, sickness, and guilt, we are still glad to see others taking a light from us and making use of us as of the disk of the moon. By this roundabout route we derive some light from our own illuminating faculty.

62. Fellowship in Joy.[5]—The snake that stings us means to hurt us and rejoices in so doing: the lowest animal can picture to itself the pain of others. But to picture to oneself the joy of others and to rejoice thereat is the highest privilege of the highest animals, and again, amongst them, is the property only of the most select specimens—accordingly a rare "human thing." Hence there have been philosophers who denied fellowship in joy.

63. Supplementary Pregnancy.—Those who have arrived at works and deeds are in an obscure way, they know not how, all the more pregnant with them, as if to prove supplementarily that these are their children and not those of chance.

64. Hard-hearted from Vanity.—Just as justice is so often a cloak for weakness, so men who are fairly intelligent, but weak, sometimes attempt dissimulation from ambitious motives and purposely show themselves unjust and hard, in order to leave behind them the impression of strength.

65. Humiliation.—If in a large sack of profit we find a single grain of humiliation we still make a wry face even at our good luck.

66. Extreme Herostratism.[6]—There might be Herostratuses who set fire to their own temple, in which their images are honoured.

67. A World of Diminutives.—The fact that all that is weak and in need of help appeals to the heart induces in us the habit of designating by diminutive and softening terms all that appeals to our hearts—and accordingly making such things weak and clinging to our imaginations.

68. The Bad Characteristic of Sympathy.—Sympathy has a peculiar impudence for its companion. For, wishing to help at all costs, sympathy is in no perplexity either as to the means of assistance or as to the nature and cause of the disease, and goes on courageously administering all its quack medicines to restore the health and reputation of the patient.

69. Importunacy.—There is even an importunacy in relation to works, and the act of associating oneself from early youth on an intimate footing with the illustrious works of all times evinces an entire absence of shame.—Others are only importunate from ignorance, not knowing with whom they have to do—for instance classical scholars young and old in relation to the works of the Greeks.

70. The Will is Ashamed of the Intellect.—In all coolness we make reasonable plans against our passions. But we make the most serious mistake in this connection in being often ashamed, when the design has to be carried out, of the coolness and calculation with which we conceived it. So we do just the unreasonable thing, from that sort of defiant magnanimity that every passion involves.

71. Why the Sceptics Offend Morality.—He who takes his morality solemnly and seriously is enraged against the sceptics in the domain of morals. For where he lavishes all his force, he wishes others to marvel but not to investigate and doubt. Then there are natures whose last shred of morality is just the belief in morals. They behave in the same way towards sceptics, if possible still more passionately.

72. Shyness.—All moralists are shy, because they know they are confounded with spies and traitors, so soon as their penchant is noticed. Besides, they are generally conscious of being impotent in action, for in the midst of work the motives of their activity almost withdraw their attention from the work.

73. A Danger to Universal Morality.—People who are at the same time noble and honest come to deify every devilry that brings out their honesty, and to suspend for a time the balance of their moral judgment.

74. The Saddest Error.—It is an unpardonable offence when one discovers that where one was convinced of being loved, one is only regarded as a household utensil and decoration, whereby the master of the house can find an outlet for his vanity before his guests.

75. Love and Duality.—What else is love but understanding and rejoicing that another lives, works, and feels in a different and opposite way to ourselves? That love may be able to bridge over the contrasts by joys, we must not remove or deny those contrasts. Even self-love presupposes an irreconcileable duality (or plurality) in one person.

76. Signs from Dreams.—What one sometimes does not know and feel accurately in waking hours—whether one has a good or a bad conscience as regards some person—is revealed completely and unambiguously by dreams.

77. Debauchery.—Not joy but joylessness is the mother of debauchery.

78. Reward and Punishment.—No one accuses without an underlying notion of punishment and revenge, even when he accuses his fate or himself. All complaint is accusation, all self-congratulation is praise. Whether we do one or the other, we always make some one responsible.

79. Doubly Unjust.—We sometimes advance truth by a twofold injustice: when we see and represent consecutively the two sides of a case which we are not in a position to see together, but in such a way that every time we mistake or deny the other side, fancying that what we see is the whole truth.

80. Mistrust.—Self-mistrust does not always proceed uncertainly and shyly, but sometimes in a furious rage, having worked itself into a frenzy in order not to tremble.

81. Philosophy of Parvenus.—If you want to be a personality you must even hold your shadow in honour.

82. Knowing how to Wash Oneself Clean.—We must know how to emerge cleaner from unclean conditions, and, if necessary, how to wash ourselves even with dirty water.

83. Letting Yourself Go.—The more you let yourself go, the less others let you go.

84. The Innocent Rogue.—There is a slow, gradual path to vice and rascality of every description. In the end, the traveller is quite abandoned by the insect-swarms of a bad conscience, and although a thorough scoundrel he walks in innocence.

85. Making Plans.—Making plans and conceiving projects involves many agreeable sentiments. He that had the strength to be nothing but a contriver of plans all his life would be a happy man. But one must occasionally have a rest from this activity by carrying a plan into execution, and then comes anger and sobriety.

86. Wherewith We See the Ideal.—Every efficient man is blocked by his efficiency and cannot look out freely from its prison. Had he not also a goodly share of imperfection, he could, by reason of his virtue, never arrive at an intellectual or moral freedom. Our shortcomings are the eyes with which we see the ideal.

87. Dishonest Praise.—Dishonest praise causes many more twinges of conscience than dishonest blame, probably only because we have exposed our

capacity for judgment far more completely through excessive praise than through excessive and unjust blame.

88. How One Dies is Indifferent.—The whole way in which a man thinks of death during the prime of his life and strength is very expressive and significant for what we call his character. But the hour of death itself, his behaviour on the death-bed, is almost indifferent. The exhaustion of waning life, especially when old people die, the irregular or insufficient nourishment of the brain during this last period, the occasionally violent pain, the novel and untried nature of the whole position, and only too often the ebb and flow of superstitious impressions and fears, as if dying were of much consequence and meant the crossing of bridges of the most terrible kind—all this forbids our using death as a testimony concerning the living. Nor is it true that the dying man is generally more honest than the living. On the contrary, through the solemn attitude of the bystanders, the repressed or flowing streams of tears and emotions, every one is inveigled into a comedy of vanity, now conscious, now unconscious. The serious way in which every dying man is treated must have been to many a poor despised devil the highest joy of his whole life and a sort of compensation and repayment for many privations.

89. Morality and its Sacrifice.—The origin of morality may be traced to two ideas: "The community is of more value than the individual," and "The permanent interest is to be preferred to the temporary." The conclusion drawn is that the permanent interest of the community is unconditionally to be set above the temporary interest of the individual, especially his momentary well-being, but also his permanent interest and even the prolongation of his existence. Even if the individual suffers by an arrangement that suits the mass, even if he is depressed and ruined by it, morality must be maintained and the victim brought to the sacrifice. Such a trend of thought arises, however, only in those who are not the victims—for in the victim's case it enforces the claim that the individual might be worth more than the many, and that the present enjoyment, the "moment in paradise,"[7] should perhaps be rated higher than a tame succession of untroubled or comfortable circumstances. But the philosophy of the sacrificial victim always finds voice too late, and so victory remains with morals and morality: which are really nothing more than the sentiment for the whole concept of morals under which one lives and has been reared—and reared not as an individual but as a member of the whole, as a cipher in a majority. Hence it constantly happens that the individual makes himself into a majority by means of his morality.

90. The Good and the Good Conscience.—You hold that all good things have at all times had a good conscience? Science, which is certainly a very good thing,

has come into the world without such a conscience and quite free from all pathos, rather clandestinely, by roundabout ways, walking with shrouded or masked face like a sinner, and always with the feeling at least of being a smuggler. Good conscience has bad conscience for its stepping-stone, not for its opposite. For all that is good has at one time been new and consequently strange, against morals, immoral, and has gnawed like a worm at the heart of the fortunate discoverer.

91. Success Sanctifies the Intentions.—We should not shrink from treading the road to a virtue, even when we see clearly that nothing but egotism, and accordingly utility, personal comfort, fear, considerations of health, reputation, or glory, are the impelling motives. These motives are styled ignoble and selfish. Very well, but if they stimulate us to some virtue—for example, self-denial, dutifulness, order, thrift, measure, and moderation—let us listen to them, whatever their epithets may be! For if we reach the goal to which they summon us, then the virtue we have attained, by means of the pure air it makes us breathe and the spiritual well-being it communicates, ennobles the remoter impulses of our action, and afterwards we no longer perform those actions from the same coarse motives that inspired us before.—Education should therefore force the virtues on the pupil, as far as possible, according to his disposition. Then virtue, the sunshine and summer atmosphere of the soul, can contribute her own share of work and add mellowness and sweetness.

92. Dabblers in Christianity, not Christians.—So that is your Christianity!—To annoy humanity you praise "God and His Saints," and again when you want to praise humanity you go so far that God and His Saints must be annoyed.—I wish you would at least learn Christian manners, as you are so deficient in the civility of the Christian heart.

93. The Religious and Irreligious Impression of Nature.—A true believer must be to us an object of veneration, but the same holds good of a true, sincere, convinced unbeliever. With men of the latter stamp we are near to the high mountains where mighty rivers have their source, and with believers we are under vigorous, shady, restful trees.

94. Judicial Murder.—The two greatest judicial murders[8] in the world's history are, to speak without exaggeration, concealed and well-concealed suicide. In both cases a man willed to die, and in both cases he let his breast be pierced by the sword in the hand of human injustice.

95. "Love."—The finest artistic conception wherein Christianity had the advantage over other religious systems lay in one word—Love. Hence it became the lyric religion (whereas in its two other creations Semitism bestowed heroico-epical religions upon the world). In the word "love" there is so much

meaning, so much that stimulates and appeals to memory and hope, that even the meanest intelligence and the coldest heart feel some glimmering of its sense. The cleverest woman and the lowest man think of the comparatively unselfish moments of their whole life, even if with them Eros never soared high: and the vast number of beings who miss love from their parents or children or sweethearts, especially those whose sexual instincts have been refined away, have found their heart's desire in Christianity.

96. The Fulfilment of Christianity.—In Christianity there is also an Epicurean trend of thought, starting from the idea that God can only demand of man, his creation and his image, what it is possible for man to fulfil, and accordingly that Christian virtue and perfection are attainable and often attained. Now, for instance, the belief in loving one's enemies—even if it is only a belief or fancy, and by no means a psychological reality (a real love)—gives unalloyed happiness, so long as it is genuinely believed. (As to the reason of this, psychologist and Christian might well differ.) Hence earthly life, through the belief, I mean the fancy, that it satisfies not only the injunction to love our enemies, but all the other injunctions of Christianity, and that it has really assimilated and embodied in itself the Divine perfection according to the command, "Be perfect as your Father in heaven is perfect," might actually become a holy life. Thus error can make Christ's promise come true.

97. Of the Future of Christianity.—We may be allowed to form a conjecture as to the disappearance of Christianity and as to the places where it will be the slowest to retreat, if we consider where and for what reasons Protestantism spread with such startling rapidity. As is well known, Protestantism promised to do far more cheaply all that the old Church did, without costly masses, pilgrimages, and priestly pomp and circumstance. It spread particularly among the Northern nations, which were not so deeply rooted as those of the South in the old Church's symbolism and love of ritual. In the South the more powerful pagan religion survived in Christianity, whereas in the North Christianity meant an opposition to and a break with the old-time creed, and hence was from the first more thoughtful and less sensual, but for that very reason, in times of peril, more fanatical and more obstinate. If from the standpoint of thought we succeed in uprooting Christianity, we can at once know the point where it will begin to disappear—the very point at which it will be most stubborn in defence. In other places it will bend but not break, lose its leaves but burst into leaf afresh, because the senses, and not thought, have gone over to its side. But it is the senses that maintain the belief that with all its expensive outlay the Church is more cheaply and conveniently managed than under the stern conditions of work and wages. Yet what does one hold leisure (or semi-idleness) to be worth, when once one has

become accustomed to it? The senses plead against a dechristianised world, saying that there would be too much work to do in it and an insufficient supply of leisure. They take the part of magic—that is, they let God work himself (oremus nos, Deus laboret).

98. Theatricality and Honesty of Unbelievers.—There is no book that contains in such abundance or expresses so faithfully all that man occasionally finds salutary—ecstatic inward happiness, ready for sacrifice or death in the belief in and contemplation of his truth—as the book that tells of Christ. From that book a clever man may learn all the means whereby a book can be made into a world-book, a vade-mecum for all, and especially that master-means of representing everything as discovered, nothing as future and uncertain. All influential books try to leave the same impression, as if the widest intellectual horizon were circumscribed here and as if about the sun that shines here every constellation visible at present or in the future must revolve.—Must not then all purely scientific books be poor in influence on the same grounds as such books are rich in influence? Is not the book fated to live humble and among humble folk, in order to be crucified in the end and never resurrected? In relation to what the religious inform us of their "knowledge" and their "holy spirit," are not all upright men of science "poor in spirit"? Can any religion demand more self-denial and draw the selfish out of themselves more inexorably than science?—This and similar things we may say, in any case with a certain theatricality, when we have to defend ourselves against believers, for it is impossible to conduct a defence without a certain amount of theatricality. But between ourselves our language must be more honest, and we employ a freedom that those believers are not even allowed, in their own interests, to understand. Away, then, with the monastic cowl of self-denial, with the appearance of humility! Much more and much better—so rings our truth! If science were not linked with the pleasure of knowledge, the utility of the thing known, what should we care for science? If a little faith, love, and hope did not lead our souls to knowledge, what would attract us to science? And if in science the ego means nothing, still the inventive, happy ego, every upright and industrious ego, means a great deal in the republic of the men of science. The homage of those who pay homage, the joy of those whom we wish well or honour, in some cases glory and a fair share of immortality, is the personal reward for every suppression of personality: to say nothing here of meaner views and rewards, although it is just on this account that the majority have sworn and always continue to swear fidelity to the laws of the republic and of science. If we had not remained in some degree unscientific, what would science matter to us? Taking everything together and speaking in plain language: "To a purely knowing being knowledge would

be indifferent."—Not the quality but the quantity of faith and devoutness distinguishes us from the pious, the believers. We are content with less. But should one of them cry out to us: "Be content and show yourselves contented!" we could easily answer: "As a matter of fact, we do not belong to the most discontented class. But you, if your faith makes you happy, show yourselves to be happy. Your faces have always done more harm to your faith than our reasons! If that glad message of your Bible were written in your faces, you would not need to demand belief in the authority of that book in such stiff-necked fashion. Your words, your actions should continually make the Bible superfluous—in fact, through you a new Bible should continually come into being. As it is, your apologia for Christianity is rooted in your unchristianity, and with your defence you write your own condemnation. If you, however, should wish to emerge from your dissatisfaction with Christianity, you should ponder over the experience of two thousand years, which, clothed in the modest form of a question, may be voiced as follows: 'If Christ really intended to redeem the world, may he not be said to have failed?' "

99. The Poet as Guide to the Future.—All the surplus poetical force that still exists in modern humanity, but is not used under our conditions of life, should (without any deduction) be devoted to a definite goal—not to depicting the present nor to reviving and summarising the past, but to pointing the way to the future. Nor should this be so done as if the poet, like an imaginative political economist, had to anticipate a more favourable national and social state of things and picture their realisation. Rather will he, just as the earlier poets portrayed the images of the Gods, portray the fair images of men. He will divine those cases where, in the midst of our modern world and reality (which will not be shirked or repudiated in the usual poetic fashion), a great, noble soul is still possible, where it may be embodied in harmonious, equable conditions, where it may become permanent, visible, and representative of a type, and so, by the stimulus to imitation and envy, help to create the future. The poems of such a poet would be distinguished by appearing secluded and protected from the heated atmosphere of the passions. The irremediable failure, the shattering of all the strings of the human instrument, the scornful laughter and gnashing of teeth, and all tragedy and comedy in the usual old sense, would appear by the side of this new art as mere archaic lumber, a blurring of the outlines of the world-picture. Strength, kindness, gentleness, purity, and an unsought, innate moderation in the personalities and their action: a levelled soil, giving rest and pleasure to the foot: a shining heaven mirrored in faces and events: science and art welded into a new unity: the mind living together with her sister, the soul, without arrogance or jealousy, and enticing from contrasts the grace of

seriousness, not the impatience of discord—all this would be the general environment, the background on which the delicate differences of the embodied ideals would make the real picture, that of ever-growing human majesty. Many roads to this poetry of the future start from Goethe, but the quest needs good pathfinders and above all a far greater strength than is possessed by modern poets, who unscrupulously represent the half-animal and the immaturity and intemperance that are mistaken by them for power and naturalness.

100. The Muse as Penthesilea.[9]—"Better to rot than to be a woman without charm." When once the Muse thinks thus, the end of her art is again at hand. But it can be a tragic and also a comic finale.

101. The Circuitous Path to the Beautiful.—If the beautiful is to be identified with that which gives pleasure—and thus sang the Muses once—the useful is often the necessary circuitous path to the beautiful, and has a perfect right to spurn the short-sighted censure of men who live for the moment, who will not wait, and who think that they can reach all good things without ever taking a circuitous path.

102. An Excuse for many a Transgression.—The ceaseless desire to create, the eternal looking outward of the artist, hinders him from becoming better and more beautiful as a personality: unless his craving for glory be great enough to compel him to exhibit in his relations with other men a growth corresponding to the growing beauty and greatness of his works. In any case he has but a limited measure of strength, and how could the proportion of strength that he spends on himself be of any benefit to his work—or vice versa?

103. Satisfying the Best People.—If we have satisfied the best people of our time with our art, it is a sign that we shall not satisfy the best people of the succeeding period. We have indeed "lived for all time," and the applause of the best people ensures our fame.[10]

104. Of One Substance.—If we are of one substance with a book or a work of art, we think in our heart of hearts that it must be excellent, and are offended if others find it ugly, over-spiced, or pretentious.

105. Speech and Emotion.—That speech is not given to us to communicate our emotions may be seen from the fact that all simple men are ashamed to seek for words to express their deeper feelings. These feelings are expressed only in actions, and even here such men blush if others seem to divine their motives. After all, among poets, to whom God generally denies this shame, the more noble are more monosyllabic in the language of emotion, and evince a certain constraint: whereas the real poets of emotion are for the most part shameless in practical life.

106. A Mistake about a Privation.—He that has not for a long time been completely weaned from an art, and is still always at home in it, has no idea how small a privation it is to live without that art.

107. Three-quarter Strength.—A work that is meant to give an impression of health should be produced with three-quarters, at the most, of the strength of its creator. If he has gone to his farthest limit, the work excites the observer and disconcerts him by its tension. All good things have something lazy about them and lie like cows in the meadow.

108. Refusing to have Hunger as a Guest.—As refined fare serves a hungry man as well as and no better than coarser food, the more pretentious artist will not dream of inviting the hungry man to his meal.

109. Living without Art and Wine.—It is with works of art as with wine—it is better if one can do without both and keep to water, and if from the inner fire and inner sweetness of the soul the water spontaneously changes again into wine.

110. The Pirate-Genius.—The pirate-genius in art, who even knows how to deceive subtle minds, arises when some one unscrupulously and from youth upwards regards all good things, that are not protected by law, as the property of a particular person, as his legitimate spoil. Now all the good things of past ages and masters lie free around us, hedged about and protected by the reverential awe of the few who know them. To these few our robber-genius, by the force of his impudence, bids defiance and accumulates for himself a wealth that once more calls forth homage and awe.

111. To the Poets of Great Towns.—In the gardens of modern poetry it will clearly be observed that the sewers of great towns are too near. With the fragrance of flowers is mingled something that betrays abomination and putrescence. With pain I ask: "Must you poets always request wit and dirt to stand godfather, when an innocent and beautiful sensation has to be christened by you? Are you obliged to dress your noble goddess in a hood of devilry and caricature? But whence this necessity, this obligation?" The reason is—because you live too near the sewers.

112. Of the Salt of Speech.—No one has ever explained why the Greek writers, having at command such an unparalleled wealth and power of language, made so sparing a use of their resources that every post-classical Greek book appears by comparison crude, over-coloured, and extravagant. It is said that towards the North Polar ice and in the hottest countries salt is becoming less and less used, whereas on the other hand the dwellers on the plains and by the coast in the more temperate zones use salt in great abundance. Is it possible that the Greeks from a twofold reason—because their intellect was colder and clearer but their fundamental passionate nature far more tropical than ours—did not need salt and spice to the same extent that we do?

113. The Freest Writer.—In a book for free spirits one cannot avoid mention of Laurence Sterne, the man whom Goethe honoured as the freest spirit of his century. May he be satisfied with the honour of being called the freest writer of all times, in comparison with whom all others appear stiff, square-toed, intolerant, and downright boorish! In his case we should not speak of the clear and rounded but of "the endless melody"—if by this phrase we arrive at a name for an artistic style in which the definite form is continually broken, thrust aside and transferred to the realm of the indefinite, so that it signifies one and the other at the same time. Sterne is the great master of double entendre, this phrase being naturally used in a far wider sense than is commonly done when one applies it to sexual relations. We may give up for lost the reader who always wants to know exactly what Sterne thinks about a matter, and whether he be making a serious or a smiling face (for he can do both with one wrinkling of his features; he can be and even wishes to be right and wrong at the same moment, to interweave profundity and farce). His digressions are at once continuations and further developments of the story, his maxims contain a satire on all that is sententious, his dislike of seriousness is bound up with a disposition to take no matter merely externally and on the surface. So in the proper reader he arouses a feeling of uncertainty whether he be walking, lying, or standing, a feeling most closely akin to that of floating in the air. He, the most versatile of writers, communicates something of this versatility to his reader. Yes, Sterne unexpectedly changes the parts, and is often as much reader as author, his book being like a play within a play, a theatre audience before another theatre audience. We must surrender at discretion to the mood of Sterne, although we can always expect it to be gracious. It is strangely instructive to see how so great a writer as Diderot has affected this double entendre of Sterne's—to be equally ambiguous throughout is just the Sternian super-humour. Did Diderot imitate, admire, ridicule, or parody Sterne in his Jacques le Fataliste? One cannot be exactly certain, and this uncertainty was perhaps intended by the author. This very doubt makes the French unjust to the work of one of their first masters, one who need not be ashamed of comparison with any of the ancients or moderns. For humour (and especially for this humorous attitude towards humour itself) the French are too serious. Is it necessary to add that of all great authors Sterne is the worst model, in fact the inimitable author, and that even Diderot had to pay for his daring? What the worthy Frenchmen and before them some Greeks and Romans aimed at and attained in prose is the very opposite of what Sterne aims at and attains. He raises himself as a masterly exception above all that artists in writing demand of themselves—propriety, reserve, character, steadfastness of purpose, comprehensiveness, perspicuity, good deportment in gait and feature.

Unfortunately Sterne the man seems to have been only too closely related to Sterne the writer. His squirrel-soul sprang with insatiable unrest from branch to branch; he knew what lies between sublimity and rascality; he had sat on every seat, always with unabashed watery eyes and mobile play of feature. He was—if language does not revolt from such a combination—of a hard-hearted kindness, and in the midst of the joys of a grotesque and even corrupt imagination he showed the bashful grace of innocence. Such a carnal and spiritual hermaphroditism, such untrammelled wit penetrating into every vein and muscle, was perhaps never possessed by any other man.

114. A Choice Reality.—Just as the good prose writer only takes words that belong to the language of daily intercourse, though not by a long way all its words—whence arises a choice style—so the good poet of the future will only represent the real and turn his eyes away from all fantastic, superstitious, half-voiced, forgotten stories, to which earlier poets devoted their powers. Only reality, though by a long way not every reality—but a choice reality.

115. Degenerate Species of Art.—Side by side with the genuine species of art, those of great repose and great movement, there are degenerate species—weary, blasé art and excited art. Both would have their weakness taken for strength and wish to be confounded with the genuine species.

116. A Hero Impossible from Lack of Colour.—The typical poets and artists of our age like to compose their pictures upon a background of shimmering red, green, grey, and gold, on the background of nervous sensuality—a condition well understood by the children of this century. The drawback comes when we do not look at these pictures with the eyes of our century. Then we see that the great figures painted by these artists have something flickering, tremulous, and dizzy about them, and accordingly we do not ascribe to them heroic deeds, but at best mock-heroic, swaggering misdeeds.

117. Overladen Style.—The overladen style is a consequence of the impoverishment of the organising force together with a lavish stock of expedients and intentions. At the beginnings of art the very reverse conditions sometimes appear.

118. Pulchrum est paucorum hominum.—History and experience tell us that the significant grotesqueness that mysteriously excites the imagination and carries one beyond everyday reality, is older and grows more luxuriantly than the beautiful and reverence for the beautiful in art: and that it begins to flourish exceedingly when the sense for beauty is on the wane. For the vast majority of mankind this grotesque seems to be a higher need than the beautiful, presumably because it contains a coarser narcotic.

119. Origins of Taste in Works of Art.—If we consider the primary germs of the artistic sense, and ask ourselves what are the various kinds of joy produced by the firstlings of art—as, for example, among savage tribes—we find first of all the joy of understanding what another means. Art in this case is a sort of conundrum, which causes its solver pleasure in his own quick and keen perceptions.—Then the roughest works of art remind us of the pleasant things we have actually experienced, and so give joy—as, for example, when the artist alludes to a chase, a victory, a wedding.—Again, the representation may cause us to feel excited, touched, inflamed, as for instance in the glorification of revenge and danger. Here the enjoyment lies in the excitement itself, in the victory over tedium.—The memory, too, of unpleasant things, so far as they have been overcome or make us appear interesting to the listener as subjects for art (as when the singer describes the mishaps of a daring seaman), can inspire great joy, the credit for which is given to art.—A more subtle variety is the joy that arises at the sight of all that is regular and symmetrical in lines, points, and rhythms. For by a certain analogy is awakened the feeling for all that is orderly and regular in life, which one has to thank alone for all well-being. So in the cult of symmetry we unconsciously do homage to rule and proportion as the source of our previous happiness, and the joy in this case is a kind of hymn of thanksgiving. Only when a certain satiety of the last-mentioned joy arises does a more subtle feeling step in, that enjoyment might even lie in a violation of the symmetrical and regular. This feeling, for example, impels us to seek reason in apparent unreason, and the sort of æsthetic riddle-guessing that results is in a way the higher species of the first-named artistic joy.—He who pursues this speculation still further will know what kind of hypotheses for the explanation of æsthetic phenomena are hereby fundamentally rejected.

120. Not too Near.—It is a disadvantage for good thoughts when they follow too closely on one another, for they hide the view from each other. That is why great artists and writers have made an abundant use of the mediocre.

121. Roughness and Weakness.—Artists of all periods have made the discovery that in roughness lies a certain strength, and that not every one can be rough who wants to be: also that many varieties of weakness have a powerful effect on the emotions. From this source are derived many artistic substitutes, which not even the greatest and most conscientious artists can abstain from using.

122. Good Memory.—Many a man fails to become a thinker for the sole reason that his memory is too good.

123. Arousing instead of Appeasing Hunger.—Great artists fancy that they have taken full possession of a soul. In reality, and often to their painful

disappointment, that soul has only been made more capacious and insatiable, so that a dozen greater artists could plunge into its depths without filling it up.

124. Artists' Anxiety.—The anxiety lest people may not believe that their figures are alive can mislead many artists of declining taste to portray these figures so that they appear as if mad. From the same anxiety, on the other hand, Greek artists of the earliest ages gave even dead and sorely wounded men that smile which they knew as the most vivid sign of life—careless of the actual forms bestowed by nature on life at its last gasp.

125. The Circle must be Completed.—He who follows a philosophy or a genre of art to the end of its career and beyond, understands from inner experience why the masters and disciples who come after have so often turned, with a depreciatory gesture, into a new groove. The circle must be described—but the individual, even the greatest, sits firm on his point of the circumference, with an inexorable look of obstinacy, as if the circle ought never to be completed.

126. The Older Art and the Soul of the Present.—Since every art becomes more and more adapted to the expression of spiritual states, of the more lively, delicate, energetic, and passionate states, the later masters, spoilt by these means of expression, do not feel at their ease in the presence of the old-time works of art. They feel as if the ancients had merely been lacking in the means of making their souls speak clearly, also perhaps in some necessary technical preliminaries. They think that they must render some assistance in this quarter, for they believe in the similarity or even unity of all souls. In truth, however, measure, symmetry, a contempt for graciousness and charm, an unconscious severity and morning chilliness, an evasion of passion, as if passion meant the death of art—such are the constituents of sentiment and morality in all old masters, who selected and arranged their means of expression not at random but in a necessary connection with their morality. Knowing this, are we to deny those that come after the right to animate the older works with their soul? No, for these works can only survive through our giving them our soul, and our blood alone enables them to speak to us. The real "historic" discourse would talk ghostly speech to ghosts. We honour the great artists less by that barren timidity that allows every word, every note to remain intact than by energetic endeavours to aid them continually to a new life.—True, if Beethoven were suddenly to come to life and hear one of his works performed with that modern animation and nervous refinement that bring glory to our masters of execution, he would probably be silent for a long while, uncertain whether he should raise his hand to curse or to bless, but perhaps say at last: "Well, well! That is neither I nor not-I, but a third thing—it seems to me, too, something right, if not just the right thing. But you must know yourselves

what to do, as in any case it is you who have to listen. As our Schiller says, 'the living man is right.' So have it your own way, and let me go down again."

127. Against the Disparagers of Brevity.—A brief dictum may be the fruit and harvest of long reflection. The reader, however, who is a novice in this field and has never considered the case in point, sees something embryonic in all brief dicta, not without a reproachful hint to the author, requesting him not to serve up such raw and ill-prepared food.

128. Against the Short-Sighted.—Do you think it is piece-work because it is (and must be) offered you in pieces?

129. Readers of Aphorisms.—The worst readers of aphorisms are the friends of the author, if they make a point of referring the general to the particular instance to which the aphorism owes its origin. This namby-pamby attitude brings all the author's trouble to naught, and instead of a philosophic lesson and a philosophic frame of mind, they deservedly gain nothing but the satisfaction of a vulgar curiosity.

130. Readers' Insults.—The reader offers a two-fold insult to the author by praising his second book at the expense of his first (or vice versa) and by expecting the author to be grateful to him on that account.

131. The Exciting Element in the History of Art.—We fall into a state of terrible tension when we follow the history of an art—as, for example, that of Greek oratory—and, passing from master to master, observe their increasing precautions to obey the old and the new laws and all these self-imposed limitations. We see that the bow must snap, and that the so-called "loose" composition, with the wonderful means of expression smothered and concealed (in this particular case the florid style of Asianism), was once necessary and almost beneficial.

132. To the Great in Art.—That enthusiasm for some object which you, O great man, introduce into this world causes the intelligence of the many to be stunted. The knowledge of this fact spells humiliation. But the enthusiast wears his hump with pride and pleasure, and you have the consolation of feeling that you have increased the world's happiness.

133. Conscienceless Æsthetes.—The real fanatics of an artistic school are perhaps those utterly inartistic natures that are not even grounded in the elements of artistic study and creation, but are impressed with the strongest of all the elementary influences of an art. For them there is no æsthetic conscience—hence nothing to hold them back from fanaticism.

134. How the Soul should be Moved by the New Music.—The artistic purpose followed by the new music, in what is now forcibly but none too lucidly termed "endless melody," can be understood by going into the sea, gradually losing one's firm tread on the bottom, and finally surrendering unconditionally to the fluid

element. One has to swim. In the previous, older music one was forced, with delicate or stately or impassioned movement, to dance. The measure necessary for dancing, the observance of a distinct balance of time and force in the soul of the hearer, imposed a continual self-control. Through the counteraction of the cooler draught of air which came from this caution and the warmer breath of musical enthusiasm, that music exercised its spell.—Richard Wagner aimed at a different excitation of the soul, allied, as above said, to swimming and floating. This is perhaps the most essential of his innovations. His famous method, originating from this aim and adapted to it—the "endless melody"—strives to break and sometimes even to despise all mathematical equilibrium of time and force. He is only too rich in the invention of such effects, which sound to the old school like rhythmic paradoxes and blasphemies. He dreads petrifaction, crystallisation, the development of music into the architectural. He accordingly sets up a three-time rhythm in opposition to the double-time, not infrequently introduces five-time and seven-time, immediately repeats a phrase, but with a prolation, so that its time is again doubled and trebled. From an easy-going imitation of such art may arise a great danger to music, for by the side of the superabundance of rhythmic emotion demoralisation and decadence lurk in ambush. The danger will become very great if such music comes to associate itself more and more closely with a quite naturalistic art of acting and pantomime, trained and dominated by no higher plastic models; an art that knows no measure in itself and can impart no measure to the kindred element, the all-too-womanish nature of music.

135. Poet and Reality.—The Muse of the poet who is not in love with reality will not be reality, and will bear him children with hollow eyes and all too tender bones.

136. Means and End.—In art the end does not justify the means, but holy means can justify the end.

137. The Worst Readers.—The worst readers are those who act like plundering soldiers. They take out some things that they might use, cover the rest with filth and confusion, and blaspheme about the whole.

138. Signs of a Good Writer.—Good writers have two things in common: they prefer being understood to being admired, and they do not write for the critical and over-shrewd reader.

139. The Mixed Species.—The mixed species in art bear witness to their authors' distrust of their own   strength. They seek auxiliary powers, advocates, hiding-places—such is the case with the poet who calls in philosophy, the musician who calls in the drama, and the thinker who calls in rhetoric to his aid.

140. Shutting One's Mouth.—When his book opens its mouth, the author must shut his.

141. Badges of Rank.—All poets and men of letters who are in love with the superlative want to do more than they can.

142. Cold Books.—The deep thinker reckons on readers who feel with him the happiness that lies in deep thinking. Hence a book that looks cold and sober, if seen in the right light, may seem bathed in the sunshine of spiritual cheerfulness and become a genuine soul-comforter.

143. A Knack of the Slow-Witted.—The slow-witted thinker generally allies himself with loquacity and ceremoniousness. By the former he thinks he is gaining mobility and fluency, by the latter he gives his peculiarity the appearance of being a result of free will and artistic purpose, with a view to dignity, which needs slow movement.

144. Le Style Baroque.[11]—He who as thinker and writer is not born or trained to dialectic and the consecutive arrangement of ideas, will unconsciously turn to the rhetoric and dramatic forms. For, after all, his object is to make himself understood and to carry the day by force, and he is indifferent whether, as shepherd, he honestly guides to himself the hearts of his fellow-men, or, as robber, he captures them by surprise. This is true of the plastic arts as of music: where the feeling of insufficient dialectic or a deficiency in expression or narration, together with an urgent, over-powerful impulse to form, gives birth to that species of style known as "baroque." Only the ill-educated and the arrogant will at once find a depreciatory force in this word. The baroque style always arises at the time of decay of a great art, when the demands of art in classical expression have become too great. It is a natural phenomenon which will be observed with melancholy—for it is a forerunner of the night—but at the same time with admiration for its peculiar compensatory arts of expression and narration. To this style belongs already a choice of material and subjects of the highest dramatic tension, at which the heart trembles even when there is no art, because heaven and hell are all too near the emotions: then, the oratory of strong passion and gestures, of ugly sublimity, of great masses, in fact of absolute quantity per se (as is shown in Michael Angelo, the father or grandfather of the Italian baroque stylists): the lights of dusk, illumination and conflagration playing upon those strongly moulded forms: ever-new ventures in means and aims, strongly underscored by artists for artists, while the layman must fancy he sees an unconscious overflowing of all the horns of plenty of an original nature-art: all these characteristics that constitute the greatness of that style are neither possible nor permitted in the earlier ante-classical and classical periods of a branch of art. Such luxuries hang long on the tree like forbidden fruit. Just now, when music

is passing into this last phase, we may learn to know the phenomenon of the baroque style in peculiar splendour, and, by comparison, find much that is instructive for earlier ages. For from Greek times onward there has often been a baroque style, in poetry, oratory, prose writing, sculpture, and, as is well known, in architecture. This style, though wanting in the highest nobility,—the nobility of an innocent, unconscious, triumphant perfection,—has nevertheless given pleasure to many of the best and most serious minds of their time. Hence, as aforesaid, it is presumptuous to depreciate it without reserve, however happy we may feel because our taste for it has not made us insensible to the purer and greater style.

145. The Value of Honest Books.—Honest books make the reader honest, at least by exciting his hatred and aversion, which otherwise cunning cleverness knows so well how to conceal. Against a book, however, we let ourselves go, however restrained we may be in our relations with men.

146. How Art makes Partisans.—Individual fine passages, an exciting general tenor, a moving and absorbing finale—so much of a work of art is accessible even to most laymen. In an art period when it is desired to win over the great majority of the laymen to the side of the artists and to make a party perhaps for the very preservation of art, the creative artist will do well to offer nothing more than the above. Then he will not be a squanderer of his strength, in spheres where no one is grateful to him. For to perform the remaining functions, the imitation of Nature in her organic development and growth, would in that case be like sowing seeds in water.

147. Becoming Great to the Detriment of History.—Every later master who leads the taste of art-lovers into his channel unconsciously gives rise to a selection and revaluation of the older masters and their works. Whatever in them is conformable and akin to him, and anticipates and foreshadows him, appears henceforth as the only important element in them and their works—a fruit in which a great error usually lies hidden like a worm.

148. How an Epoch becomes Lured to Art.—If we teach people by all the enchantments of artists and thinkers to feel reverence for their defects, their intellectual poverty, their absurd infatuations and passions (as it is quite possible to do); if we show them only the lofty side of crime and folly, only the touching and appealing element in weakness and flabbiness and blind devotion (that too has often enough been done):—we have employed the means for inspiring even an unphilosophical and inartistic age with an ecstatic love of philosophy and art (especially of thinkers and artists as personalities) and, in the worst case, perhaps with the only means of defending the existence of such tender and fragile beings.

149. Criticism and Joy.—Criticism, one-sided and unjust as well as intelligent criticism, gives so much pleasure to him who exercises it that the world is indebted to every work and every action that inspires much criticism and many critics. For criticism draws after it a glittering train of joyousness, wit, self-admiration, pride, instruction, designs of improvement.—The God of joy created the bad and the mediocre for the same reason that he created the good.

150. Beyond his Limits.—When an artist wants to be more than an artist—for example, the moral awakener of his people—he at last falls in love, as a punishment, with a monster of moral substance. The Muse laughs, for, though a kind-hearted Goddess, she can also be malignant from jealousy. Milton and Klopstock are cases in point.

151. A Glass Eye.—The tendency of a talent towards moral subjects, characters, motives, towards the "beautiful soul" of the work of art, is often only a glass eye put on by the artist who lacks a beautiful soul. It may result, though rarely, that his eye finally becomes living Nature, if indeed it be Nature with a somewhat troubled look. But the ordinary result is that the whole world thinks it sees Nature where there is only cold glass.

152. Writing and Desire for Victory.—Writing should always indicate a victory, indeed a conquest of oneself which must be communicated to others for their behoof. There are, however, dyspeptic authors who only write when they cannot digest something, or when something has remained stuck in their teeth. Through their anger they try unconsciously to disgust the reader too, and to exercise violence upon him—that is, they desire victory, but victory over others.

153. A Good Book Needs Time.—Every good book tastes bitter when it first comes out, for it has the defect of newness. Moreover, it suffers damage from its living author, if he is well known and much talked about. For all the world is accustomed to confuse the author with his work. Whatever of profundity, sweetness, and brilliance the work may contain must be developed as the years go by, under the care of growing, then old, and lastly traditional reverence. Many hours must pass, many a spider must have woven its web about the book. A book is made better by good readers and clearer by good opponents.

154. Extravagance as an Artistic Means.—Artists well understand the idea of using extravagance as an artistic means in order to convey an impression of wealth. This is one of those innocent wiles of soul-seduction that the artist must know, for in his world, which has only appearance in view, the means to appearance need not necessarily be genuine.

155. The Hidden Barrel-Organ.—Genius, by virtue of its more ample drapery, knows better than talent how to hide its barrel-organ. Yet after all it too can only play its seven old pieces over and over again.

156. The Name on the Title-Page.—It is now a matter of custom and almost of duty for the author's name to appear on the book, and this is a main cause of the fact that books have so little influence. If they are good, they are worth more than the personalities of their authors, of which they are the quintessences. But as soon as the author makes himself known on the title-page, the quintessence, from the reader's point of view, becomes diluted with the personal, the most personal element, and the aim of the book is frustrated. It is the ambition of the intellect no longer to appear individual.

157. The Most Cutting Criticism.—We make the most cutting criticism of a man or a book when we indicate his or its ideal.

158. Little or no Love.—Every good book is written for a particular reader and men of his stamp, and for that very reason is looked upon unfavourably by all other readers, by the vast majority. Its reputation accordingly rests on a narrow basis and must be built up by degrees.—The mediocre and bad book is mediocre and bad because it seeks to please, and does please, a great number.

159. Music and Disease.—The danger of the new music lies in the fact that it puts the cup of rapture and exaltation to the lips so invitingly, and with such a show of moral ecstasy, that even the noble and temperate man always drinks a drop too much. This minimum of intemperance, constantly repeated, can in the end bring about a deeper convulsion and destruction of mental health than any coarse excess could do. Hence nothing remains but some day to fly from the grotto of the nymph, and through perils and billowy seas to forge one's way to the smoke of Ithaca and the embraces of a simpler and more human spouse.

160. Advantage for Opponents.—A book full of intellect communicates something thereof even to its opponents.

161. Youth and Criticism.—To criticise a book means, for the young, not to let oneself be touched by a single productive thought therefrom, and to protect one's skin with hands and feet. The youngster lives in opposition to all novelty that he cannot love in the lump, in a position of self-defence, and in this connection he commits, as often as he can, a superfluous sin.

162. Effect of Quantity.—The greatest paradox in the history of poetic art lies in this: that in all that constitutes the greatness of the old poets a man may be a barbarian, faulty and deformed from top to toe, and still remain the greatest of poets. This is the case with Shakespeare, who, as compared with Sophocles, is like a mine of immeasurable wealth in gold, lead, and rubble, whereas Sophocles is not merely gold, but gold in its noblest form, one that almost makes us forget the money-value of the metal. But quantity in its highest intensity has the same effect as quality. That is a good thing for Shakespeare.

163. All Beginning is Dangerous.—The Poet can choose whether to raise emotion from one grade to another, and so finally to exalt it to a great height—or to try a surprise attack, and from the start to pull the bell-rope with might and main. Both processes have their danger—in the first case his hearer may run away from him through boredom, in the second through terror.

164. In Favour of Critics.—Insects sting, not from malice, but because they too want to live. It is the same with our critics—they desire our blood, not our pain.

165. Success of Aphorisms.—The inexperienced, when an aphorism at once illuminates their minds with its naked truth, always think that it is old and well known. They look askance at the author, as if he had wanted to steal the common property of all, whereas they enjoy highly spiced half-truths, and give the author to understand as much. He knows how to appreciate the hint, and easily guesses thereby where he has succeeded and failed.

166. The Desire for Victory.—An artist who exceeds the limit of his strength in all that he undertakes will end by carrying the multitude along with him through the spectacle of violent wrestling that he affords. Success is not always the accompaniment only of victory, but also of the desire for victory.

167. Sibi Scribere.—The sensible author writes for no other posterity than his own—that is, for his age—so as to be able even then to take pleasure in himself.

168. Praise of the Aphorism.—A good aphorism is too hard for the tooth of time, and is not worn away by all the centuries, although it serves as food for every epoch. Hence it is the greatest paradox in literature, the imperishable in the midst of change, the nourishment which always remains highly valued, as salt does, and never becomes stupid like salt.

169. The Art-Need of the Second Order.—The people may have something of what can be called art-need, but it is small, and can be cheaply satisfied. On the whole, the remnant of art (it must be honestly confessed) suffices for this need. Let us consider, for example, the kind of melodies and songs in which the most vigorous, unspoiled, and true-hearted classes of the population find genuine delight; let us live among shepherds, cowherds, peasants, huntsmen, soldiers, and sailors, and give ourselves the answer. And in the country town, just in the houses that are the homes of inherited civic virtue, is it not the worst music at present produced that is loved and, one might say, cherished? He who speaks of deeper needs and unsatisfied yearnings for art among the people, as it is, is a crank or an impostor. Be honest! Only in exceptional men is there now an art-need in the highest sense—because art is once more on the down-grade, and human powers and hopes are for the time being directed to other matters.—Apart from this, outside the populace, there exists indeed, in the higher and highest strata of society, a broader and more comprehensive art-need, but of the second order.

Here there is a sort of artistic commune, which possibly means to be sincere. But let us look at the elements! They are in general the more refined malcontents, who attain no genuine pleasure in themselves; the cultured, who have not become free enough to dispense with the consolations of religion, and yet do not find its incense sufficiently fragrant; the half-aristocratic, who are too weak to combat by a heroic conversion or renunciation the one fundamental error of their lives or the pernicious bent of their characters; the highly gifted, who think themselves too dignified to be of service by modest activity, and are too lazy for real, self-sacrificing work; girls who cannot create for themselves a satisfactory sphere of duties; women who have tied themselves by a light-hearted or nefarious marriage, and know that they are not tied securely enough; scholars, physicians, merchants, officials who specialised too early and never gave their lives a free enough scope—who do their work efficiently, it is true, but with a worm gnawing at their hearts; finally, all imperfect artists—these are nowadays the true needers of art! What do they really desire from art? Art is to drive away hours and moments of discomfort, boredom, half-bad conscience, and, if possible, transform the faults of their lives and characters into faults of world-destiny. Very different were the Greeks, who realised in their art the outflow and overflow of their own sense of well-being and health, and loved to see their perfection once more from a standpoint outside themselves. They were led to art by delight in themselves; our contemporaries—by disgust of themselves.

170. The Germans in the Theatre.—The real theatrical talent of the Germans was Kotzebue. He and his Germans, those of higher as well as those of middle-class society, were necessarily associated, and his contemporaries should have said of him in all seriousness, "in him we live and move and have our being." Here was nothing—no constraint, pretence, or half-enjoyment: what he could and would do was understood. Yes, until now the honest theatrical success on the German stage has been in the hands of the shamefaced or unashamed heirs of Kotzebue's methods and influence—that is, as far as comedy still flourishes at all. The result is that much of the Germanism of that age, sometimes far off from the great towns, still survives. Good-natured; incontinent in small pleasures; always ready for tears; with the desire, in the theatre at any rate, to be able to get rid of their innate sobriety and strict attention to duty and exercise; a smiling, nay, a laughing indulgence; confusing goodness and sympathy and welding them into one, as is the essential characteristic of German sentimentality; exceedingly happy at a noble, magnanimous action; for the rest, submissive towards superiors, envious of each other, and yet in their heart of hearts thoroughly self-satisfied—such were they and such was he.—The second dramatic talent was Schiller. He discovered a class of hearers which had hitherto

never been taken into consideration: among the callow German youth of both sexes. His poetry responded to their higher, nobler, more violent if more confused emotions, their delight in the jingle of moral words (a delight that begins to disappear when we reach the thirties). Thus he won for himself, by virtue of the passionateness and partisanship of the young, a success which gradually reacted with advantage upon those of riper years. Generally speaking, Schiller rejuvenated the Germans. Goethe stood and still stands above the Germans in every respect. To them he will never belong. How could a nation in well-being and well-wishing come up to the intellectuality of Goethe? Beethoven composed and Schopenhauer philosophised above the heads of the Germans, and it was above their heads, in the same way, that Goethe wrote his Tasso, his Iphigenie. He was followed by a small company of highly cultured persons, who were educated by antiquity, life, and travel, and had grown out of German ways of thought. He himself did not wish it to be otherwise.—When the Romantics set up their well-conceived Goethe cult; when their amazing skill in appreciation was passed on to the disciples of Hegel, the real educators of the Germans of this century; when the awakening national ambition turned out advantageous to the fame of the German poets; when the real standard of the nation, as to whether it could honestly find enjoyment in anything, became inexorably subordinated to the judgment of individuals and to that national ambition,—that is, when people began to enjoy by compulsion,—then arose that false, spurious German culture which was ashamed of Kotzebue; which brought Sophocles, Calderon, and even the Second Part of Goethe's Faust on the stage; and which, on account of its foul tongue and congested stomach, no longer knows now what it likes and what it finds tedious.—Happy are those who have taste, even if it be a bad taste! Only by this characteristic can one be wise as well as happy. Hence the Greeks, who were very refined in such matters, designated the sage by a word that means "man of taste," and called wisdom, artistic as well as scientific, "taste" (sophia).

171. Music as a Late-Comer in every Culture.—Among all the arts that are accustomed to grow on a definite culture-soil and under definite social and political conditions, music is the last plant to come up, arising in the autumn and fading-season of the culture to which it belongs. At the same time, the first signs and harbingers of a new spring are usually already noticeable, and sometimes music, like the language of a forgotten age, rings out into a new, astonished world, and comes too late. In the art of the Dutch and Flemish musicians the soul of the Christian middle ages at last found its fullest tone: their sound-architecture is the posthumous but legitimate and equal sister of Gothic. Not until Handel's music was heard the note of the best in the soul of Luther and his kin, the great Judæo-heroical impulse that created the whole Reformation

movement. Mozart first expressed in golden melody the age of Louis xiv. and the art of Racine and Claude Lorrain. The eighteenth century—that century of rhapsody, of broken ideals and transitory happiness—only sang itself out in the music of Beethoven and Rossini. A lover of sentimental similes might say that all really important music was a swan-song.—Music is, in fact, not a universal language for all time, as is so often said in its praise, but responds exactly to a particular period and warmth of emotion which involves a quite definite, individual culture, determined by time and place, as its inner law. The music of Palestrina would be quite unintelligible to a Greek; and again, what would the music of Rossini convey to Palestrina?—It may be that our most modern German music, with all its pre-eminence and desire of pre-eminence, will soon be no longer understood. For this music sprang from a culture that is undergoing a rapid decay, from the soil of that epoch of reaction and restoration in which a certain Catholicism of feeling, as well as a delight in all indigenous, national, primitive manners, burst into bloom and scattered a blended perfume over Europe. These two emotional tendencies, adopted in their greatest strength and carried to their farthest limits, found final expression in the music of Wagner. Wagner's predilection for the old native sagas, his free idealisation of their unfamiliar gods and heroes,—who are really sovereign beasts of prey with occasional fits of thoughtfulness, magnanimity, and boredom,—his re-animation of those figures, to which he gave in addition the mediæval Christian thirst for ecstatic sensuality and spiritualisation—all this Wagnerian give-and-take with regard to materials, souls, figures, and words—would clearly express the spirit of his music, if it could not, like all music, speak quite unambiguously of itself. This spirit wages the last campaign of reaction against the spirit of illumination which passed into this century from the last, and also against the super-national ideas of French revolutionary romanticism and of English and American insipidity in the reconstruction of state and society.—But is it not evident that the spheres of thought and emotion apparently suppressed by Wagner and his school have long since acquired fresh strength, and that his late musical protest against them generally rings into ears that prefer to hear different and opposite notes; so that one day that high and wonderful art will suddenly become unintelligible and will be covered by the spider's web of oblivion?—In considering this state of affairs we must not let ourselves be led astray by those transitory fluctuations which arise like a reaction within a reaction, as a temporary sinking of the mountainous wave in the midst of the general upheaval. Thus, this decade of national war, ultramontane martyrdom, and socialistic unrest may, in its remoter after-effect, even aid the Wagnerian art to acquire a sudden halo, without guaranteeing that it "has a future" or that it has the future. It is in the very nature of music that the fruits of its great culture-vintage should lose their taste and wither earlier than the fruits of the plastic arts or those that grow on the tree of knowledge. Among all the products of the human artistic sense ideas are the most solid and lasting.

172. The Poet no longer a Teacher.—Strange as it may sound to our time, there were once poets and artists whose soul was above the passions with their delights and convulsions, and who therefore took their pleasure in purer materials, worthier men, more delicate complications and dénouements. If the artists of our day for the most part unfetter the will, and so are under certain circumstances for that very reason emancipators of life, those were tamers of the will, enchanters of animals, creators of men. In fact, they moulded, re-moulded, and new-moulded life, whereas the fame of poets of our day lies in unharnessing, unchaining, and shattering.—The ancient Greeks demanded of the poet that he should be the teacher of grown men. How ashamed the poet would be now if this demand were made of him! He is not even a good student of himself, and so never himself becomes a good poem or a fine picture. Under the most favourable circumstances he remains the shy, attractive ruin of a temple, but at the same time a cavern of cravings, overgrown like a ruin with flowers, nettles, and poisonous weeds, inhabited and haunted by snakes, worms, spiders, and birds; an object for sad reflection as to why the noblest and most precious must grow up at once like a ruin, without the past and future of perfection.

173. Looking Forward and Backward.—An art like that which streams out of Homer, Sophocles, Theocritus, Calderon, Racine, Goethe, as the superabundance of a wise and harmonious conduct of life—that is the true art, at which we grasp when we have ourselves become wiser and more harmonious. It is not that barbaric, if ever so delightful, outpouring of hot and highly coloured things from an undisciplined, chaotic soul, which is what we understood by "art" in our youth. It is obvious from the nature of the case that for certain periods of life an art of overstrain, excitement, antipathy to the orderly, monotonous, simple, logical, is an inevitable need, to which artists must respond, lest the soul of such periods should unburden itself in other ways, through all kinds of disorder and impropriety. Hence youths as they generally are, full, fermenting, tortured above all things by boredom, and women who lack work that fully occupies their soul, require that art of delightful disorder. All the more violently on that account are they inflamed with a desire for satisfaction without change, happiness without stupor and intoxication.

174. Against the Art of Works of Art.—Art is above all and first of all meant to embellish life, to make us ourselves endurable and if possible agreeable in the eyes of others. With this task in view, art moderates us and holds us in restraint, creates forms of intercourse, binds over the uneducated to laws of decency,

cleanliness, politeness, well-timed speech and silence. Hence art must conceal or transfigure everything that is ugly—the painful, terrible, and disgusting elements which in spite of every effort will always break out afresh in accordance with the very origin of human nature. Art has to perform this duty especially in regard to the passions and spiritual agonies and anxieties, and to cause the significant factor to shine through unavoidable or unconquerable ugliness. To this great, super-great task the so-called art proper, that of works of art, is a mere accessary. A man who feels within himself a surplus of such powers of embellishment, concealment, and transfiguration will finally seek to unburden himself of this surplus in works of art. The same holds good, under special circumstances, of a whole nation.—But as a rule we nowadays begin art at the end, hang on to its tail, and think that works of art constitute art proper, and that life should be improved and transformed by this means—fools that we are! If we begin a dinner with dessert, and try sweet after sweet, small wonder that we ruin our digestions and even our appetites for the good, hearty, nourishing meal to which art invites us!

175. Continued Existence of Art.—Why, really, does a creative art nowadays continue to exist? Because the majority who have hours of leisure (and such an art is for them only) think that they cannot fill up their time without music, theatres and picture-galleries, novels and poetry. Granted that one could keep them from this indulgence, either they would strive less eagerly for leisure, and the invidious sight of the rich would be less common (a great gain for the stability of society), or they would have leisure, but would learn to reflect on what can be learnt and unlearnt: on their work, for instance, their associations, the pleasure they could bestow. All the world, with the exception of the artist, would in both cases reap the advantage.—Certainly, there are many vigorous, sensible readers who could take objection to this. Still, it must be said on behalf of the coarse and malignant that the author himself is concerned with this protest, and that there is in his book much to be read that is not actually written down therein.

176. The Mouthpiece of the Gods.—The poet expresses the universal higher opinions of the nation, he is its mouthpiece and flute; but by virtue of metre and all other artistic means he so expresses them that the nation regards them as something quite new and wonderful, and believes in all seriousness that he is the mouthpiece of the Gods. Yes, under the clouds of creation the poet himself forgets whence he derives all his intellectual wisdom—from father and mother, from teachers and books of all kinds, from the street and particularly from the priest. He is deceived by his own art, and really believes, in a naïve period, that a God is speaking through him, that he is creating in a state of religious inspiration. As a matter of fact, he is only saying what he has learnt, a medley of

popular wisdom and popular foolishness. Hence, so far as a poet is really vox populi he is held to be vox dei.

177. What all Art wants to Do and Cannot.—The last and hardest task of the artist is the presentment of what remains the same, reposes in itself, is lofty and simple and free from the bizarre. Hence the noblest forms of moral perfection are rejected as inartistic by weaker artists, because the sight of these fruits is too painful for their ambition. The fruit gleams at them from the topmost branches of art, but they lack the ladder, the courage, the grip to venture so high. In himself a Phidias is quite possible as a poet, but, if modern strength be taken into consideration, almost solely in the sense that to God nothing is impossible. The desire for a poetical Claude Lorrain is already an immodesty at present, however earnestly one man's heart may yearn for such a consummation.—The presentment of the highest man, the most simple and at the same time the most complete, has hitherto been beyond the scope of all artists. Perhaps, however, the Greeks, in the ideal of Athene, saw farther than any men did before or after their time.

178. Art and Restoration.—The retrograde movements in history, the so-called periods of restoration, which try to revive intellectual and social conditions that existed before those immediately preceding,—and seem really to succeed in giving them a brief resurrection,—have the charm of sentimental recollection, ardent longing for what is almost lost, hasty embracing of a transitory happiness. It is on account of this strange trend towards seriousness that in such transient and almost dreamy periods art and poetry find a natural soil, just as the tenderest and rarest plants grow on mountain-slopes of steep declivity.—Thus many a good artist is unwittingly impelled to a "restoration" way of thinking in politics and society, for which, on his own account, he prepares a quiet little corner and garden. Here he collects about himself the human remains of the historical epoch that appeals to him, and plays his lyre to many who are dead, half-dead, and weary to death, perhaps with the above-mentioned result of a brief resurrection.

179. Happiness of the Age.—In two respects our age is to be accounted happy. With respect to the past, we enjoy all cultures and their productions, and nurture ourselves on the noblest blood of all periods. We stand sufficiently near to the magic of the forces from whose womb these periods are born to be able in passing to submit to their spell with pleasure and terror; whereas earlier cultures could only enjoy themselves, and never looked beyond themselves, but were rather overarched by a bell of broader or narrower dome, through which indeed light streamed down to them, but which their gaze could not pierce. With respect to the future, there opens out to us for the first time a mighty, comprehensive vista of human and economic purposes engirdling the whole inhabited globe. At the

same time, we feel conscious of a power ourselves to take this new task in hand without presumption, without requiring supernatural aids. Yes, whatever the result of our enterprise, however much we may have overestimated our strength, at any rate we need render account to no one but ourselves, and mankind can henceforth begin to do with itself what it will.—There are, it is true, peculiar human bees, who only know how to suck the bitterest and worst elements from the chalice of every flower. It is true that all flowers contain something that is not honey, but these bees may be allowed to feel in their own way about the happiness of our time, and continue to build up their hive of discomfort.

180. A Vision.—Hours of instruction and meditation for adults, even the most mature, and such institutions visited without compulsion but in accordance with the moral injunction of the whole community; the churches as the meeting-places most worthy and rich in memories for the purpose; at the same time daily festivals in honour of the reason that is attained and attainable by man; a newer and fuller budding and blooming of the ideal of the teacher, in which the clergyman, the artist and the physician, the man of science and the sage are blended, and their individual virtues should come to the fore as a collective virtue in their teaching itself, in their discourses, in their method—this is my ever-recurring vision, of which I firmly believe that it has raised a corner of the veil of the future.

181. Education a Distortion.—The extraordinary haphazardness of the whole system of education, which leads every adult to say nowadays that his sole educator was chance, and the weathercock-nature of educational methods and aims, may be explained as follows. The oldest and the newest culture-powers, as in a turbulent mass-meeting, would rather be heard than understood, and wish to prove at all costs by their outcries and clamourings that they still exist or already exist. The poor teachers and educators are first dazed by this senseless noise, then become silent and finally apathetic, allowing anything to be done to them just as they in their turn allow anything to be done to their pupils. They are not trained themselves, so how are they to train others? They are themselves no straight-growing, vigorous, succulent trees, and he who wishes to attach himself to them must wind and bend himself and finally become distorted and deformed as they.

182. Philosophers and Artists of the Age.—Rhapsody and frigidity, burning desires and waning of the heart's glow—this wretched medley is to be found in the picture of the highest European society of the present day. There the artist thinks that he is achieving a great deal when through his art he lights the torch of the heart as well as the torch of desire. The philosopher has the same notion, when

in the chilliness of his heart, which he has in common with his age, he cools hot desires in himself and his following by his world-denying judgments.

183. Not To Be a Soldier of Culture Without Necessity.—At last people are learning what it costs us so dear not to know in our youth—that we must first do superior actions and secondly seek the superior wherever and under whatever names it is to be found; that we must at once go out of the way of all badness and mediocrity without fighting it; and that even doubt as to the excellence of a thing (such as quickly arises in one of practised taste) should rank as an argument against it and a reason for completely avoiding it. We must not shrink from the danger of occasionally making a mistake and confounding the less accessible good with the bad and imperfect. Only he who can do nothing better should attack the world's evils as the soldier of culture. But those who should support culture and spread its teachings ruin themselves if they go about armed, and by precautions, night-watches, and bad dreams turn the peace of their domestic and artistic life into sinister unrest.

184. How Natural History Should Be Expounded.—Natural history, like the history of the war and victory of moral and intellectual forces in the campaign against anxiety, self-delusion, laziness, superstition, folly, should be so expounded that every reader or listener may be continually aroused to strive after mental and physical health and soundness, after the feeling of joy, and be awakened to the desire to be the heir and continuator of mankind, to an ever nobler adventurous impulse. Hitherto natural history has not found its true language, because the inventive and eloquent artists—who are needed for this purpose—never rid themselves of a secret mistrust of it, and above all never wish to learn from it a thorough lesson. Nevertheless it must be conceded to the English that their scientific manuals for the lower strata of the people have made admirable strides towards that ideal. But then such books are written by their foremost men of learning, full, complete, and inspiring natures, and not, as among us, by mediocre investigators.

185. Genius in Humanity.—If genius, according to Schopenhauer's observation, lies in the coherent and vivid recollection of our own experience, a striving towards genius in humanity collectively might be deduced from the striving towards knowledge of the whole historic past—which is beginning to mark off the modern age more and more as compared with earlier ages and has for the first time broken down the barriers between nature and spirit, men and animals, morality and physics. A perfectly conceived history would be cosmic self-consciousness.

186. The Cult of Culture.—On great minds is bestowed the terrifying all-too-human of their natures, their blindnesses, deformities, and extravagances,

so that their more powerful, easily all-too-powerful influence may be continually held within bounds through the distrust aroused by such qualities. For the sum-total of all that humanity needs for its continued existence is so comprehensive, and demands powers so diverse and so numerous, that for every one-sided predilection, whether in science or politics or art or commerce, to which such natures would persuade us, mankind as a whole has to pay a heavy price. It has always been a great disaster to culture when human beings are worshipped. In this sense we may understand the precept of Mosaic law which forbids us to have any other gods but God.—Side by side with the cult of genius and violence we must always place, as its complement and remedy, the cult of culture. This cult can find an intelligent appreciation even for the material, the inferior, the mean, the misunderstood, the weak, the imperfect, the one-sided, the incomplete, the untrue, the apparent, even the wicked and horrible, and can grant them the concession that all this is necessary. For the continued harmony of all things human, attained by amazing toil and strokes of luck, and just as much the work of Cyclopes and ants as of geniuses, shall never be lost. How, indeed, could we dispense with that deep, universal, and often uncanny bass, without which, after all, melody cannot be melody?

187. The Antique World and Pleasure.—The man of the antique world understood better how to rejoice, we understand better how to grieve less. They continually found new motives for feeling happy, for celebrating festivals, being inventive with all their wealth of shrewdness and reflection. We, on the other hand, concentrate our intellect rather on the solving of problems which have in view painlessness and the removal of sources of discomfort. With regard to suffering existence, the ancients sought to forget or in some way to convert the sensation into a pleasant one, thus trying to supply palliatives. We attack the causes of suffering, and on the whole prefer to use prophylactics.—Perhaps we are only building upon a foundation whereon a later age will once more set up the temple of joy.

188. The Muses as Liars.—"We know how to tell many lies," so sang the Muses once, when they revealed themselves to Hesiod.—The conception of the artist as deceiver, once grasped, leads to important discoveries.

189. How Paradoxical Homer can be.—Is there anything more desperate, more horrible, more incredible, shining over human destiny like a winter sun, than that idea of Homer's: "So the decree of the Gods willed it, and doomed man to perish, that it might be a matter for song even to distant generations"?

In other words, we suffer and perish so that poets may not lack material, and this is the dispensation of those very Gods of Homer who seem much concerned about the joyousness of generations to come, but very little about us men of the present. To think that such ideas should ever have entered the head of a Greek!

190. Supplementary Justification of Existence.—Many ideas have come into the world as errors and fancies but have turned out truths, because men have afterwards given them a genuine basis to rest upon.

191. Pro and Con Necessary.—He who has not realised that every great man must not only be encouraged but also, for the sake of the common welfare, opposed, is certainly still a great child—or himself a great man.

192. Injustice of Genius.—Genius is most unjust towards geniuses, if they be contemporary. Either it thinks it has no need of them and considers them superfluous (for it can do without them), or their influence crosses the path of its electric current, in which case it even calls them pernicious.

193. The Saddest Destiny of a Prophet.—He has worked twenty years to convince his contemporaries, and succeeds at last, but in the meantime his adversaries have also succeeded—he is no longer convinced of himself.

194. Three Thinkers like one Spider.—In every philosophical school three thinkers follow one another in this relation: the first produces from himself sap and seed, the second draws it out in threads and spins a cunning web, the third waits in this web for the victims who are caught in it—and tries to live upon this philosophy.

195. From Association with Authors.—It is as bad a habit to go about with an author grasping him by the nose as grasping him by the horn (and every author has his horn).

196. A Team of Two.—Vagueness of thought and outbursts of sentimentality are as often wedded to the reckless desire to have one's own way by hook or by crook, to make oneself alone of any consequence, as a genuinely helpful, gracious, and kindly spirit is wedded to the impulse towards clearness and purity of thought and towards emotional moderation and self-restraint.

197. Binding and Separating Forces.—Surely it is in the heads of men that there arises the force that binds them—an understanding of their common interest or the reverse; and in their hearts the force that separates them—a blind choosing and groping in love and hate, a devotion to one at the expense of all, and a consequent contempt for the common utility.

198. Marksmen and Thinkers.—There are curious marksmen who miss their mark, but leave the shooting-gallery with secret pride in the fact that their bullet at any rate flew very far (beyond the mark, it is true), or that it did not hit the mark but hit something else. There are thinkers of the same stamp.

199. Attack from Two Sides.—We act as enemies towards an intellectual tendency or movement when we are superior to it and disapprove of its aim, or

when its aim is too high and unrecognisable to our eye—in other words, when it is superior to us. So the same party may be attacked from two sides, from above and from below. Not infrequently the assailants, from common hatred, form an alliance which is more repulsive than all that they hate.

200. Original.—Original minds are distinguished not by being the first to see a new thing, but by seeing the old, well-known thing, which is seen and overlooked by every one, as something new. The first discoverer is usually that quite ordinary and unintellectual visionary—chance.

201. Error of Philosophers.—The philosopher believes that the value of his philosophy lies in the whole, in the structure. Posterity finds it in the stone with which he built and with which, from that time forth, men will build oftener and better—in other words, in the fact that the structure may be destroyed and yet have value as material.

202. Wit.—Wit is the epitaph of an emotion.

203. The Moment before Solution.—In science it occurs every day and every hour that a man, immediately before the solution, remains stuck, being convinced that his efforts have been entirely in vain—like one who, in untying a noose, hesitates at the moment when it is nearest to coming loose, because at that very moment it looks most like a knot.

204. Among the Visionaries.—The thoughtful man, and he who is sure of his intelligence, may profitably consort with visionaries for a decade and abandon himself in their torrid zone to a moderate insanity. He will thus have travelled a good part of the road towards that cosmopolitanism of the intellect which can say without presumption, "Nothing intellectual is alien to me."

205. Keen Air.—The best and healthiest element in science as amid the mountains is the keen air that plays about it.—Intellectual molly-coddles (such as artists) dread and abuse science on account of this atmosphere.

206. Why Savants are Nobler than Artists.—Science requires nobler natures than does poetry; natures that are more simple, less ambitious, more restrained, calmer, that think less of posthumous fame and can bury themselves in studies which, in the eye of the many, scarcely seem worthy of such a sacrifice of personality. There is another loss of which they are conscious. The nature of their occupation, its continual exaction of the greatest sobriety, weakens their will; the fire is not kept up so vigorously as on the hearths of poetic minds. As such, they often lose their strength and prime earlier than artists do—and, as has been said, they are aware of their danger. Under all circumstances they seem less gifted because they shine less, and thus they will always be rated below their value.

207. How Far Piety Obscures.—In later centuries the great man is credited with all the great qualities and virtues of his century. Thus all that is best is continually

obscured by piety, which treats the picture as a sacred one, to be surrounded with all manner of votive offerings. In the end the picture is completely veiled and covered by the offerings, and thenceforth is more an object of faith than of contemplation.

208. Standing on One's Head.—If we make truth stand on its head, we generally fail to notice that our own head, too, is not in its right position.

209. Origin and Utility of Fashion.—The obvious satisfaction of the individual with his own form excites imitation and gradually creates the form of the many—that is, fashion. The many desire, and indeed attain, that same comforting satisfaction with their own form. Consider how many reasons every man has for anxiety and shy self-concealment, and how, on this account, three-fourths of his energy and goodwill is crippled and may become unproductive! So we must be very grateful to fashion for unfettering that three-fourths and communicating self-confidence and the power of cheerful compromise to those who feel themselves bound to each other by its law. Even foolish laws give freedom and calm of the spirit, so long as many persons have submitted to their sway.

210. Looseners of Tongues.—The value of many men and books rests solely on their faculty for compelling all to speak out the most hidden and intimate things. They are looseners of tongues and crowbars to open the most stubborn teeth. Many events and misdeeds which are apparently only sent as a curse to mankind possess this value and utility.

211. Intellectual Freedom of Domicile.[12]—Who of us could dare to call himself a "free spirit" if he could not render homage after his fashion, by taking on his own shoulders a portion of that burden of public dislike and abuse, to men to whom this name is attached as a reproach? We might as well call ourselves in all seriousness "spirits free of domicile" (Freizügig) (and without that arrogant or high-spirited defiance) because we feel the impulse to freedom (Zug zur Freiheit) as the strongest instinct of our minds and, in contrast to fixed and limited minds, practically see our ideal in an intellectual nomadism—to use a modest and almost depreciatory expression.

212. Yes, the Favour of the Muses!—What Homer says on this point goes right to our heart, so true, so terrible is it:

"The Muse loved him with all her heart and gave him good and evil, for she took away his eyes and vouchsafed him sweet song."

This is an endless text for thinking men: she gives good and evil, that is her manner of loving with all her heart and soul! And each man will interpret specially for himself why we poets and thinkers have to give up our eyes in her service.[13]

213. Against the Cultivation of Music.—The artistic training of the eye from childhood upwards by means of drawing, painting, landscape-sketching, figures, scenes, involves an estimable gain in life, making the eyesight keen, calm, and enduring in the observation of men and circumstances. No similar secondary advantage arises from the artistic cultivation of the ear, whence public schools will generally do well to give the art of the eye a preference over that of the ear.

214. The Discoverers of Trivialities.—Subtle minds, from which nothing is farther than trivialities, often discover a triviality after taking all manner of circuitous routes and mountain paths, and, to the astonishment of the non-subtle, rejoice exceedingly.

215. Morals of Savants.—A regular and rapid advance in the sciences is only possible when the individual is compelled to be not so distrustful as to test every calculation and assertion of others, in fields which are remote from his own. A necessary condition, however, is that every man should have competitors in his own sphere, who are extremely distrustful and keep a sharp eye upon him. From this juxtaposition of "not too distrustful" and "extremely distrustful" arises sincerity in the republic of learning.

216. Reasons for Sterility.—There are highly gifted minds which are always sterile only because, from temperamental weakness, they are too impatient to wait for their pregnancy.

217. The Perverted World of Tears.—The manifold discomforts which the demands of higher culture cause to man finally pervert his nature to such an extent that he usually keeps himself stoical and unbending. Thus he has tears in reserve only for rare occasions of happiness, so that many must weep even at the enjoyment of painlessness—only when happy does his heart still beat.

218. The Greeks as Interpreters.—When we speak of the Greeks we unwittingly speak of to-day and yesterday; their universally known history is a blank mirror, always reflecting something that is not in the mirror itself. We enjoy the freedom of speaking about them in order to have the right of being silent about others—so that these Greeks themselves may whisper something in the ear of the reflective reader. Thus the Greeks facilitate to modern men the communication of much that is debatable and hard to communicate.

219. Of the Acquired Character of the Greeks.—We are easily led astray by the renowned Greek clearness, transparency, simplicity, and order, by their crystal-like naturalness and crystal-like art, into believing that all these gifts were bestowed on the Greeks—for instance, that they could not but write well, as Lichtenberg expressed it on one occasion. Yet no statement could be more hasty and more untenable. The history of prose from Gorgias to Demosthenes shows a course of toiling and wrestling towards light from the obscure, overloaded, and

tasteless, reminding one of the labour of heroes who had to construct the first roads through forest and bog. The dialogue of tragedy was the real achievement of the dramatist, owing to its uncommon clearness and precision, whereas the national tendency was to riot in symbolism and innuendo, a tendency expressly fostered by the great choral lyric. Similarly it was the achievement of Homer to liberate the Greeks from Asiatic pomp and gloom, and to have attained the clearness of architecture in details great and small. Nor was it by any means thought easy to say anything in a pure and illuminating style. How else should we account for the great admiration for the epigram of Simonides, which shows itself so simple, with no gilded points or arabesques of wit, but says all that it has to say plainly and with the calm of the sun, not with the straining after effect of the lightning. Since the struggle towards light from an almost native twilight is Greek, a thrill of jubilation runs through the people when they hear a laconic sentence, the language of elegy or the maxims of the Seven Wise Men. Hence they were so fond of giving precepts in verse, a practice that we find objectionable. This was the true Apolline task of the Hellenic spirit, with the aim of rising superior to the perils of metre and the obscurity which is otherwise characteristic of poetry. Simplicity, flexibility, and sobriety were wrestled for and not given by nature to this people. The danger of a relapse into Asianism constantly hovered over the Greeks, and really overtook them from time to time like a murky, overflowing tide of mystical impulses, primitive savagery and darkness. We see them plunge in; we see Europe, as it were, flooded, washed away—for Europe was very small then; but they always emerge once more to the light, good swimmers and divers that they are, those fellow-countrymen of Odysseus.

220. The Pagan Characteristic.—Perhaps there is nothing more astonishing to the observer of the Greek world than to discover that the Greeks from time to time held festivals, as it were, for all their passions and evil tendencies alike, and in fact even established a kind of series of festivals, by order of the State, for their "all-too-human." This is the pagan characteristic of their world, which Christianity has never understood and never can understand, and has always combated and despised.—They accepted this all-too-human as unavoidable, and preferred, instead of railing at it, to give it a kind of secondary right by grafting it on to the usages of society and religion. All in man that has power they called divine, and wrote it on the walls of their heaven. They do not deny this natural instinct that expresses itself in evil characteristics, but regulate and limit it to definite cults and days, so as to turn those turbulent streams into as harmless a course as possible, after devising sufficient precautionary measures. That is the root of all the moral broad-mindedness of antiquity. To the wicked, the dubious, the backward, the animal element, as to the barbaric, pre-Hellenic and Asiatic,

which still lived in the depths of Greek nature, they allowed a moderate outflow, and did not strive to destroy it utterly. The whole system was under the domain of the State, which was built up not on individuals or castes, but on common human qualities. In the structure of the State the Greeks show that wonderful sense for typical facts which later on enabled them to become investigators of Nature, historians, geographers, and philosophers. It was not a limited moral law of priests or castes, which had to decide about the constitution of the State and State worship, but the most comprehensive view of the reality of all that is human. Whence do the Greeks derive this freedom, this sense of reality? Perhaps from Homer and the poets who preceded him. For just those poets whose nature is generally not the most wise or just possess, in compensation, that delight in reality and activity of every kind, and prefer not to deny even evil. It suffices for them if evil moderates itself, does not kill or inwardly poison everything—in other words, they have similar ideas to those of the founders of Greek constitutions, and were their teachers and forerunners.

221. Exceptional Greeks.—In Greece, deep, thorough, serious minds were the exception. The national instinct tended rather to regard the serious and thorough as a kind of grimace. To borrow forms from a foreign source, not to create but to transform into the fairest shapes—that is Greek. To imitate, not for utility but for artistic illusion, ever and anon to gain the mastery over forced seriousness, to arrange, beautify, simplify—that is the continual task from Homer to the Sophists of the third and fourth centuries of our era, who are all outward show, pompous speech, declamatory gestures, and address themselves to shallow souls that care only for appearance, sound, and effect. And now let us estimate the greatness of those exceptional Greeks, who created science! Whoever tells of them, tells the most heroic story of the human mind!

222. Simplicity not the First nor the Last Thing in Point of Time.—In the history of religious ideas many errors about development and false gradations are made in matters which in reality are not consecutive outgrowths but contemporary yet separate phenomena. In particular, simplicity has still far too much the reputation of being the oldest, the initial thing. Much that is human arises by subtraction and division, and not merely by doubling, addition, and unification.—For instance, men still believe in a gradual development of the idea of God from those unwieldy stones and blocks of wood up to the highest forms of anthropomorphism. Yet the fact is that so long as divinity was attributed to and felt in trees, logs of wood, stones, and beasts, people shrank from humanising their forms as from an act of godlessness. First of all, poets, apart from all considerations of cult and the ban of religious shame, have had to make the inner imagination of man accustomed and compliant to this notion. Wherever more

pious periods and phases of thought gained the upper hand, this liberating influence of poets fell into the background, and sanctity remained, after as before, on the side of the monstrous, uncanny, quite peculiarly inhuman. And then, much of what the inner imagination ventures to picture to itself would exert a painful influence if externally and corporeally represented. The inner eye is far bolder and more shameless than the outer (whence the well-known difficulty and, to some extent, impossibility, of working epic material into dramatic form). The religious imagination for a long time entirely refuses to believe in the identity of God with an image: the image is meant to fix the numen of the Deity, actually and specifically, although in a mysterious and not altogether intelligible way. The oldest image of the Gods is meant to shelter and at the same time to hide[14] the God—to indicate him but not to expose him to view. No Greek really looked upon his Apollo as a pointed pillar of wood, his Eros as a lump of stone. These were symbols, which were intended to inspire dread of the manifestation of the God. It was the same with those blocks of wood out of which individual limbs, generally in excessive number, were fashioned with the scantiest of carving—as, for instance, a Laconian Apollo with four hands and four ears. In the incomplete, symbolical, or excessive lies a terrible sanctity, which is meant to prevent us from thinking of anything human or similar to humanity. It is not an embryonic stage of art in which such things are made—as if they were not able to speak more plainly and portray more sensibly in the age when such images were honoured! Rather, men are afraid of just one thing—direct speaking out. Just as the cella hides and conceals in a mysterious twilight, yet not completely, the holy of holies, the real numen of the Deity; just as, again, the peripteric temple hides the cella, protecting it from indiscreet eyes as with a screen and a veil, yet not completely—so it is with the image of the Deity, and at the same time the concealment of the Deity.—Only when outside the cult, in the profane world of athletic contest, the joy in the victor had risen so high that the ripples thus started reacted upon the lake of religious emotion, was the statue of the victor set up before the temple. Then the pious pilgrim had to accustom his eye and his soul, whether he would or no, to the inevitable sight of human beauty and super-strength, so that the worship of men and Gods melted into each other from physical and spiritual contact. Then too for the first time the fear of really humanising the figures of the Gods is lost, and the mighty arena for great plastic art is opened—even now with the limitation that wherever there is to be adoration the primitive form and ugliness are carefully preserved and copied. But the Hellene, as he dedicates and makes offerings, may now with religious sanction indulge in his delight in making God become a man.

223. Whither We must Travel.—Immediate self-observation is not enough, by a long way, to enable us to learn to know ourselves. We need history, for the past continues to flow through us in a hundred channels. We ourselves are, after all, nothing but our own sensation at every moment of this continued flow. Even here, when we wish to step down into the stream of our apparently most peculiar and personal development, Heraclitus' aphorism, "You cannot step twice into the same river," holds good.—This is a piece of wisdom which has, indeed, gradually become trite, but nevertheless has remained as strong and true as it ever was. It is the same with the saying that, in order to understand history, we must scrutinise the living remains of historical periods; that we must travel, as old Herodotus travelled, to other nations, especially to those so-called savage or half-savage races in regions where man has doffed or not yet donned European garb. For they are ancient and firmly established steps of culture on which we can stand. There is, however, a more subtle art and aim in travelling, which does not always necessitate our passing from place to place and going thousands of miles away. Very probably the last three centuries, in all their colourings and refractions of culture, survive even in our vicinity, only they have to be discovered. In some families, or even in individuals, the strata are still superimposed on each other, beautifully and perceptibly; in other places there are dispersions and displacements of the structure which are harder to understand. Certainly in remote districts, in less known mountain valleys, circumscribed communities have been able more easily to maintain an admirable pattern of a far older sentiment, a pattern that must here be investigated. On the other hand, it is improbable that such discoveries will be made in Berlin, where man comes into the world washed-out and sapless. He who after long practice of this art of travel has become a hundred-eyed Argus will accompany his Io—I mean his ego—everywhere, and in Egypt and Greece, Byzantium and Rome, France and Germany, in the age of wandering or settled races, in Renaissance or Reformation, at home and abroad, in sea, forest, plant, and mountain, will again light upon the travel-adventure of this ever-growing, ever-altered ego.—Thus self-knowledge becomes universal knowledge as regards the entire past, and, by another chain of observation, which can only be indicated here, self-direction and self-training in the freest and most far-seeing spirits might become universal direction as regards all future humanity.

224. Balm and Poison.—We cannot ponder too deeply on this fact: Christianity is the religion of antiquity grown old; it presupposes degenerate old culture-stocks, and on them it had, and still has, power to work like balm. There are periods when ears and eyes are full of slime, so that they can no longer hear the voice of reason and philosophy or see the wisdom that walks in bodily shape,

whether it bears the name of Epictetus or of Epicurus. Then, perhaps, the erection of the martyr's cross and the "trumpet of the last judgment" may have the effect of still inspiring such races to end their lives decently. If we think of Juvenal's Rome, of that poisonous toad with the eyes of Venus, we understand what it means to make the sign of the Cross before the world, we honour the silent Christian community and are grateful for its having stifled the Greco-Roman Empire. If, indeed, most men were then born in spiritual slavery, with the sensuality of old men, what a pleasure to meet beings who were more soul than body, and who seemed to realise the Greek idea of the shades of the under-world—shy, scurrying, chirping, kindly creatures, with a reversion on the "better life," and therefore so unassuming, so secretly scornful, so proudly patient!—This Christianity, as the evening chime of the good antiquity, with cracked, weary and yet melodious bell, is balm in the ears even to one who only now traverses those centuries historically. What must it have been to those men themselves!—To young and fresh barbarian nations, on the other hand, Christianity is a poison. For to implant the teaching of sinfulness and damnation in the heroic, childlike, and animal soul of the old Germans is nothing but poisoning. An enormous chemical fermentation and decomposition, a medley of sentiments and judgments, a rank growth of adventurous legend, and hence in the long run a fundamental weakening of such barbarian peoples, was the inevitable result. True, without this weakening what should we have left of Greek culture, of the whole cultured past of the human race? For the barbarians untouched by Christianity knew very well how to make a clean sweep of old cultures, as was only too clearly shown by the heathen conquerors of Romanised Britain. Thus Christianity, against its will, was compelled to aid in making "the antique world" immortal.—There remains, however, a counter-question and the possibility of a counter-reckoning. Without this weakening through the poisoning referred to, would any of those fresh stocks—the Germans, for instance—have been in a position gradually to find by themselves a higher, a peculiar, a new culture, of which the most distant conception would therefore have been lost to humanity?—In this, as in every case, we do not know, Christianly speaking, whether God owes the devil or the devil God more thanks for everything having turned out as it has.

225. Faith makes Holy and Condemns.—A Christian who happened upon forbidden paths of thought might well ask himself on some occasion whether it is really necessary that there should be a God, side by side with a representative Lamb, if faith in the existence of these beings suffices to produce the same influences? If they do exist after all, are they not superfluous beings? For all that is given by the Christian religion to the human soul, all that is beneficent,

consoling, and edifying, just as much as all that depresses and crushes, emanates from that faith and not from the objects of that faith. It is here as in another well-known case—there were indeed no witches, but the terrible effects of the belief in witches were the same as if they really had existed. For all occasions where the Christian awaits the immediate intervention of a God, though in vain (for there is no God), his religion is inventive enough to find subterfuges and reasons for tranquillity. In so far Christianity is an ingenious religion.—Faith, indeed, has up to the present not been able to move real mountains, although I do not know who assumed that it could. But it can put mountains where there are none.

226. The Tragi-Comedy of Regensburg.—Here and there we see with terrible clearness the harlequinade of Fortune, how she fastens the rope, on which she wills that succeeding centuries should dance, on to a few days, one place, the condition and opinions of one brain. Thus the fate of modern German history lies in the days of that disputation at Regensburg: the peaceful settlement of ecclesiastical and moral affairs, without religious wars or a counter-reformation, and also the unity of the German nation, seemed assured: the deep, gentle spirit of Contarini hovered for one moment over the theological squabble, victorious, as representative of the riper Italian piety, reflecting the morning glory of intellectual freedom. But Luther's hard head, full of suspicions and strange misgivings, showed resistance. Because justification by grace appeared to him his greatest motto and discovery, he did not believe the phrase in the mouth of Italians; whereas, in point of fact, as is well known, they had invented it much earlier and spread it throughout Italy in deep silence. In this apparent agreement Luther saw the tricks of the devil, and hindered the work of peace as well as he could, thereby advancing to a great extent the aims of the Empire's foes.—And now, in order to have a still stronger idea of the dreadful farcicality of it all, let us add that none of the principles about which men then disputed in Regensburg—neither that of original sin, nor that of redemption by proxy, nor that of justification by faith—is in any way true or even has any connection with truth: that they are now all recognised as incapable of being discussed. Yet on this account the world was set on fire—that is to say, by opinions which correspond to no things or realities; whereas as regards purely philological questions—as, for instance, that of the sacramental words in the Eucharist—discussion at any rate is permitted, because in this case the truth can be said. But "where nothing is, even truth has lost her right."[15]—Lastly, it only remains to be said that it is true these principles give rise to sources of power so mighty that without them all the mills of the modern world could not be driven with such force. And it is

primarily a matter of force, only secondarily of truth (and perhaps not even secondarily)—is it not so, my dear up-to-date friends?

227. Goethe's Errors.—Goethe is a signal exception among great artists in that he did not live within the limited confines of his real capacity, as if that must be the essential, the distinctive, the unconditional, and the last thing in him and for all the world. Twice he intended to possess something higher than he really possessed—and went astray in the second half of his life, where he seems quite convinced that he is one of the great scientific discoverers and illuminators. So too in the first half of his life he demanded of himself something higher than the poetic art seemed to him—and here already he made a mistake. That nature wished to make him a plastic artist,—this was his inwardly glowing and scorching secret, which finally drove him to Italy, that he might give vent to his mania in this direction and make to it every possible sacrifice. At last, shrewd as he was, and honestly averse to any mental perversion in himself, he discovered that a tricksy elf of desire had attracted him to the belief in this calling, and that he must free himself of the greatest passion of his heart and bid it farewell. The painful conviction, tearing and gnawing at his vitals, that it was necessary to bid farewell, finds full expression in the character of Tasso. Over Tasso, that Werther intensified, hovers the premonition of something worse than death, as when one says: "Now it is over, after this farewell: how shall I go on living without going mad?" These two fundamental errors of his life gave Goethe, in face of a purely literary attitude towards poetry (the only attitude then known to the world), such an unembarrassed and apparently almost arbitrary position. Not to speak of the period when Schiller (poor Schiller, who had no time himself and left no time to others) drove away his shy dread of poetry, his fear of all literary life and craftsmanship, Goethe appears like a Greek who now and then visits his beloved, doubting whether she be not a Goddess to whom he can give no proper name. In all his poetry one notices the inspiring neighbourhood of plastic art and Nature. The features of these figures that floated before him—and perhaps he always thought he was on the track of the metamorphoses of one Goddess—became, without his will or knowledge, the features of all the children of his art. Without the extravagances of error he would not have been Goethe—that is, the only German artist in writing who has not yet become out of date—just because he desired as little to be a writer as a German by vocation.

228. Travellers and their Grades.—Among travellers we may distinguish five grades. The first and lowest grade is of those who travel and are seen—they become really travelled and are, as it were, blind. Next come those who really see the world. The third class experience the results of their seeing. The fourth weave their experience into their life and carry it with them henceforth. Lastly, there are

some men of the highest strength who, as soon as they have returned home, must finally and necessarily work out in their lives and productions all the things seen that they have experienced and incorporated in themselves.—Like these five species of travellers, all mankind goes through the whole pilgrimage of life, the lowest as purely passive, the highest as those who act and live out their lives without keeping back any residue of inner experiences.

229. In Climbing Higher.—So soon as we climb higher than those who hitherto admired us, we appear to them as sunken and fallen. For they imagined that under all circumstances they were on the heights in our company (maybe also through our agency).

230. Measure and Moderation.—Of two quite lofty things, measure and moderation, it is best never to speak. A few know their force and significance, from the mysterious paths of inner experiences and conversions: they honour in them something quite godlike, and are afraid to speak aloud. All the rest hardly listen when they are spoken about, and think the subjects under discussion are tedium and mediocrity. We must perhaps except those who have once heard a warning note from that realm but have stopped their ears against the sound. The recollection of it makes them angry and exasperated.

231. Humanity of Friendship and Comradeship.—"If thou wilt take the left hand, then I will go to the right,"[16] that feeling is the hall-mark of humanity in intimate intercourse, and without that feeling every friendship, every band of apostles or disciples, sooner or later becomes a fraud.

232. The Profound.—Men of profound thought appear to themselves in intercourse with others like comedians, for in order to be understood they must always simulate superficiality.

233. For the Scorners of "Herd-Humanity."—He who regards human beings as a herd, and flies from them as fast as he can, will certainly be caught up by them and gored upon their horns.

234. The Main Transgression against the Vain.—In society, he who gives another an opportunity of favourably setting forth his knowledge, sentiments, and experience sets himself above him. Unless he is felt by the other to be a superior being without limitation, he is guilty of an attack upon his vanity, while what he aimed at was the gratification of the other man's vanity.

235. Disappointment.—When a long life of action distinguished by speeches and writings gives publicity to a man's personality, personal intercourse with him is generally disappointing on two grounds. Firstly, one expects too much from a brief period of intercourse (namely, all that the thousand and one opportunities of life can alone bring out). Secondly, no recognised person gives himself the

trouble to woo recognition in individual cases. He is too careless, and we are at too high a tension.

236. Two Sources of Kindness.—To treat all men with equal good-humour, and to be kind without distinction of persons, may arise as much from a profound contempt for mankind as from an ingrained love of humanity.

237. The Wanderer in the Mountains to Himself.—There are certain signs that you have gone farther and higher. There is a freer, wider prospect before you, the air blows cooler yet milder in your face (you have unlearned the folly of confounding mildness with warmth), your gait is more firm and vigorous, courage and discretion have waxed together. On all these grounds your journey may now be more lonely and in any case more perilous than heretofore, if indeed not to the extent believed by those who from the misty valley see you, the roamer, striding on the mountains.

238. With the Exception of Our Neighbour.—I admit that my head is set wrong on my neck only, for every other man, as is well known, knows better than I what I should do or leave alone. The only one who cannot help me is myself, poor beggar! Are we not all like statues on which false heads have been placed? Eh, dear neighbour?—Ah no; you, just you, are the exception!

239. Caution.—We must either not go about at all with people who are lacking in the reverence for personalities, or inexorably fetter them beforehand with the manacles of convention.

240. The Wish to Appear Vain.—In conversation with strangers or little-known acquaintances, to express only selected thoughts, to speak of one's famous acquaintances, and important experiences and travels, is a sign that one is not proud, or at least would not like to appear proud. Vanity is the polite mask of pride.

241. Good Friendship.—A good friendship arises when the one man deeply respects the other, more even than himself; loves him also, though not so much as himself; and finally, to facilitate intercourse, knows how to add the delicate bloom and veneer of intimacy, but at the same time wisely refrains from a true, real intimacy, from the confounding of meum and tuum.

242. Friends as Ghosts.—If we change ourselves vitally, our friends, who have not changed, become ghosts of our own past: their voice sounds shadowy and dreadful to us, as if we heard our own voice speaking, but younger, harder, less mellow.

243. One Eye and Two Glances.—The same people whose eyes naturally plead for favours and indulgences are accustomed, from their frequent humiliations and cravings for revenge, to assume a shameless glance as well.

244. The Haze of Distance.—A child throughout life—that sounds very touching, but is only the verdict from the distance. Seen and known close at hand, he is always called "puerile throughout life."

245. Advantage and Disadvantage in the Same Misunderstanding.—The mute perplexity of the subtle brain is usually understood by the non-subtle as a silent superiority, and is much dreaded whereas the perception of perplexity would produce good will.

246. The Sage giving Himself out to be a Fool.—The philanthropy of the sage sometimes makes him decide to pretend to be excited, enraged, or delighted, so that he may not hurt his surroundings by the coldness and rationality of his true nature.

247. Forcing Oneself to Attention.—So soon as we note that any one in intercourse and conversation with us has to force himself to attention, we have adequate evidence that he loves us not, or loves us no longer.

248. The Way to a Christian Virtue.—Learning from one's enemies is the best way to love them, for it inspires us with a grateful mood towards them.

249. Stratagem of the Importunate.—The importunate man gives us gold coins as change for our convention coins, and thereby tries to force us afterwards to treat our convention as an oversight and him as an exception.

250. Reason for Dislike.—We become hostile to many an artist or writer, not because we notice in the end that he has duped us, but because he did not find more subtle means necessary to entrap us.

251. In Parting.—Not by the way one soul approaches another, but by the way it separates, do I recognise its relationship and homogeneity with the other.

252. Silentium.—We must not speak about our friends, or we renounce the sentiment of friendship.

253. Impoliteness.—Impoliteness is often the sign of a clumsy modesty, which when taken by surprise loses its head and would fain hide the fact by means of rudeness.

254. Honesty's Miscalculation.—Our newest acquaintances are sometimes the first to learn what we have hitherto kept dark. We have the foolish notion that our proof of confidence is the strongest fetter wherewith to hold them fast. But they do not know enough about us to feel so strongly the sacrifice involved in our speaking out, and betray our secrets to others without any idea of betrayal. Hereby we possibly lose our old friends.

255. In the Ante-Chamber of Favour.—All men whom we let stand long in the ante-chamber of our favour get into a state of fermentation or become bitter.

256. Warning to the Despised.—When we have sunk unmistakably in the estimation of mankind we should cling tooth and nail to modesty in intercourse,

or we shall betray to others that we have sunk in our own estimation as well. Cynicism in intercourse is a sign that a man, when alone, treats himself too as a dog.

257. Ignorance often Ennobles.—With regard to the respect of those who pay respect, it is an advantage ostensibly not to understand certain things. Ignorance, too, confers privileges.

258. The Opponent of Grace.—The impatient and arrogant man does not care for grace, feeling it to be a corporeal, visible reproach against himself. For grace is heartfelt toleration in movement and gesture.

259. On Seeing Again.—When old friends see each other again after a long separation, it often happens that they affect an interest in matters to which they have long since become indifferent. Sometimes both remark this, but dare not raise the veil—from a mournful doubt. Hence arise conversations as in the realm of the dead.

260. Making Friends only with the Industrious.—The man of leisure is dangerous to his friends, for, having nothing to do, he talks of what his friends are doing or not doing, interferes, and finally makes himself a nuisance. The clever man will only make friends with the industrious.

261. One Weapon twice as Much as Two.—It is an unequal combat when one man defends his cause with head and heart, the other with head alone. The first has sun and wind against him, as it were, and his two weapons interfere with each other: he loses the prize—in the eyes of truth. True, the victory of the second, with his one weapon, is seldom a victory after the hearts of all the other spectators, and makes him unpopular.

262. Depth and Troubled Waters.—The public easily confounds him who fishes in troubled waters with him who pumps up from the depths.

263. Demonstrating One's Vanity to Friend and Foe.—Many a man, from vanity, maltreats even his friends, when in the presence of witnesses to whom he wishes to make his own preponderance clear. Others exaggerate the merits of their enemies, in order to point proudly to the fact that they are worthy of such foes.

264. Cooling Off.—The over-heating of the heart is generally allied with illness of the head and judgment. He who is concerned for a time with the health of his head must know what he has to cool, careless of the future of his heart. For if we are capable at all of giving warmth, we are sure to become warm again and then have our summer.

265. Mingled Feelings.—Towards science women and self-seeking artists entertain a feeling that is composed of envy and sentimentality.

266. Where Danger is Greatest.—We seldom break our leg so long as life continues a toilsome upward climb. The danger comes when we begin to take things easily and choose the convenient paths.

267. Not too Early.—We must beware of becoming sharp too early, or we shall also become thin too early.

268. Joy in Refractoriness.—The good teacher knows cases where he is proud that his pupil remains true to himself in opposition to him—at times when the youth must not understand the man or would be harmed by understanding him.

269. The Experiment of Honesty.—Young men, who wish to be more honest than they have been, seek as victim some one acknowledged to be honest, attacking him first with an attempt to reach his height by abuse—with the underlying notion that this first experiment at any rate is void of danger. For just such a one has no right to chastise the impudence of the honest man.

270. The Eternal Child.—We think, short-sighted that we are, that fairy-tales and games belong to childhood. As if at any age we should care to live without fairy-tales and games! Our words and sentiments are indeed different, but the essential fact remains the same, as is proved by the child himself looking on games as his work and fairy-tales as his truth. The shortness of life ought to preserve us from a pedantic distinction between the different ages—as if every age brought something new—and a poet ought one day to portray a man of two hundred, who really lives without fairy-tales and games.

271. Every Philosophy is the Philosophy of a Period of Life.—The period of life in which a philosopher finds his teaching is manifested by his teaching; he cannot avoid that, however elevated above time and hour he may feel himself. Thus, Schopenhauer's philosophy remains a mirror of his hot and melancholy youth—it is no mode of thought for older men. Plato's philosophy reminds one of the middle thirties, when a warm and a cold current generally rush together, so that spray and delicate clouds and, under favourable circumstances and glimpses of sunshine, enchanting rainbow-pictures result.

272. Of the Intellect of Women.—The intellectual strength of a woman is best proved by the fact that she offers her own intellect as a sacrifice out of love for a man and his intellect, and that nevertheless in the new domain, which was previously foreign to her nature, a second intellect at once arises as an aftergrowth, to which the man's mind impels her.

273. Raising and Lowering in the Sexual Domain.—The storm of desire will sometimes carry a man up to a height where all desire is silenced, where he really loves and lives in a better state of being rather than in a better state of choice. On the other hand, a good woman, from true love, often climbs down to desire, and

lowers herself in her own eyes. The latter action in particular is one of the most pathetic sensations which the idea of a good marriage can involve.

274. Man Promises, Woman Fulfils.—By woman Nature shows how far she has hitherto achieved her task of fashioning humanity, by man she shows what she has had to overcome and what she still proposes to do for humanity.—The most perfect woman of every age is the holiday-task of the Creator on every seventh day of culture, the recreation of the artist from his work.

275. Transplanting.—If we have spent our intellect in order to gain mastery over the intemperance of the passions, the sad result often follows that we transfer the intemperance to the intellect, and from that time forth are extravagant in thought and desire of knowledge.

276. Laughter as Treachery.—How and when a woman laughs is a sign of her culture, but in the ring of laughter her nature reveals itself, and in highly cultured women perhaps even the last insoluble residue of their nature. Hence the psychologist will say with Horace, though from different reasons: "Ridete puellae."

277. From the Youthful Soul.—Youths varyingly show devotion and impudence towards the same person, because at bottom they only despise or admire themselves in that other person, and between the two feelings but stagger to and fro in themselves, so long as they have not found in experience the measure of their will and ability.

278. For the Amelioration of the World.—If we forbade the discontented, the sullen, and the atrabilious to propagate, we might transform the world into a garden of happiness.—This aphorism belongs to a practical philosophy for the female sex.

279. Not to Distrust your Emotions.—The feminine phrase "Do not distrust your emotions" does not mean much more than "Eat what tastes good to you." This may also, especially for moderate natures, be a good everyday rule. But other natures must live according to another maxim: "You must eat not only with your mouth but also with your brain, in order that the greediness of your mouth may not prove your undoing."

280. A Cruel Fancy of Love.—Every great love involves the cruel thought of killing the object of love, so that it may be removed once for all from the mischievous play of change. For love is more afraid of change than of destruction.

281. Doors.—In everything that is learnt or experienced, the child, just like the man, sees doors; but for the former they are places to go to, for the latter to go through.

282. Sympathetic Women.—The sympathy of women, which is talkative, takes the sick-bed to market.

283. Early Merit.—He who acquires merit early in life tends to forget all reverence for age and old people, and accordingly, greatly to his disadvantage, excludes himself from the society of the mature, those who confer maturity. Thus in spite of his early merit he remains green, importunate, and boyish longer than others.

284. Souls All of a Piece.—Women and artists think that where we do not contradict them we cannot. Reverence on ten counts and silent disapproval on ten others appears to them an impossible combination, because their souls are all of a piece.

285. Young Talents.—With respect to young talents we must strictly follow Goethe's maxim, that we should often avoid harming error in order to avoid harming truth. Their condition is like the diseases of pregnancy, and involves strange appetites. These appetites should be satisfied and humoured as far as possible, for the sake of the fruit they may be expected to produce. It is true that, as nurse of these remarkable invalids, one must learn the difficult art of voluntary self-abasement.

286. Disgust with Truth.—Women are so constituted that all truth (in relation to men, love, children, society, aim of life) disgusts them—and that they try to be revenged on every one who opens their eyes.

287. The Source of Great Love.—Whence arises the sudden passion of a man for a woman, a passion so deep, so vital? Least of all from sensuality only: but when a man finds weakness, need of help, and high spirits united in the same creature, he suffers a sort of overflowing of soul, and is touched and offended at the same moment. At this point arises the source of great love.

288. Cleanliness.—In the child, the sense for cleanliness should be fanned into a passion, and then later on he will raise himself, in ever new phases, to almost every virtue, and will finally appear, in compensation for all talent, as a shining cloud of purity, temperance, gentleness, and character, happy in himself and spreading happiness around.

289. Of Vain Old Men.—Profundity of thought belongs to youth, clarity of thought to old age. When, in spite of this, old men sometimes speak and write in the manner of the profound, they do so from vanity, imagining that they thereby assume the charm of juvenility, enthusiasm, growth, apprehensiveness, hopefulness.

290. Enjoyment of Novelty.—Men use a new lesson or experience later on as a ploughshare or perhaps also as a weapon, women at once make it into an ornament.

291. How both Sexes behave when in the Right.—If it is conceded to a woman that she is right, she cannot deny herself the triumph of setting her heel on the neck of the vanquished; she must taste her victory to the full. On the other hand, man towards man in such a case is ashamed of being right. But then man is accustomed to victory; with woman it is an exception.

292. Abnegation in the Will to Beauty.—In order to become beautiful, a woman must not desire to be considered pretty. That is to say, in ninety-nine out of a hundred cases where she could please she must scorn and put aside all thoughts of pleasing. Only then can she ever reap the delight of him whose soul's portal is wide enough to admit the great.

293. Unintelligible, Unendurable.—A youth cannot understand that an old man has also had his delights, his dawns of feeling, his changings and soarings of thought. It offends him to think that such things have existed before. But it makes him very bitter to hear that, to become fruitful, he must lose those buds and dispense with their fragrance.

294. The Party with the Air of Martyrdom.—Every party that can assume an air of martyrdom wins good-natured souls over to its side and thereby itself acquires an air of good nature—greatly to its advantage.

295. Assertions surer than Arguments.—An assertion has, with the majority of men at any rate, more effect than an argument, for arguments provoke mistrust. Hence demagogues seek to strengthen the arguments of their party by assertions.

296. The Best Concealers.—All regularly successful men are profoundly cunning in making their faults and weaknesses look like manifestations of strength. This proves that they must know their defects uncommonly well.

297. From Time to Time.—He sat in the city gateway and said to one who passed through that this was the city gate. The latter replied that this was true, but that one must not be too much in the right if one expected to be thanked for it. "Oh," answered the other, "I don't want thanks, but from time to time it is very pleasant not merely to be in the right but to remain in the right."

298. Virtue was not Invented by the Germans.—Goethe's nobleness and freedom from envy, Beethoven's fine hermitical resignation, Mozart's cheerfulness and grace of heart, Handel's unbending manliness and freedom under the law, Bach's confident and luminous inner life, such as does not even need to renounce glamour and success—are these qualities peculiarly German?—If they are not, they at least prove to what goal Germans should strive and to what they can attain.

299. Pia Fraus or Something Else.—I hope I am mistaken, but I think that in Germany of to-day a twofold sort of hypocrisy is set up as the duty of the moment for every one. From imperial-political misgivings Germanism is demanded, and

from social apprehensions Christianity—but both only in words and gestures, and particularly in ability to keep silent. It is the veneer that nowadays costs so much and is paid for so highly; and for the benefit of the spectators the face of the nation assumes German and Christian wrinkles.

300. How far even in the Good the Half may be More than the Whole.—In all things that are constructed to last and demand the service of many hands, much that is less good must be made a rule, although the organiser knows what is better and harder very well. He will calculate that there will never be a lack of persons who can correspond to the rule, and he knows that the middling good is the rule.—The youth seldom sees this point, and as an innovator thinks how marvellously he is in the right and how strange is the blindness of others.

301. The Partisan.—The true partisan learns nothing more, he only experiences and judges. It is significant that Solon, who was never a partisan but pursued his aims above and apart from parties or even against them, was the father of that simple phrase wherein lies the secret of the health and vitality of Athens: "I grow old, but I am always learning."

302. What is German according to Goethe.—They are really intolerable people of whom one cannot even accept the good, who have freedom of disposition but do not remark that they are lacking in freedom of taste and spirit. Yet just this, according to Goethe's well-weighed judgment, is German.—His voice and his example indicate that the German should be more than a German if he wishes to be useful or even endurable to other nations—and which direction his striving should take, in order that he may rise above and beyond himself.

303. When it is Necessary to Remain Stationary.—When the masses begin to rage, and reason is under a cloud, it is a good thing, if the health of one's soul is not quite assured, to go under a doorway and look out to see what the weather is like.

304. The Revolution-Spirit and the Possession-Spirit.—The only remedy against Socialism that still lies in your power is to avoid provoking Socialism—in other words, to live in moderation and contentment, to prevent as far as possible all lavish display, and to aid the State as far as possible in its taxing of all superfluities and luxuries. You do not like this remedy? Then, you rich bourgeois who call yourselves "Liberals," confess that it is your own inclination that you find so terrible and menacing in Socialists, but allow to prevail in yourselves as unavoidable, as if with you it were something different. As you are constituted, if you had not your fortune and the cares of maintaining it, this bent of yours would make Socialists of you. Possession alone differentiates you from them. If you wish to conquer the assailants of your prosperity, you must first conquer yourselves.—And if that prosperity only meant well-being, it would not be so

external and provocative of envy; it would be more generous, more benevolent, more compensatory, more helpful. But the spurious, histrionic element in your pleasures, which lie more in the feeling of contrast (because others have them not, and feel envious) than in feelings of realised and heightened power—your houses, dresses, carriages, shops, the demands of your palates and your tables, your noisy operatic and musical enthusiasm; lastly your women, formed and fashioned but of base metal, gilded but without the ring of gold, chosen by you for show and considering themselves meant for show—these are the things that spread the poison of that national disease, which seizes the masses ever more and more as a Socialistic heart-itch, but has its origin and breeding-place in you. Who shall now arrest this epidemic?

305. Party Tactics.—When a party observes that a previous member has changed from an unqualified to a qualified adherent, it endures it so ill that it irritates and mortifies him in every possible way with the object of forcing him to a decisive break and making him an opponent. For the party suspects that the intention of finding a relative value in its faith, a value which admits of pro and con, of weighing and discarding, is more dangerous than downright opposition.

306. For the Strengthening of Parties.—Whoever wishes to strengthen a party internally should give it an opportunity of being forcibly treated with obvious injustice. The party thus acquires a capital of good conscience, which hitherto it perhaps lacked.

307. To Provide for One's Past.—As men after all only respect the old-established and slowly developed, he who would survive after his death must not only provide for posterity but still more for the past. Hence tyrants of every sort (including tyrannical artists and politicians) like to do violence to history, so that history may seem a preparation and a ladder up to them.

308. Party Writers.—The beating of drums, which delights young writers who serve a party, sounds to him who does not belong to the party like a rattling of chains, and excites sympathy rather than admiration.

309. Taking Sides against Ourselves.—Our followers never forgive us for taking sides against ourselves, for we seem in their eyes not only to be spurning their love but to be exposing them to the charge of lack of intelligence.

310. Danger in Wealth.—Only a man of intellect should hold property: otherwise property is dangerous to the community. For the owner, not knowing how to make use of the leisure which his possessions might secure to him, will continue to strive after more property. This strife will be his occupation, his strategy in the war with ennui. So in the end real wealth is produced from the moderate property that would be enough for an intellectual man. Such wealth, then, is the glittering outcrop of intellectual dependence and poverty, but it looks

quite different from what its humble origin might lead one to expect, because it can mask itself with culture and art—it can, in fact, purchase the mask. Hence it excites envy in the poor and uncultured—who at bottom always envy culture and see no mask in the mask—and gradually paves the way for a social revolution. For a gilded coarseness and a histrionic blowing of trumpets in the pretended enjoyment of culture inspires that class with the thought, "It is only a matter of money," whereas it is indeed to some extent a matter of money, but far more of intellect.

311. Joy in Commanding and Obeying.—Commanding is a joy, like obeying; the former when it has not yet become a habit, the latter just when it has become a habit. Old servants under new masters advance each other mutually in giving pleasure.

312. Ambition for a Forlorn Hope.—There is an ambition for a forlorn hope which forces a party to place itself at the post of extreme danger.

313. When Asses are Needed.—We shall not move the crowd to cry "Hosanna!" until we have ridden into the city upon an ass.

314. Party Usage.—Every party attempts to represent the important elements that have sprung up outside it as unimportant, and if it does not succeed, it attacks those elements the more bitterly, the more excellent they are.

315. Becoming Empty.—Of him who abandons himself to the course of events, a smaller and smaller residue is continually left. Great politicians may therefore become quite empty men, although they were once full and rich.

316. Welcome Enemies.—The Socialistic movements are nowadays becoming more and more agreeable rather than terrifying to the dynastic governments, because by these movements they are provided with a right and a weapon for making exceptional rules, and can thus attack their real bogies, democrats and anti-dynasts.—Towards all that such governments professedly detest they feel a secret cordiality and inclination. But they are compelled to draw the veil over their soul.

317. Possession Possesses.—Only up to a certain point does possession make men feel freer and more independent; one step farther, and possession becomes lord, the possessor a slave. The latter must sacrifice his time, his thoughts to the former, and feels himself compelled to an intercourse, nailed to a spot, incorporated with the State—perhaps quite in conflict with his real and essential needs.

318. Of the Mastery of Them that Know.—It is easy, ridiculously easy, to set up a model for the choice of a legislative body. First of all the honest and reliable men of the nation, who at the same time are masters and experts in some one

branch, have to become prominent by mutual scenting-out and recognition. From these, by a narrower process of selection, the learned and expert of the first rank in each individual branch must again be chosen, also by mutual recognition and guarantee. If the legislative body be composed of these, it will finally be necessary, in each individual case, that only the voices and judgments of the most specialised experts should decide; the honesty of all the rest should have become so great that it is simply a matter of decency to leave the voting also in the hands of these men. The result would be that the law, in the strictest sense, would emanate from the intelligence of the most intelligent.—As things now are, voting is done by parties, and at every division there must be hundreds of uneasy consciences among the ill-taught, the incapable of judgment, among those who merely repeat, imitate, and go with the tide. Nothing lowers the dignity of a new law so much as this inherent shamefaced feeling of insincerity that necessarily results at every party division. But, as has been said, it is easy, ridiculously easy, to set up such a model: no power on earth is at present strong enough to realise such an ideal—unless the belief in the highest utility of knowledge, and of those that know, at last dawns even upon the most hostile minds and is preferred to the prevalent belief in majorities. In the sense of such a future may our watchword be: "More reverence for them that know, and down with all parties!"

319. Of the "Nation of Thinkers" (or of Bad Thinking).—The vague, vacillating, premonitory, elementary, intuitive elements—to choose obscure names for obscure things—that are attributed to the German nature would be, if they really still existed, a proof that our culture has remained several stages behind and is still surrounded by the spell and atmosphere of the Middle Ages.—It is true that in this backwardness there are certain advantages: by these qualities the Germans (if, as has been said before, they still possess them) would possess the capacity, which other nations have now lost, for doing certain things and particularly for understanding certain things. Much undoubtedly is lost if the lack of sense—which is just the common factor in all those qualities—is lost. Here too, however, there are no losses without the highest compensatory gains, so that no reason is left for lamenting, granting that we do not, like children, and gourmands, wish to enjoy at once the fruits of all seasons of the year.

320. Carrying Coals to Newcastle.—The governments of the great States have two instruments for keeping the people dependent, in fear and obedience: a coarser, the army, and a more refined, the school. With the aid of the former they win over to their side the ambition of the higher strata and the strength of the lower, so far as both are characteristic of active and energetic men of moderate or inferior gifts. With the aid of the latter they win over gifted poverty, especially the intellectually pretentious semi-poverty of the middle classes. Above

all, they make teachers of all grades into an intellectual court looking unconsciously "towards the heights." By putting obstacle after obstacle in the way of private schools and the wholly distasteful individual tuition they secure the disposal of a considerable number of educational posts, towards which numerous hungry and submissive eyes are turned to an extent five times as great as can ever be satisfied. These posts, however, must support the holder but meagrely, so that he maintains a feverish thirst for promotion and becomes still more closely attached to the views of the government. For it is always more advantageous to foster moderate discontent than contentment, the mother of courage, the grandmother of free thought and exuberance. By means of this physically and mentally bridled body of teachers, the youth of the country is as far as possible raised to a certain level of culture that is useful to the State and arranged on a suitable sliding-scale. Above all, the immature and ambitious minds of all classes are almost imperceptibly imbued with the idea that only a career which is recognised and hall-marked by the State can lead immediately to social distinction. The effect of this belief in government examinations and titles goes so far that even men who have remained independent and have risen by trade or handicraft still feel a pang of discontent in their hearts until their position too is marked and acknowledged by a gracious bestowal of rank and orders from above—until one becomes a "somebody." Finally the State connects all these hundreds of offices and posts in its hands with the obligation of being trained and hallmarked in these State schools if one ever wishes to enter this charmed circle. Honour in society, daily bread, the possibility of a family, protection from above, the feeling of community in a common culture—all this forms a network of hopes into which every young man walks: how should he feel the slightest breath of mistrust? In the end, perhaps, the obligation of being a soldier for one year has become with every one, after the lapse of a few generations, an unreflecting habit, an understood thing, with an eye to which we construct the plan of our lives quite early. Then the State can venture on the master-stroke of weaving together school and army, talent, ambition and strength by means of common advantages—that is, by attracting the more highly gifted on favourable terms to the army and inspiring them with the military spirit of joyful obedience; so that finally, perhaps, they become attached permanently to the flag and endow it by their talents with an ever new and more brilliant lustre. Then nothing more is wanted but an opportunity for great wars. These are provided from professional reasons (and so in all innocence) by diplomats, aided by newspapers and Stock Exchanges. For "the nation," as a nation of soldiers, need never be supplied with a good conscience in war—it has one already.

321. The Press.—If we consider how even to-day all great political transactions glide upon the stage secretly and stealthily; how they are hidden by unimportant events, and seem small when close at hand; how they only show their far-reaching effect, and leave the soil still quaking, long after they have taken place;—what significance can we attach to the Press in its present position, with its daily expenditure of lung-power in order to bawl, to deafen, to excite, to terrify? Is it anything more than an everlasting false alarm, which tries to lead our ears and our wits into a false direction?

322. After a Great Event.—A nation and a man whose soul has come to light through some great event generally feel the immediate need of some act of childishness or coarseness, as much from shame as for purposes of recreation.

323. To be a Good German means to de-Germanise Oneself.—National differences consist, far more than has hitherto been observed, only in the differences of various grades of culture, and are only to a very small extent permanent (nor even that in a strict sense). For this reason all arguments based on national character are so little binding on one who aims at the alteration of convictions—in other words, at culture. If, for instance, we consider all that has already been German, we shall improve upon the hypothetical question, "What is German?" by the counter-question, "What is now German?" and every good German will answer it practically, by overcoming his German characteristics. For when a nation advances and grows, it bursts the girdle previously given to it by its national outlook. When it remains stationary or declines, its soul is surrounded by a fresh girdle, and the crust, as it becomes harder and harder, builds a prison around, with walls growing ever higher. Hence if a nation has much that is firmly established, this is a sign that it wishes to petrify and would like to become nothing but a monument. This happened, from a definite date, in the case of Egypt. So he who is well-disposed towards the Germans may for his part consider how he may more and more grow out of what is German. The tendency to be un-German has therefore always been a mark of efficient members of our nation.

324. Foreignisms.—A foreigner who travelled in Germany found favour or the reverse by certain assertions of his, according to the districts in which he stayed. All intelligent Suabians, he used to say, are coquettish.—The other Suabians still believed that Uhland was a poet and Goethe immoral.—The best about German novels now in vogue was that one need not read them, for one knew already what they contained.—The native of Berlin seemed more good-humoured than the South German, for he was all too fond of mocking, and so could endure mockery himself, which the South German could not.—The intellect of the Germans was kept down by their beer and their newspapers: he recommended them tea and pamphlets, of course as a cure.—He advised us to contemplate the different

nations of worn-out Europe and see how well each displayed some particular quality of old age, to the delight of those who sit before the great spectacle: how the French successfully represent the cleverness and amiability of old age, the English the experience and reserve, the Italians the innocence and candour. Can the other masks of old age be wanting? Where is the proud old man, the domineering old man, the covetous old man?—The most dangerous region in Germany was Saxony and Thuringia: nowhere else was there more mental nimbleness, more knowledge of men, side by side with freedom of thought; and all this was so modestly veiled by the ugly dialect and the zealous officiousness of the inhabitants that one hardly noticed that one here had to deal with the intellectual drill-sergeants of Germany, her teachers for good or evil.—The arrogance of the North Germans was kept in check by their tendency to obey, that of the South Germans by their tendency—to make themselves comfortable.—It appeared to him that in their women German men possessed awkward but self-opinionated housewives, who belauded themselves so perseveringly that they had almost persuaded the world, and at any rate their husbands, of their peculiarly German housewifely virtue.—When the conversation turned on Germany's home and foreign policy, he used to say (he called it "betray the secret") that Germany's greatest statesman did not believe in great statesmen.—The future of Germany he found menaced and menacing, for Germans had forgotten how to enjoy themselves (an art that the Italians understood so well), but, by the great games of chance called wars and dynastic revolutions, had accustomed themselves to emotionalism, and consequently would one day have an émeute. For that is the strongest emotion that a nation can procure for itself.—The German Socialist was all the more dangerous because impelled by no definite necessity: his trouble lay in not knowing what he wanted; so, even if he attained many of his objects, he would still pine away from desire in the midst of delights, just like Faust, but presumably like a very vulgar Faust. "For the Faust-Devil," he finally exclaimed, "by whom cultured Germans were so much plagued, was exorcised by Bismarck; but now the Devil has entered into the swine,[17] and is worse than ever!"

325. Opinions.—Most men are nothing and count for nothing until they have arrayed themselves in universal convictions and public opinions. This is in accordance with the tailors' philosophy, "The apparel makes the man." Of exceptional men, however, it must be said, "The wearer primarily makes the apparel." Here opinions cease to be public, and become something else than masks, ornament, and disguise.

326. Two Kinds of Sobriety.—In order not to confound the sobriety arising from mental exhaustion with that arising from moderation, one must remark that the former is peevish, the latter cheerful.

327. Debasement of Joy.—To call a thing good not a day longer than it appears to us good, and above all not a day earlier—that is the only way to keep joy pure. Otherwise, joy all too easily becomes insipid and rotten to the taste, and counts, for whole strata of the people, among the adulterated foodstuffs.

328. The Scapegoat of Virtue.—When a man does his very best, those who mean well towards him, but are not capable of appreciating him, speedily seek a scapegoat to immolate, thinking it is the scapegoat of sin—but it is the scapegoat of virtue.

329. Sovereignty.—To honour and acknowledge even the bad, when it pleases one, and to have no conception of how one could be ashamed of being pleased thereat, is the mark of sovereignty in things great and small.

330. Influence a Phantom, not a Reality.—The man of mark gradually learns that so far as he has influence he is a phantom in other brains, and perhaps he falls into a state of subtle vexation of soul, in which he asks himself whether he must not maintain this phantom of himself for the benefit of his fellow-men.

331. Giving and Taking.—When one takes away (or anticipates) the smallest thing that another possesses, the latter is blind to the fact that he has been given something greater, nay, even the greatest thing.

332. Good Ploughland.—All rejection and negation betoken a deficiency in fertility. If we were good ploughland, we should allow nothing to be unused or lost, and in every thing, event, or person we should welcome manure, rain, or sunshine.

333. Intercourse as an Enjoyment.—If a man renounces the world and intentionally lives in solitude, he may come to regard intercourse with others, which he enjoys but seldom, as a special delicacy.

334. To Know how to Suffer in Public.—We must advertise our misfortunes and from time to time heave audible sighs and show visible marks of impatience. For if we could let others see how assured and happy we are in spite of pain and privation, how envious and ill-tempered they would become at the sight!—But we must take care not to corrupt our fellow-men; besides, if they knew the truth, they would levy a heavy toll upon us. At any rate our public misfortune is our private advantage.

335. Warmth on the Heights.—On the heights it is warmer than people in the valleys suppose, especially in winter. The thinker recognises the full import of this simile.

336. To Will the Good and be Capable of the Beautiful.—It is not enough to practise the good one must have willed it, and, as the poet says, include the Godhead in our will. But the beautiful we must not will, we must be capable of it, in innocence and blindness, without any psychical curiosity. He that lights his lantern to find perfect men should remember the token by which to know them. They are the men who always act for the sake of the good and in so doing always attain to the beautiful without thinking of the beautiful. Many better and nobler men, from impotence or from want of beauty in their souls, remain unrefreshing and ugly to behold, with all their good will and good works. They rebuff and injure even virtue through the repulsive garb in which their bad taste arrays her.

337. Danger of Renunciation.—We must beware of basing our lives on too narrow a foundation of appetite. For if we renounce all the joys involved in positions, honours, associations, revels, creature comforts, and arts, a day may come when we perceive that this repudiation has led us not to wisdom but to satiety of life.

338. Final Opinion on Opinions.—Either we should hide our opinions or hide ourselves behind our opinions. Whoever does otherwise, does not know the way of the world, or belongs to the order of pious fire-eaters.

339. "Gaudeamus Igitur."—Joy must contain edifying and healing forces for the moral nature of man. Otherwise, how comes it that our soul, as soon as it basks in the sunshine of joy, unconsciously vows to itself, "I will be good!" "I will become perfect!" and is at once seized by a premonition of perfection that is like a shudder of religious awe?

340. To One who is Praised.—So long as you are praised, believe that you are not yet on your own course but on that of another.

341. Loving the Master.—The apprentice and the master love the master in different ways.

342. All-too-Beautiful and Human.—"Nature is too beautiful for thee, poor mortal," one often feels. But now and then, at a profound contemplation of all that is human, in its fulness, vigour, tenderness, and complexity, I have felt as if I must say, in all humility, "Man also is too beautiful for the contemplation of man!" Nor did I mean the moral man alone, but every one.

343. Real and Personal Estate.—When life has treated us in true robber fashion, and has taken away all that it could of honour, joys, connections, health, and property of every kind, we perhaps discover in the end, after the first shock, that we are richer than before. For now we know for the first time what is so peculiarly ours that no robber hand can touch it, and perhaps, after all the plunder and devastation, we come forward with the airs of a mighty real estate owner.

344. Involuntarily Idealised.—The most painful feeling that exists is finding out that we are always taken for something higher than we really are. For we must thereby confess to ourselves, "There is in you some element of fraud—your speech, your expression, your bearing, your eye, your dealings; and this deceitful something is as necessary as your usual honesty, but constantly destroys its effect and its value."

345. Idealist and Liar.—We must not let ourselves be tyrannised even by that finest faculty of idealising things: otherwise, truth will one day part company from us with the insulting remark: "Thou arch-liar, what have I to do with thee?"

346. Being Misunderstood.—When one is misunderstood generally, it is impossible to remove a particular misunderstanding. This point must be recognised, to save superfluous expenditure of energy in self-defence.

347. The Water-Drinker Speaks.—Go on drinking your wine, which has refreshed you all your life—what affair is it of yours if I have to be a water-drinker? Are not wine and water peaceable, brotherly elements, that can live side by side without mutual recriminations?

348. From Cannibal Country.—In solitude the lonely man is eaten up by himself, among crowds by the many. Choose which you prefer.

349. The Freezing-Point of the Will.—"Some time the hour will come at last, the hour that will envelop you in the golden cloud of painlessness; when the soul enjoys its own weariness and, happy in patient playing with patience, resembles the waves of a lake, which on a quiet summer day, in the reflection of a many-hued evening sky, sip and sip at the shore and again are hushed—without end, without purpose, without satiety, without need—all calm rejoicing in change, all ebb and flow of Nature's pulse." Such is the feeling and talk of all invalids, but if they attain that hour, a brief period of enjoyment is followed by ennui. But this is the thawing-wind of the frozen will, which awakes, stirs, and once more begets desire upon desire.—Desire is a sign of convalescence or recovery.

350. The Disclaimed Ideal.—It happens sometimes by an exception that a man only reaches the highest when he disclaims his ideal. For this ideal previously drove him onward too violently, so that in the middle of the track he regularly got out of breath and had to rest.

351. A Treacherous Inclination.—It should be regarded as a sign of an envious but aspiring man, when he feels himself attracted by the thought that with regard to the eminent there is but one salvation—love.

352. Staircase Happiness.—Just as the wit of many men does not keep pace with opportunity (so that opportunity has already passed through the door while wit still waits on the staircase outside), so others have a kind of staircase happiness, which walks too slowly to keep pace with swift-footed Time. The best that it can

enjoy of an experience, of a whole span of life, falls to its share long afterwards, often only as a weak, spicy fragrance, giving rise to longing and sadness—as if "it might have been possible"—some time or other—to drink one's fill of this element: but now it is too late.

353. Worms.—The fact that an intellect contains a few worms does not detract from its ripeness.

354. The Seat of Victory.—A good seat on horseback robs an opponent of his courage, the spectator of his heart—why attack such a man? Sit like one who has been victorious!

355. Danger in Admiration.—From excessive admiration for the virtues of others one can lose the sense of one's own, and finally, through lack of practice, lose these virtues themselves, without retaining the alien virtues as compensation.

356. Uses of Sickliness.—He who is often ill not only has a far greater pleasure in health, on account of his so often getting well, but acquires a very keen sense of what is healthy or sickly in actions and achievements, both his own and others'. Thus, for example, it is just the writers of uncertain health—among whom, unfortunately, nearly all great writers must be classed—who are wont to have a far more even and assured tone of health in their writings, because they are better versed than are the physically robust in the philosophy of psychical health and convalescence and in their teachers—morning, sunshine, forest, and fountain.

357. Disloyalty a Condition of Mastery.—It cannot be helped—every master has but one pupil, and he becomes disloyal to him, for he also is destined for mastery.

358. Never in Vain.—In the mountains of truth you never climb in vain. Either you already reach a higher point to-day, or you exercise your strength in order to be able to climb higher to-morrow.

359. Through Grey Window-Panes.—Is what you see through this window of the world so beautiful that you do not wish to look through any other window—ay, and even try to prevent others from so doing?

360. A Sign of Radical Changes.—When we dream of persons long forgotten or dead, it is a sign that we have suffered radical changes, and that the soil on which we live has been completely undermined. The dead rise again, and our antiquity becomes modernity.

361. Medicine of the Soul.—To lie still and think little is the cheapest medicine for all diseases of the soul, and, with the aid of good-will, becomes pleasanter every hour that it is used.

362. Intellectual Order of Precedence.—You rank far below others when you try to establish the exception and they the rule.

363. The Fatalist.—You must believe in fate—science can compel you thereto. All that develops in you out of that belief—cowardice, devotion or loftiness, and uprightness—bears witness to the soil in which the grain was sown, but not to the grain itself, for from that seed anything and everything can grow.

364. The Reason for Much Fretfulness.—He that prefers the beautiful to the useful in life will undoubtedly, like children who prefer sweetmeats to bread, destroy his digestion and acquire a very fretful outlook on the world.

365. Excess as a Remedy.—We can make our own talent once more acceptable to ourselves by honouring and enjoying the opposite talent for some time to excess.—Using excess as a remedy is one of the more refined devices in the art of life.

366. "Will a Self."—Active, successful natures act, not according to the maxim, "Know thyself," but as if always confronted with the command, "Will a self, so you will become a self."—Fate seems always to have left them a choice. Inactive, contemplative natures, on the other hand, reflect on how they have chosen their self "once for all" at their entry into life.

367. To Live as Far as Possible without a Following.—How small is the importance of followers we first grasp when we have ceased to be the followers of our followers.

368. Obscuring Oneself.—We must understand how to obscure ourselves in order to get rid of the gnat-swarms of pestering admirers.

369. Ennui.—There is an ennui of the most subtle and cultured brains, to which the best that the world can offer has become stale. Accustomed to eat ever more and more recherché fare and to feel disgust at coarser diet, they are in danger of dying of hunger. For the very best exists but in small quantities, and has sometimes become inaccessible or hard as stone, so that even good teeth can no longer bite it.

370. The Danger in Admiration.—The admiration of a quality or of an art may be so strong as to deter us from aspiring to possess that quality or art.

371. What is Required of Art.—One man wants to enjoy himself by means of art, another for a time to get out of or above himself.—To meet both requirements there exists a twofold species of artists.

372. Secessions.—Whoever secedes from us offends not us, perhaps, but certainly our adherents.

373. After Death.—It is only long after the death of a man that we find it inconceivable that he should be missed—in the case of really great men, only after decades. Those who are honest usually think when any one dies that he is not much missed, and that the pompous funeral oration is a piece of hypocrisy.

Necessity first teaches the necessariness of an individual, and the proper epitaph is a belated sigh.

374. Leaving in Hades.—We must leave many things in the Hades of half-conscious feeling, and not try to release them from their shadow-existence, or else they will become, as thoughts and words, our demoniacal tyrants, with cruel lust after our blood.

375. Near to Beggary.—Even the richest intellect sometimes mislays the key to the room in which his hoarded treasures repose. He is then like the poorest of the poor, who must beg to get a living.

376. Chain-Thinkers.—To him who has thought a great deal, every new thought that he hears or reads at once assumes the form of a chain.

377. Pity.—In the gilded sheath of pity is sometimes hidden the dagger of envy.

378. What is Genius?—To aspire to a lofty aim and to will the means to that aim.

379. Vanity of Combatants.—He who has no hope of victory in a combat, or who is obviously worsted, is all the more desirous that his style of fighting should be admired.

380. The Philosophic Life Misinterpreted.—At the moment when one is beginning to take philosophy seriously, the whole world fancies that one is doing the reverse.

381. Imitation.—By imitation, the bad gains, the good loses credit—especially in art.

382. Final Teaching of History.—"Oh that I had but lived in those times!" is the exclamation of foolish and frivolous men. At every period of history that we seriously review, even if it be the most belauded era of the past, we shall rather cry out at the end, "Anything but a return to that! The spirit of that age would oppress you with the weight of a hundred atmospheres, the good and beautiful in it you would not enjoy, its evil you could not digest." Depend upon it, posterity will pass the same verdict on our own epoch, and say that it was unbearable, that life under such conditions was intolerable. "And yet every one can endure his own times?" Yes, because the spirit of his age not only lies upon him but is in him. The spirit of the age offers resistance to itself and can bear itself.

383. Greatness as a Mask.—By greatness in our comportment we embitter our foes; by envy that we do not conceal we almost reconcile them to us. For envy levels and makes equal; it is an unconscious, plaintive variety of modesty.—It may be indeed that here and there, for the sake of the above-named advantage, envy has been assumed as a mask by those who are not envious. Certainly, however, greatness in comportment is often used as the mask of envy by ambitious men

who would rather suffer drawbacks and embitter their foes than let it be seen that they place them on an equal footing with themselves.

384. Unpardonable.—You gave him an opportunity of displaying the greatness of his character, and he did not make use of the opportunity. He will never forgive you for that.

385. Contrasts.—The most senile thought ever conceived about men lies in the famous saying, "The ego is always hateful," the most childish in the still more famous saying, "Love thy neighbour as thyself."—With the one knowledge of men has ceased, with the other it has not yet begun.

386. A Defective Ear.—"We still belong to the mob so long as we always shift the blame on to others; we are on the track of wisdom when we always make ourselves alone responsible; but the wise man finds no one to blame, neither himself nor others."—Who said that? Epictetus, eighteen hundred years ago.—The world has heard but forgotten the saying.—No, the world has not heard and not forgotten it: everything is not forgotten. But we had not the necessary ear, the ear of Epictetus.—So he whispered it into his own ear?—Even so: wisdom is the whispering of the sage to himself in the crowded market-place.

387. A Defect of Standpoint, not of Vision.—We always stand a few paces too near ourselves and a few paces too far from our neighbour. Hence we judge him too much in the lump, and ourselves too much by individual, occasional, insignificant features and circumstances.

388. Ignorance about Weapons.—How little we care whether another knows a subject or not!—whereas he perhaps sweats blood at the bare idea that he may be considered ignorant on the point. Yes, there are exquisite fools, who always go about with a quiverful of mighty, excommunicatory utterances, ready to shoot down any one who shows freely that there are matters in which their judgment is not taken into account.

389. At the Drinking-Table of Experience.—People whose innate moderation leads them to drink but the half of every glass, will not admit that everything in the world has its lees and sediment.

390. Singing-Birds.—The followers of a great man often put their own eyes out, so that they may be the better able to sing his praise.

391. Beyond our Ken.—The good generally displeases us when it is beyond our ken.

392. Rule as Mother or as Child.—There is one condition that gives birth to rules, another to which rules give birth.

393. Comedy.—We sometimes earn honour or love for actions and achievements which we have long since sloughed as the snake sloughs his skin. We are hereby easily seduced into becoming the comic actors of our own past,

and into throwing the old skin once more about our shoulders—and that not merely from vanity, but from good-will towards our admirers.

394. A Mistake of Biographers.—The small force that is required to launch a boat into the stream must not be confounded with the force of the stream that carries the boat along. Yet this mistake is made in nearly all biographies.

395. Not Buying too Dear.—The things that we buy too dear we generally turn to bad use, because we have no love for them but only a painful recollection. Thus they involve a twofold drawback.

396. The Philosophy that Society always Needs.—The pillars of the social structure rest upon the fundamental fact that every one cheerfully contemplates all that he is, does, and attempts, his sickness or health, his poverty or affluence, his honour or insignificance, and says to himself, "After all, I would not change places with any one!"—Whoever wishes to add a stone to the social structure should always try to implant in mankind this cheerful philosophy of contentment and refusal to change places.

397. The Mark of a Noble Soul.—A noble soul is not that which is capable of the highest flights, but that which rises little and falls little, living always in a free and bright atmosphere and altitude.

398. Greatness and its Contemplator.—The noblest effect of greatness is that it gives the contemplator a power of vision that magnifies and embellishes.

399. Being Satisfied.—We show that we have attained maturity of understanding when we no longer go where rare flowers lurk under the thorniest hedges of knowledge, but are satisfied with gardens, forests, meadows, and ploughlands, remembering that life is too short for the rare and uncommon.

400. Advantage in Privation.—He who always lives in the warmth and fulness of the heart, and, as it were, in the summer air of the soul, cannot form an idea of that fearful delight which seizes more wintry natures, who for once in a way are kissed by the rays of love and the milder breath of a sunny February day.

401. Recipe for the Sufferer.—You find the burden of life too heavy? Then you must increase the burden of your life. When the sufferer finally thirsts after and seeks the river of Lethe, then he must become a hero to be certain of finding it.

402. The Judge.—He who has seen another's ideal becomes his inexorable judge, and as it were his evil conscience.

403. The Utility of Great Renunciation.—The useful thing about great renunciation is that it invests us with that youthful pride through which we can thenceforth easily demand of ourselves small renunciations.

404. How Duty Acquires a Glamour.—You can change a brazen duty into gold in the eyes of all by always performing something more than you have promised.

405. Prayer to Mankind.—"Forgive us our virtues"—so should we pray to mankind.

406. They that Create and They that Enjoy.—Every one who enjoys thinks that the principal thing to the tree is the fruit, but in point of fact the principal thing to it is the seed.—Herein lies the difference between them that create and them that enjoy.

407. The Glory of all Great Men.—What is the use of genius if it does not invest him who contemplates and reveres it with such freedom and loftiness of feeling that he no longer has need of genius?—To make themselves superfluous is the glory of all great men.

408. The Journey to Hades.—I too have been in the underworld, even as Odysseus, and I shall often be there again. Not sheep alone have I sacrificed, that I might be able to converse with a few dead souls, but not even my own blood have I spared. There were four pairs who responded to me in my sacrifice: Epicurus and Montaigne, Goethe and Spinoza, Plato and Rousseau, Pascal and Schopenhauer. With them I have to come to terms. When I have long wandered alone, I will let them prove me right or wrong; to them will I listen, if they prove each other right or wrong. In all that I say, conclude, or think out for myself and others, I fasten my eyes on those eight and see their eyes fastened on mine.—May the living forgive me if I look upon them at times as shadows, so pale and fretful, so restless and, alas! so eager for life. Those eight, on the other hand, seem to me so living that I feel as if even now, after their death, they could never become weary of life. But eternal vigour of life is the important point: what matters "eternal life," or indeed life at all?

Part II. The Wanderer And His Shadow.

The Shadow: It is so long since I heard you speak that I should like to give you an opportunity of talking.

The Wanderer: I hear a voice—where? whose? I almost fancied that I heard myself speaking, but with a voice yet weaker than my own.

The Shadow (after a pause): Are you not glad to have an opportunity of speaking?

The Wanderer: By God and everything else in which I disbelieve, it is my shadow that speaks. I hear it, but I do not believe it.

The Shadow: Let us assume that it exists, and think no more about it. In another hour all will be over.

The Wanderer: That is just what I thought when in a forest near Pisa I saw first two and then five camels.

The Shadow: It is all the better if we are both equally forbearing towards each other when for once our reason is silent. Thus we shall avoid losing our tempers in conversation, and shall not at once apply mutual thumb-screws in the event of any word sounding for once unintelligible to us. If one does not know exactly how to answer, it is enough to say something. Those are the reasonable terms on which I hold conversation with any person. During a long talk the wisest of men becomes a fool once and a simpleton thrice.

The Wanderer: Your moderation is not flattering to those to whom you confess it.

The Shadow: Am I, then, to flatter?

The Wanderer: I thought a man's shadow was his vanity. Surely vanity would never say, "Am I, then, to flatter?"

The Shadow: Nor does human vanity, so far as I am acquainted with it, ask, as I have done twice, whether it may speak. It simply speaks.

The Wanderer: Now I see for the first time how rude I am to you, my beloved shadow. I have not said a word of my supreme delight in hearing and not merely seeing you. You must know that I love shadows even as I love light. For the existence of beauty of face, clearness of speech, kindliness and firmness of character, the shadow is as necessary as the light. They are not opponents—rather do they hold each other's hands like good friends; and when the light vanishes, the shadow glides after it.

The Shadow: Yes, and I hate the same thing that you hate—night. I love men because they are votaries of life. I rejoice in the gleam of their eyes when they recognise and discover, they who never weary of recognising and discovering. That shadow which all things cast when the sunshine of knowledge falls upon them—that shadow too am I.

The Wanderer: I think I understand you, although you have expressed yourself in somewhat shadowy terms. You are right. Good friends give to each other here and there, as a sign of mutual understanding, an obscure phrase which to any third party is meant to be a riddle. And we are good friends, you and I. So enough of preambles! Some few hundred questions oppress my soul, and the time for you to answer them is perchance but short. Let us see how we may come to an understanding as quickly and peaceably as possible.

The Shadow: But shadows are more shy than men. You will not reveal to any man the manner of our conversation?

The Wanderer: The manner of our conversation? Heaven preserve me from wire-drawn, literary dialogues! If Plato had found less pleasure in spinning them out, his readers would have found more pleasure in Plato. A dialogue that in real life is a source of delight, when turned into writing and read, is a picture with nothing but false perspectives. Everything is too long or too short.—Yet perhaps I may reveal the points on which we have come to an understanding?

The Shadow: With that I am content. For every one will only recognise your views once more, and no one will think of the shadow.

The Wanderer: Perhaps you are wrong, my friend! Hitherto they have observed in my views more of the shadow than of me.

The Shadow: More of the shadow than of the light? Is that possible?

The Wanderer: Be serious, dear fool! My very first question demands seriousness.

1. Of the Tree of Knowledge.—Probability, but no truth; the semblance of freedom, but no freedom—these are the two fruits by virtue of which the tree of knowledge cannot be confounded with the tree of life.

2. The World's Reason.—That the world is not the abstract essence of an eternal reasonableness is sufficiently proved by the fact that that bit of the world which we know—I mean our human reason—is none too reasonable. And if this is not eternally and wholly wise and reasonable, the rest of the world will not be so either. Here the conclusion a minori ad majus, a parte ad totum holds good, and that with decisive force.

3. "In the Beginning was."—To glorify the origin—that is the metaphysical after-shoot which sprouts again at the contemplation of history, and absolutely makes us imagine that in the beginning of things lies all that is most valuable and essential.

4. Standard for the Value of Truth.—The difficulty of climbing mountains is no gauge of their height. Yet in the case of science it is different!—we are told by certain persons who wish to be considered "the initiated,"—the difficulty in finding truth is to determine the value of truth! This insane morality originates in the idea that "truths" are really nothing more than gymnastic appliances, with which we have to exercise ourselves until we are thoroughly tired. It is a morality for the athletes and gymnasts of the intellect.

5. Use of Words and Reality.—There exists a simulated contempt for all the things that mankind actually holds most important, for all everyday matters. For instance, we say "we only eat to live"—an abominable lie, like that which speaks of the procreation of children as the real purpose of all sexual pleasure. Conversely, the reverence for "the most important things" is hardly ever quite genuine. The priests and metaphysicians have indeed accustomed us to a hypocritically exaggerated use of words regarding these matters, but they have not altered the feeling that these most important things are not so important as those despised "everyday matters." A fatal consequence of this twofold hypocrisy is that we never make these everyday matters (such as eating, housing, clothes, and

intercourse) the object of a constant unprejudiced and universal reflection and revision, but, as such a process appears degrading, we divert from them our serious intellectual and artistic side. Hence in such matters habit and frivolity win an easy victory over the thoughtless, especially over inexperienced youth. On the other hand, our continual transgressions of the simplest laws of body and mind reduce us all, young and old, to a disgraceful state of dependence and servitude—I mean to that fundamentally superfluous dependence upon physicians, teachers and clergymen, whose dead-weight still lies heavy upon the whole of society.

6. Earthly Infirmities and their Main Cause.—If we look about us, we are always coming across men who have eaten eggs all their lives without observing that the oblong-shaped taste the best; who do not know that a thunder-storm is beneficial to the stomach; that perfumes are most fragrant in cold, clear air; that our sense of taste varies in different parts of our mouths; that every meal at which we talk well or listen well does harm to the digestion. If we are not satisfied with these examples of defective powers of observation, we shall concede all the more readily that the everyday matters are very imperfectly seen and rarely observed by the majority. Is this a matter of indifference?—Let us remember, after all, that from this defect are derived nearly all the bodily and spiritual infirmities of the individual. Ignorance of what is good and bad for us, in the arrangement of our mode of life, the division of our day, the selection of our friends and the time we devote to them, in business and leisure, commanding and obeying, our feeling for nature and for art, our eating, sleeping, and meditation; ignorance and lack of keen perceptions in the smallest and most ordinary details—this it is that makes the world "a vale of tears" for so many. Let us not say that here as everywhere the fault lies with human unreason. Of reason there is enough and to spare, but it is wrongly directed and artificially diverted from these little intimate things. Priests and teachers, and the sublime ambition of all idealists, coarser and subtler, din it even into the child's ears that the means of serving mankind at large depend upon altogether different things—upon the salvation of the soul, the service of the State, the advancement of science, or even upon social position and property; whereas the needs of the individual, his requirements great and small during the twenty-four hours of the day, are quite paltry or indifferent.—Even Socrates attacked with all his might this arrogant neglect of the human for the benefit of humanity, and loved to indicate by a quotation from Homer the true sphere and conception of all anxiety and reflection: "All that really matters," he said, "is the good and evil hap I find at home."

7. Two Means of Consolation.—Epicurus, the soul-comforter of later antiquity, said, with that marvellous insight which to this very day is so rarely to be found,

that for the calming of the spirit the solution of the final and ultimate theoretical problems is by no means necessary. Hence, instead of raising a barren and remote discussion of the final question, whether the Gods existed, it sufficed him to say to those who were tormented by "fear of the Gods": "If there are Gods, they do not concern themselves with us." The latter position is far stronger and more favourable, for, by conceding a few points to the other, one makes him readier to listen and to take to heart. But as soon as he sets about proving the opposite (that the Gods do concern themselves with us), into what thorny jungles of error must the poor man fall, quite of his own accord, and without any cunning on the part of his interlocutor! The latter must only have enough subtlety and humanity to conceal his sympathy with this tragedy. Finally, the other comes to feel disgust—the strongest argument against any proposition—disgust with his own hypothesis. He becomes cold, and goes away in the same frame of mind as the pure atheist who says, "What do the Gods matter to me? The devil take them!"—In other cases, especially when a half-physical, half-moral assumption had cast a gloom over his spirit, Epicurus did not refute the assumption. He agreed that it might be true, but that there was a second assumption to explain the same phenomenon, and that it could perhaps be maintained in other ways. The plurality of hypotheses (for example, that concerning the origin of conscientious scruples) suffices even in our time to remove from the soul the shadows that arise so easily from pondering over a hypothesis which is isolated, merely visible, and hence overvalued a hundredfold.—Thus whoever wishes to console the unfortunate, the criminal, the hypochondriac, the dying, may call to mind the two soothing suggestions of Epicurus, which can be applied to a great number of problems. In their simplest form they would run: firstly, granted the thing is so, it does not concern us; secondly, the thing may be so, but it may also be otherwise.

8. In the Night.—So soon as night begins to fall our sensations concerning everyday matters are altered. There is the wind, prowling as if on forbidden paths, whispering as if in search of something, fretting because he cannot find it. There is the lamplight, with its dim red glow, its weary look, unwillingly fighting against night, a sullen slave to wakeful man. There are the breathings of the sleeper, with their terrible rhythm, to which an ever-recurring care seems to blow the trumpet-melody—we do not hear it, but when the sleeper's bosom heaves we feel our heart-strings tighten; and when the breath sinks and almost dies away into a deathly stillness, we say to ourselves, "Rest awhile, poor troubled spirit!" All living creatures bear so great a burden that we wish them an eternal rest; night invites to death.—If human beings were deprived of the sun and resisted night by means of moonlight and oil-lamps, what a philosophy would cast its veil over them! We

already see only too plainly how a shadow is thrown over the spiritual and intellectual nature of man by that moiety of darkness and sunlessness that envelops life.

9. Origin of the Doctrine of Free Will.—Necessity sways one man in the shape of his passions, another as a habit of hearing and obeying, a third as a logical conscience, a fourth as a caprice and a mischievous delight in evasions. These four, however, seek the freedom of their will at the very point where they are most securely fettered. It is as if the silkworm sought freedom of will in spinning. What is the reason? Clearly this, that every one thinks himself most free where his vitality is strongest; hence, as I have said, now in passion, now in duty, now in knowledge, now in caprice. A man unconsciously imagines that where he is strong, where he feels most thoroughly alive, the element of his freedom must lie. He thinks of dependence and apathy, independence and vivacity as forming inevitable pairs.—Thus an experience that a man has undergone in the social and political sphere is wrongly transferred to the ultimate metaphysical sphere. There the strong man is also the free man, there the vivid feeling of joy and sorrow, the high hopes, the keen desires, the powerful hates are the attributes of the ruling, independent natures, while the thrall and the slave live in a state of dazed oppression.—The doctrine of free will is an invention of the ruling classes.

10. Absence of Feeling of New Chains.—So long as we do not feel that we are in some way dependent, we consider ourselves independent—a false conclusion that shows how proud man is, how eager for dominion. For he hereby assumes that he would always be sure to observe and recognise dependence so soon as he suffered it, the preliminary hypothesis being that he generally lives in independence, and that, should he lose that independence for once in a way, he would immediately detect a contrary sensation.—Suppose, however, the reverse to be true—that he is always living in a complex state of dependence, but thinks himself free where, through long habit, he no longer feels the weight of the chain? He only suffers from new chains, and "free will" really means nothing more than an absence of feeling of new chains.

11. Freedom of the Will and the Isolation of Facts.—Our ordinary inaccurate observation takes a group of phenomena as one and calls them a fact. Between this fact and another we imagine a vacuum, we isolate each fact. In reality, however, the sum of our actions and cognitions is no series of facts and intervening vacua, but a continuous stream. Now the belief in free will is incompatible with the idea of a continuous, uniform, undivided, indivisible flow. This belief presupposes that every single action is isolated and indivisible; it is an atomic theory as regards volition and cognition.—We misunderstand facts as we misunderstand characters, speaking of similar characters and similar facts,

whereas both are non-existent. Further, we bestow praise and blame only on this false hypothesis, that there are similar facts, that a graduated order of species of facts exists, corresponding to a graduated order of values. Thus we isolate not only the single fact, but the groups of apparently equal facts (good, evil, compassionate, envious actions, and so forth). In both cases we are wrong.—The word and the concept are the most obvious reason for our belief in this isolation of groups of actions. We do not merely thereby designate the things; the thought at the back of our minds is that by the word and the concept we can grasp the essence of the actions. We are still constantly led astray by words and actions, and are induced to think of things as simpler than they are, as separate, indivisible, existing in the absolute. Language contains a hidden philosophical mythology, which, however careful we may be, breaks out afresh at every moment. The belief in free will—that is to say, in similar facts and isolated facts—finds in language its continual apostle and advocate.

12. The Fundamental Errors.—A man cannot feel any psychical pleasure or pain unless he is swayed by one of two illusions. Either he believes in the identity of certain facts, certain sensations, and in that case finds spiritual pleasure and pain in comparing present with past conditions and in noting their similarity or difference (as is invariably the case with recollection); or he believes in the freedom of the will, perhaps when he reflects, "I ought not to have done this," "This might have turned out differently," and from these reflections likewise he derives pleasure and pain. Without the errors that are rife in every psychical pain and pleasure, humanity would never have developed. For the root idea of humanity is that man is free in a world of bondage—man, the eternal wonder-worker, whether his deeds be good or evil—man, the amazing exception, the super-beast, the quasi-God, the mind of creation, the indispensable, the key-word to the cosmic riddle, the mighty lord of nature and despiser of nature, the creature that calls its history "the history of the world"! Vanitas vanitatum homo.

13. Repetition.—It is an excellent thing to express a thing consecutively in two ways, and thus provide it with a right and a left foot. Truth can stand indeed on one leg, but with two she will walk and complete her journey.

14. Man as the Comic Actor of the World.—It would require beings more intellectual than men to relish to the full the humorous side of man's view of himself as the goal of all existence and of his serious pronouncement that he is satisfied only with the prospect of fulfilling a world-mission. If a God created the world, he created man to be his ape, as a perpetual source of amusement in the midst of his rather tedious eternities. The music of the spheres surrounding the world would then presumably be the mocking laughter of all the other creatures

around mankind. God in his boredom uses pain for the tickling of his favourite animal, in order to enjoy his proudly tragic gestures and expressions of suffering, and, in general, the intellectual inventiveness of the vainest of his creatures—as inventor of this inventor. For he who invented man as a joke had more intellect and more joy in intellect than has man.—Even here, where our human nature is willing to humble itself, our vanity again plays us a trick, in that we men should like in this vanity at   least to be quite marvellous and incomparable. Our uniqueness in the world! Oh, what an improbable thing it is! Astronomers, who occasionally acquire a horizon outside our world, give us to understand that the drop of life on the earth is without significance for the total character of the mighty ocean of birth and decay; that countless stars present conditions for the generation of life similar to those of the earth—and yet these are but a handful in comparison with the endless number that have never known, or have long been cured, of the eruption of life; that life on each of these stars, measured by the period of its existence, has been but an instant, a flicker, with long, long intervals afterwards—and thus in no way the aim and final purpose of their existence. Possibly the ant in the forest is quite as firmly convinced that it is the aim and purpose of the existence of the forest, as we are convinced in our imaginations (almost unconsciously) that the destruction of mankind involves the destruction of the world. It is even modesty on our part to go no farther than this, and not to arrange a universal twilight of the world and the Gods as the funeral ceremony of the last man. Even to the eye of the most unbiassed astronomer a lifeless world can scarcely appear otherwise than as a shining and swinging star wherein man lies buried.

15. The Modesty of Man.—How little pleasure is enough for the majority to make them feel that life is good! How modest is man!

16. Where Indifference is Necessary.—Nothing would be more perverse than to wait for the truths that science will finally establish concerning the first and last things, and until then to think (and especially to believe) in the traditional way, as one is so often advised to do. The impulse that bids us seek nothing but certainties in this domain is a religious offshoot, nothing better—a hidden and only apparently sceptical variety of the "metaphysical need," the underlying idea being that for a long time no view of these ultimate certainties will be obtainable, and that until then the "believer" has the right not to trouble himself about the whole subject. We have no need of these certainties about the farthermost horizons in order to live a full and efficient human life, any more than the ant needs them in order to be a good ant. Rather must we ascertain the origin of that troublesome significance that we have attached to these things for so long. For this we require the history of ethical and religious sentiments, since it is only

under the influence of such sentiments that these most acute problems of knowledge have become so weighty and terrifying. Into the outermost regions to which the mental eye can penetrate (without ever penetrating into them), we have smuggled such concepts as guilt and punishment (everlasting punishment, too!). The darker those regions, the more careless we have been. For ages men have let their imaginations run riot where they could establish nothing, and have induced posterity to accept these fantasies as something serious and true, with this abominable lie as their final trump-card: that faith is worth more than knowledge. What we need now in regard to these ultimate things is not knowledge as against faith, but indifference as against faith and pretended knowledge in these matters!—Everything must lie nearer to us than what has hitherto been preached to us as the most important thing, I mean the questions: "What end does man serve?" "What is his fate after death?" "How does he make his peace with God?" and all the rest of that bag of tricks. The problems of the dogmatic philosophers, be they idealists, materialists, or realists, concern us as little as do these religious questions. They all have the same object in view—to force us to a decision in matters where neither faith nor knowledge is needed. It is better even for the most ardent lover of knowledge that the territory open to investigation and to reason should be encircled by a belt of fog-laden, treacherous marshland, a strip of ever watery, impenetrable, and indeterminable country. It is just by the comparison with the realm of darkness on the edge of the world of knowledge that the bright, accessible region of that world rises in value.—We must once more become good friends of the "everyday matters," and not, as hitherto, despise them and look beyond them at clouds and monsters of the night. In forests and caverns, in marshy tracts and under dull skies, on the lowest rungs of the ladder of culture, man has lived for æons, and lived in poverty. There he has learnt to despise the present, his neighbours, his life, and himself, and we, the inhabitants of the brighter fields of Nature and mind, still inherit in our blood some taint of this contempt for everyday matters.

17. Profound Interpretations.—He who has interpreted a passage in an author "more profoundly" than was intended, has not interpreted the author but has obscured him. Our metaphysicians are in the same relation, or even in a worse relation, to the text of Nature. For, to apply their profound interpretations, they often alter the text to suit their purpose—or, in other words, corrupt the text. A curious example of the corruption and obscuration of an author's text is furnished by the ideas of Schopenhauer on the pregnancy of women. "The sign of a continuous will to life in time," he says, "is copulation; the sign of the light of knowledge which is associated anew with this will and holds the possibility of a deliverance, and that too in the highest degree of clearness, is the renewed

incarnation of the will to life. This incarnation is betokened by pregnancy, which is therefore frank and open, and even proud, whereas copulation hides itself like a criminal." He declares that every woman, if surprised in the sexual act, would be likely to die of shame, but "displays her pregnancy without a trace of shame, nay even with a sort of pride." Now, firstly, this condition cannot easily be displayed more aggressively than it displays itself, and when Schopenhauer gives prominence only to the intentional character of the display, he is fashioning his text to suit the interpretation. Moreover, his statement of the universality of the phenomenon is not true. He speaks of "every woman." Many women, especially the younger, often appear painfully ashamed of their condition, even in the presence of their nearest kinsfolk. And when women of riper years, especially in the humbler classes, do actually appear proud of their condition, it is because they would give us to understand that they are still desirable to their husbands. That a neighbour on seeing them or a passing stranger should say or think "Can it be possible?"—that is an alms always acceptable to the vanity of women of low mental capacity. In the reverse instance, to conclude from Schopenhauer's proposition, the cleverest and most intelligent women would tend more than any to exult openly in their condition. For they have the best prospect of giving birth to an intellectual prodigy, in whom "the will" can once more "negative" itself for the universal good. Stupid women, on the other hand, would have every reason to hide their pregnancy more modestly than anything they hide.—It cannot be said that this view corresponds to reality. Granted, however, that Schopenhauer was right on the general principle that women show more self-satisfaction when pregnant than at any other time, a better explanation than this lies to hand. One might imagine the clucking of a hen even before she lays an egg, saying, "Look! look! I shall lay an egg! I shall lay an egg!"

18. The Modern Diogenes.—Before we look for man, we must have found the lantern.—Will it have to be the Cynic's lantern?

19. Immoralists.—Moralists must now put up with being rated as immoralists, because they dissect morals. He, however, who would dissect must kill, but only in order that we may know more, judge better, live better, not in order that all the world may dissect. Unfortunately, men still think that every moralist in his every action must be a pattern for others to imitate. They confound him with the preacher of morality. The older moralists did not dissect enough and preached too often, whence that confusion and the unpleasant consequences for our latter-day moralists are derived.

20. A Caution against Confusion.—There are moralists who treat the strong, noble, self-denying attitude of such beings as the heroes of Plutarch, or the pure, enlightened, warmth-giving state of soul peculiar to truly good men and women,

as difficult scientific problems. They investigate the origin of such phenomena, indicating the complex element in the apparent simplicity, and directing their gaze to the tangled skein of motives, the delicate web of conceptual illusions, and the sentiments of individuals or of groups, that are a legacy of ancient days gradually increased. Such moralists are very different from those with whom they are most commonly confounded, from those petty minds that do not believe at all in these modes of thought and states of soul, and imagine their own poverty to be hidden somewhere behind the glamour of greatness and purity. The moralists say, "Here are problems," and these pitiable creatures say, "Here are impostors and deceptions." Thus the latter deny the existence of the very things which the former are at pains to explain.

21. Man as the Measurer.—Perhaps all human morality had its origin in the tremendous excitement that seized primitive man when he discovered measure and measuring, scales and weighing (for the word Mensch [man] means "the measurer"—he wished to name himself after his greatest discovery!). With these ideas they mounted into regions that are quite beyond all measuring and weighing, but did not appear to be so in the beginning.

22. The Principle of Equilibrium.—The robber and the man of power who promises to protect a community from robbers are perhaps at bottom beings of the same mould, save that the latter attains his ends by other means than the former—that is to say, through regular imposts paid to him by the community, and no longer through forced contributions. (The same relation exists between merchant and pirate, who for a long period are one and the same person: where the one function appears to them inadvisable, they exercise the other. Even to-day mercantile morality is really nothing but a refinement on piratical morality—buying in the cheapest market, at prime cost if possible, and selling in the dearest.) The essential point is that the man of power promises to maintain the equilibrium against the robber, and herein the weak find a possibility of living. For either they must group themselves into an equivalent power, or they must subject themselves to some one of equivalent power (i.e. render service in return for his efforts). The latter course is generally preferred, because it really keeps two dangerous beings in check—the robber through the man of power, and the man of power through the standpoint of advantage; for the latter profits by treating his subjects with graciousness and tolerance, in order that they may support not only themselves but their ruler. As a matter of fact, conditions may still be hard and cruel enough, yet in comparison with the complete annihilation that was formerly always a possibility, men breathe freely.—The community is at first the organisation of the weak to counterbalance menacing forces. An organisation to outweigh those forces would be more advisable, if its members

grew strong enough to destroy the adverse power: and when it is a question of one mighty oppressor, the attempt will certainly be made. But if the one man is the head of a clan, or if he has a large following, a rapid and decisive annihilation is improbable, and a long or permanent feud is only to be expected. This feud, however, involves the least desirable condition for the community, for it thereby loses the time to provide for its means of subsistence with the necessary regularity, and sees the product of all work hourly threatened. Hence the community prefers to raise its power of attack and defence to the exact plane on which the power of its dangerous neighbour stands, and to give him to understand that an equal weight now lies in its own side of the scales—so why not be good friends?—Thus equilibrium is a most important conception for the understanding of the ancient doctrines of law and morals. Equilibrium is, in fact, the basis of justice. When justice in ruder ages says, "An eye for an eye, a tooth for a tooth," it presupposes the attainment of this equilibrium and tries to maintain it by means of this compensation; so that, when crime is committed, the injured party will not take the revenge of blind anger. By means of the jus talionis the equilibrium of the disturbed relations of power is restored, for in such primitive times an eye or an arm more means a bit more power, more weight.—In a community where all consider themselves equal, disgrace and punishment await crime—that is, violations of the principle of equilibrium. Disgrace is thrown into the scale as a counter-weight against the encroaching individual, who has gained profit by his encroachment, and now suffers losses (through disgrace) which annul and outweigh the previous profits. Punishment, in the same way, sets up a far greater counter-weight against the preponderance which every criminal hopes to obtain—imprisonment as against a deed of violence, restitution and fines as against theft. Thus the sinner is reminded that his action has excluded him from the community and from its moral advantages, since the community treats him as an inferior, a weaker brother, an outsider. For this reason punishment is not merely retaliation, but has something more, something of the cruelty of the state of nature, and of this it would serve as a reminder.

23. Whether the Adherents of the Doctrine of Free Will have a Right to Punish?—Men whose vocation it is to judge and punish try to establish in every case whether an evil-doer is really responsible for his act, whether he was able to apply his reasoning powers, whether he acted with motives and not unconsciously or under constraint. If he is punished, it is because he preferred the worse to the better motives, which he must consequently have known. Where this knowledge is wanting, man is, according to the prevailing view, not responsible—unless his ignorance, e.g. his ignorantia legis, be the consequence of an intentional neglect to learn what he ought: in that case he already preferred the worse to the better

motives at the time when he refused to learn, and must now pay the penalty of his unwise choice. If, on the other hand, perhaps through stupidity or shortsightedness, he has never seen the better motives, he is generally not punished, for people say that he made a wrong choice, he acted like a brute beast. The intentional rejection of the better reason is now needed before we treat the offender as fit to be punished. But how can any one be intentionally more unreasonable than he ought to be? Whence comes the decision, if the scales are loaded with good and bad motives? So the origin is not error or blindness, not an internal or external constraint? (It should furthermore be remembered that every so-called "external constraint" is nothing more than the internal constraint of fear and pain.) Whence? is the repeated question. So reason is not to be the cause of action, because reason cannot decide against the better motives? Thus we call "free will" to our aid. Absolute discretion is to decide, and a moment is to intervene when no motive exercises an influence, when the deed is done as a miracle, resulting from nothing. This assumed discretion is punished in a case where no discretion should rule. Reason, which knows law, prohibition, and command, should have left no choice, they say, and should have acted as a constraint and a higher power. Hence the offender is punished because he makes use of "free will"—in other words, has acted without motive where he should have been guided by motives. But why did he do it? This question must not even be asked; the deed was done without a "Why?" without motive, without origin, being a thing purposeless, unreasoned.—However, according to the above-named preliminary condition of punishability, such a deed should not be punished at all! Moreover, even this reason for punishing should not hold good, that in this case something had not been done, had been omitted, that reason had not been used at all: for at any rate the omission was unintentional, and only intentional omission is considered punishable. The offender has indeed preferred the worse to the better motives, but without motive and purpose: he has indeed failed to apply his reason, but not exactly with the object of not applying it. The very assumption made in the case of punishable crime, that the criminal intentionally renounced his reason, is removed by the hypothesis of "free will." According to your own principles, you must not punish, you adherents of the doctrine of free will!—These principles are, however, nothing but a very marvellous conceptual mythology, and the hen that hatched them has brooded on her eggs far away from all reality.

24. Judging the Criminal and his Judge.—The criminal, who knows the whole concatenation of circumstances, does not consider his act so far beyond the bounds of order and comprehension as does his judge. His punishment, however, is measured by the degree of astonishment that seizes the judge when

he finds the crime incomprehensible.—If the defending counsel's knowledge of the case and its previous history extends far enough, the so-called extenuating circumstances which he duly pleads must end by absolving his client from all guilt. Or, to put it more plainly, the advocate will, step by step, tone down and finally remove the astonishment of the judge, by forcing every honest listener to the tacit avowal, "He was bound to act as he did, and if we punished, we should be punishing eternal Necessity."—Measuring the punishment by the degree of knowledge we possess or can obtain of the previous history of the crime—is that not in conflict with all equity?

25. Exchange and Equity.—In an exchange, the only just and honest course would be for either party to demand only so much as he considers his commodity to be worth, allowance being made for trouble in acquisition, scarcity, time spent and so forth, besides the subjective value. As soon as you make your price bear a relation to the other's need, you become a refined sort of robber and extortioner.—If money is the sole medium of exchange, we must remember that a shilling is by no means the same thing in the hands of a rich heir, a farm labourer, a merchant, and a university student. It would be equitable for every one to receive much or little for his money, according as he has done much or little to earn it. In practice, as we all know, the reverse is the case. In the world of high finance the shilling of the idle rich man can buy more than that of the poor, industrious man.

26. Legal Conditions as Means.—Law, where it rests upon contracts between equals, holds good so long as the power of the parties to the contract remains equal or similar. Wisdom created law to end all feuds and useless expenditure among men on an equal footing. Quite as definite an end is put to this waste, however, when one party has become decidedly weaker than the other. Subjection enters and law ceases, but the result is the same as that attained by law. For now it is the wisdom of the superior which advises to spare the inferior and not uselessly to squander his strength. Thus the position of the inferior is often more favourable than that of the equal.—Hence legal conditions are temporary means counselled by wisdom, and not ends.

27. Explanation of Malicious Joy.—Malicious joy arises when a man consciously finds himself in evil plight and feels anxiety or remorse or pain. The misfortune that overtakes B. makes him equal to A., and A. is reconciled and no longer envious.—If A. is prosperous, he still hoards up in his memory B.'s misfortune as a capital, so as to throw it in the scale as a counter-weight when he himself suffers adversity. In this case too he feels "malicious joy" (Schadenfreude). The sentiment of equality thus applies its standard to the domain of luck and chance. Malicious joy is the commonest expression of victory and restoration of equality, even in a

higher state of civilisation. This emotion has only been in existence since the time when man learnt to look upon another as his equal—in other words, since the foundation of society.

28. The Arbitrary Element in the Award of Punishment.—To most criminals punishment comes just as illegitimate children come to women. They have done the same thing a hundred times without any bad consequences. Suddenly comes discovery, and with discovery punishment. Yet habit should make the deed for which the criminal is punished appear more excusable, for he has developed a propensity that is hard to resist. Instead of this, the criminal is punished more severely if the suspicion of habitual crime rests on him, and habit is made a valid reason against all extenuation. On the other hand, a model life, wherein crime shows up in more terrible contrast, should make the guilt appear more heavy! But here the custom is to soften the punishment. Everything is measured not from the standpoint of the criminal but from that of society and its losses and dangers. The previous utility of an individual is weighed against his one nefarious action, his previous criminality is added to that recently discovered, and punishment is thus meted out as highly as possible. But if we thus punish or reward a man's past (for in the former case the diminution of punishment is a reward) we ought to go farther back and punish and reward the cause of his past—I mean parents, teachers, society. In many instances we shall then find the judges somehow or other sharing in the guilt. It is arbitrary to stop at the criminal himself when we punish his past: if we will not grant the absolute excusability of every crime, we should stop at each individual case and probe no farther into the past—in other words, isolate guilt and not connect it with previous actions. Otherwise we sin against logic. The teachers of free will should draw the inevitable conclusion from their doctrine of "free will" and boldly decree: "No action has a past."

29. Envy and her Nobler Sister.—Where equality is really recognised and permanently established, we see the rise of that propensity that is generally considered immoral, and would scarcely be conceivable in a state of nature—envy. The envious man is susceptible to every sign of individual superiority to the common herd, and wishes to depress every one once more to the level—or raise himself to the superior plane. Hence arise two different modes of action, which Hesiod designated good and bad Eris. In the same way, in a condition of equality there arises indignation if A. is prosperous above and B. unfortunate beneath their deserts and equality. These latter, however, are emotions of nobler natures. They feel the want of justice and equity in things that are independent of the arbitrary choice of men—or, in other words, they desire the equality recognised by man to be recognised as well by Nature and chance. They are angry that men of equal merits should not have equal fortune.

30. The Envy of the Gods.—"The envy of the Gods" arises when a despised person sets himself on an equality with his superior (like Ajax), or is made equal with him by the favour of fortune (like Niobe, the too favoured mother). In the social class system this envy demands that no one shall have merits above his station, that his prosperity shall be on a level with his position, and especially that his self-consciousness shall not outgrow the limits of his rank. Often the victorious general, or the pupil who achieves a masterpiece, has experienced "the envy of the gods."

31. Vanity as an Anti-Social Aftergrowth.—As men, for the sake of security, have made themselves equal in order to found communities, but as also this conception is imposed by a sort of constraint and is entirely opposed to the instincts of the individual, so, the more universal security is guaranteed, the more do new offshoots of the old instinct for predominance appear. Such offshoots appear in the setting-up of class distinctions, in the demand for professional dignities and privileges, and, generally speaking, in vanity (manners, dress, speech, and so forth). So soon as danger to the community is apparent, the majority, who were unable to assert their preponderance in a time of universal peace, once more bring about the condition of equality, and for the time being the absurd privileges and vanities disappear. If the community, however, collapses utterly and anarchy reigns supreme, there arises the state of nature: an absolutely ruthless inequality as recounted by Thucydides in the case of Corcyra. Neither a natural justice nor a natural injustice exists.

32. Equity.—Equity is a development of justice, and arises among such as do not come into conflict with the communal equality. This more subtle recognition of the principle of equilibrium is applied to cases where nothing is prescribed by law. Equity looks forwards and backwards, its maxim being, "Do unto others as you would that they should do unto you." Aequum means: "This principle is conformable to our equality; it tones down even our small differences to an appearance of equality, and expects us to be indulgent in cases where we are not compelled to pardon."

33. Elements of Revenge.—The word "revenge" is spoken so quickly that it almost seems as if it could not contain more than one conceptual and emotional root. Hence we are still at pains to find this root. Our economists, in the same way, have never wearied of scenting a similar unity in the word "value," and of hunting after the primitive root idea of value. As if all words were not pockets, into which this or that or several things have been stuffed at once! So "revenge" is now one thing, now another, and sometimes more composite. Let us first distinguish that defensive counter-blow, which we strike, almost unconsciously, even at inanimate objects (such as machinery in motion) that have hurt us. The

notion is to set a check to the object that has hurt us, by bringing the machine to a stop. Sometimes the force of this counter-blow, in order to attain its object, will have to be strong enough to shatter the machine. If the machine be too strong to be disorganised by one man, the latter will all the same strike the most violent blow he can—as a sort of last attempt. We behave similarly towards persons who hurt us, at the immediate sensation of the hurt. If we like to call this an act of revenge, well and good: but we must remember that here self-preservation alone has set its cog-wheels of reason in motion, and that after all we do not think of the doer of the injury but only of ourselves. We act without any idea of doing injury in return, only with a view to getting away safe and sound.—It needs time to pass in thought from oneself to one's adversary and ask oneself at what point he is most vulnerable. This is done in the second variety of revenge, the preliminary idea of which is to consider the vulnerability and susceptibility of the other. The intention then is to give pain. On the other hand, the idea of securing himself against further injury is in this case so entirely outside the avenger's horizon, that he almost regularly brings about his own further injury and often foresees it in cold blood. If in the first sort of revenge it was the fear of a second blow that made the counter-blow as strong as possible, in this case there is an almost complete indifference to what one's adversary will do: the strength of the counter-blow is only determined by what he has already done to us. Then what has he done? What profit is it to us if he is now suffering, after we have suffered through him? This is a case of readjustment, whereas the first act of revenge only serves the purpose of self-preservation. It may be that through our adversary we have lost property, rank, friends, children—these losses are not recovered by revenge, the readjustment only concerns a subsidiary loss which is added to all the other losses. The revenge of readjustment does not preserve one from further injury, it does not make good the injury already suffered—except in one case. If our honour has suffered through our adversary, revenge can restore it. But in any case honour has suffered an injury if intentional harm has been done us, because our adversary proved thereby that he was not afraid of us. By revenge we prove that we are not afraid of him either, and herein lies the settlement, the readjustment. (The intention of showing their complete lack of fear goes so far in some people that the dangers of revenge—loss of health or life or other losses—are in their eyes an indispensable condition of every vengeful act. Hence they practise the duel, although the law also offers them aid in obtaining satisfaction for what they have suffered. They are not satisfied with a safe means of recovering their honour, because this would not prove their fearlessness.)—In the first-named variety of revenge it is just fear that strikes the counter-blow; in the second case it is the absence of fear, which, as has been said, wishes to manifest itself in the counter-blow.—Thus nothing appears more different than the motives of the two courses of action which are designated by the one word "revenge." Yet it often happens that the avenger is not precisely certain as to what really prompted his deed: perhaps he struck the counterblow from fear and the instinct of self-preservation, but in the background, when he has time to reflect upon the standpoint of wounded honour, he imagines that he has avenged himself for the sake of his honour—this motive is in any case more reputable than the other. An essential point is whether he sees his honour injured in the eyes of others (the world) or only in the eyes of his offenders: in the latter case he will prefer secret, in the former open revenge. Accordingly, as he enters strongly or feebly into the soul of the doer and the spectator, his revenge will be more bitter or more tame. If he is entirely lacking in this sort of imagination, he will not think at all of revenge, as the feeling of "honour" is not present in him, and accordingly cannot be wounded. In the same way, he will not think of revenge if he despises the offender and the spectator; because as objects of his contempt they cannot give him honour, and accordingly cannot rob him of honour. Finally, he will forego revenge in the not uncommon case of his loving the offender. It is true that he then suffers loss of honour in the other's eyes, and will perhaps become less worthy of having his love returned. But even to renounce all requital of love is a sacrifice that love is ready to make when its only object is to avoid hurting the beloved object: this would mean hurting oneself more than one is hurt by the sacrifice.—Accordingly, every one will avenge himself, unless he be bereft of honour or inspired by contempt or by love for the offender. Even if he turns to the law-courts, he desires revenge as a private individual; but also, as a thoughtful, prudent man of society, he desires the revenge of society upon one who does not respect it. Thus by legal punishment private honour as well as that of society is restored—that is to say, punishment is revenge. Punishment undoubtedly contains the first-mentioned element of revenge, in as far as by its means society helps to preserve itself, and strikes a counter-blow in self-defence. Punishment desires to prevent further injury, to scare other offenders. In this way the two elements of revenge, different as they are, are united in punishment, and this may perhaps tend most of all to maintain the above-mentioned confusion of ideas, thanks to which the individual avenger generally does not know what he really wants.

34. The Virtues that Damage Us.—As members of communities we think we have no right to exercise certain virtues which afford us great honour and some pleasure as private individuals (for example, indulgence and favour towards miscreants of all kinds)—in short, every mode of action whereby the advantage of society would suffer through our virtue. No bench of judges, face to face with its

conscience, may permit itself to be gracious. This privilege is reserved for the king as an individual, and we are glad when he makes use of it, proving that we should like to be gracious individually, but not collectively. Society recognises only the virtues profitable to her, or at least not injurious to her—virtues like justice, which are exercised without loss, or, in fact, at compound interest. The virtues that damage us cannot have originated in society, because even now opposition to them arises in every small society that is in the making. Such virtues are therefore those of men of unequal standing, invented by the superior individuals; they are the virtues of rulers, and the idea underlying them is: "I am mighty enough to put up with an obvious loss; that is a proof of my power." Thus they are virtues closely akin to pride.

35. The Casuistry of Advantage.—There would be no moral casuistry if there were no casuistry of advantage. The most free and refined intelligence is often incapable of choosing between two alternatives in such a way that his choice necessarily involves the greater advantage. In such cases we choose because we must, and afterwards often feel a kind of emotional sea-sickness.

36. Turning Hypocrite.—Every beggar turns hypocrite, like every one who makes his living out of indigence, be it personal or public.—The beggar does not feel want nearly so keenly as he must make others feel it, if he wishes to make a living by mendicancy.

37. A Sort of Cult of the Passions.—You hypochondriacs, you philosophic blind-worms talk of the formidable nature of human passions, in order to inveigh against the dreadsomeness of the whole world-structure. As if the passions were always and everywhere formidable! As if this sort of terror must always exist in the world!—Through a carelessness in small matters, through a deficiency in observation of self and of the rising generation, you have yourselves allowed your passions to develop into such unruly monsters that you are frightened now at the mere mention of the word "passion"! It rests with you and it rests with us to divest the passions of their formidable features and so to dam them that they do not become devastating floods.—We must not exalt our errors into eternal fatalities. Rather shall we honestly endeavour to convert all the passions of humanity into sources of joy.[18]

38. The Sting of Conscience.—The sting of conscience, like the gnawing of a dog at a stone, is mere foolishness.

39. Origin of Rights.—Rights may be traced to traditions, traditions to momentary agreements. At some time or other men were mutually content with the consequences of making an agreement, and, again, too indolent formally to renew it. Thus they went on living as if it had constantly been renewed, and gradually, when oblivion cast its veil over the origin, they thought they possessed

a sacred, unalterable foundation on which every generation would be compelled to build. Tradition was now a constraint, even if it no more involved the profit originally derived from making the agreement.—Here the weak have always found their strong fortress. They are inclined to immortalise the momentary agreement, the single act of favour shown towards them.

40. The Significance of Oblivion in Moral Sentiment.—The same actions that in primitive society first aimed at the common advantage were later on performed from other motives: from fear or reverence of those who demanded and recommended them; or from habit, because men had seen them done about them from childhood upwards; or from kindness, because the practising of them caused delight and approving looks on all sides; or from vanity, because they were praised. Such actions, in which the fundamental motive, that of utility, has been forgotten, are then called moral; not, indeed, because they are done from those other motives, but because they are not done with a conscious purpose of utility.—Whence the hatred of utility that suddenly manifests itself here, and by which all praiseworthy actions formally exclude all actions for the sake of utility?—Clearly society, the rallying-point of all morality and of all maxims in praise of moral action, has had to battle too long and too fiercely with the selfishness and obstinacy of the individual not to rate every motive morally higher than utility. Hence it looks as if morals had not sprung from utility, whereas in fact morals are originally the public utility, which had great difficulty in prevailing over the interests of the unit and securing a loftier reputation.

41. The Heirs to the Wealth of Morality.—Even in the domain of morals there is an inherited wealth, which is owned by the gentle, the good-tempered, the compassionate, the indulgent. They have inherited from their forefathers their gentle mode of action, but not common sense (the source of that mode of action). The pleasant thing about this wealth is that one must always bestow and communicate a portion of it, if its presence is to be felt at all. Thus this wealth unconsciously aims at bridging the gulf between the morally rich and the morally poor, and, what is its best and most remarkable feature, not for the sake of a future mean between rich and poor, but for the sake of a universal prosperity and superfluity.—Such may be the prevailing view of inherited moral wealth, but it seems to me that this view is maintained more in majorem gloriam of morality than in honour of truth. Experience at least establishes a maxim which must serve, if not as a refutation, at any rate as an important check upon that generalisation. Without the most exquisite intelligence, says experience, without the most refined capacity for choice and a strong propensity to observe the mean, the morally rich will become spendthrifts of morality. For by abandoning themselves without restraint to their compassionate, gentle, conciliatory,

harmonising instincts, they make all about them more careless, more covetous, and more sentimental. The children of these highly moral spendthrifts easily and (sad to relate) at best become pleasant but futile wasters.

42. The Judge and Extenuating Circumstances.—"One should behave as a man of honour even towards the devil and pay his debts," said an old soldier, when the story of Faust had been related to him in rather fuller detail. "Hell is the right place for Faust!" "You are terrible, you men!" cried his wife; "how can that be? After all, his only fault was having no ink in his ink-stand! It is indeed a sin to write with blood, but surely for that such a handsome man ought not to burn in Hell-fire?"

43. Problem of the Duty of Truth.—Duty is an imperious sentiment that forces us to action. We call it good, and consider it outside the pale of discussion. The origin, limits, and justification of duty we will not debate or allow to be debated. But the thinker considers everything an evolution and every evolution a subject for discussion, and is accordingly without duty so long as he is merely a thinker. As such, he would not recognise the duty of seeing and speaking the truth; he would not feel the sentiment at all. He asks, whence comes it and whither will it go? But even this questioning appears to him questionable. Surely, however, the consequence would be that the thinker's machinery would no longer work properly if he could really feel himself unencumbered by duty in the search for knowledge? It would appear, then, that for fuel the same element is necessary as must be investigated by means of the machine.—Perhaps the formula will be: granted there were a duty of recognising truth, what is then the truth in regard to every other kind of duty?—But is not a hypothetical sense of duty a contradiction in terms?

44. Grades of Morals.—Morality is primarily a means of preserving the community and saving it from destruction. Next it is a means of maintaining the community on a certain plane and in a certain degree of benevolence. Its motives are fear and hope, and these in a more coarse, rough, and powerful form, the more the propensity towards the perverse, one-sided, and personal still persists. The most terrible means of intimidation must be brought into play so long as milder forms have no effect and that twofold species of preservation cannot be attained. (The strongest intimidation, by the way, is the invention of a hereafter with a hell everlasting.) For this purpose we must have racks and torturers of the soul. Further grades of morality, and accordingly means to the end referred to, are the commandments of a God (as in the Mosaic law). Still further and higher are the commandments of an absolute sense of duty with a "Thou shalt"—all rather roughly hewn yet broad steps, because on the finer, narrower steps men cannot yet set their feet. Then comes a morality of inclination, of taste, finally of

insight—which is beyond all the illusory motives of morality, but has convinced itself that humanity for long periods could be allowed no other.

45. The Morality of Pity in the Mouths of The Intemperate.—All those who are not sufficiently masters of themselves and do not know morality as a self-control and self-conquest continuously exercised in things great and small, unconsciously come to glorify the good, compassionate, benevolent impulses of that instinctive morality which has no head, but seems merely to consist of a heart and helpful hands. It is to their interest even to cast suspicion upon a morality of reason and to set up the other as the sole morality.

46. Sewers of the Soul.—Even the soul must have its definite sewers, through which it can allow its filth to flow off: for this purpose it may use persons, relations, social classes, its native country, or the world, or finally—for the wholly arrogant (I mean our modern "pessimists")—le bon Dieu.

47. A Kind of Rest and Contemplation.—Beware lest your rest and contemplation resemble that of a dog before a butcher's stall, prevented by fear from advancing and by greed from retiring, and opening its eyes wide as though they were mouths.

48. Prohibitions without Reasons.—A prohibition, the reason of which we do not understand or admit, is almost a command, not only for the stiff-necked but for the thirster after knowledge. We at once make an experiment in order to learn why the prohibition was made. Moral prohibitions, like those of the Decalogue, are only suited to ages when reason lies vanquished. Nowadays a prohibition like "Thou shalt not kill," "Thou shalt not commit adultery," laid down without reasons, would have an injurious rather than a beneficial effect.

49. Character Portrait.—What sort of a man is it that can say of himself: "I despise very easily, but never hate. I at once find out in every man something which can be honoured and for which I honour him: the so-called amiable qualities attract me but little"?

50. Pity and Contempt.—The expression of pity is regarded as a sign of contempt, because one has clearly ceased to be an object of fear as soon as one becomes an object of pity. One has sunk below the level of the equilibrium. For this equilibrium does not satisfy human vanity, which is only satisfied by the feeling that one is imposing respect and awe. Hence it is difficult to explain why pity is so highly prized, just as we need to explain why the unselfish man, who is originally despised or feared as being artful, is praised.

51. The Capacity of Being Small.—We must be as near to flowers, grasses, and butterflies as a child, that is, not much bigger than they. We adults have grown up beyond them and have to stoop to them. I think the grasses hate us when we

confess our love for them.—He who would have a share in all good things must understand at times how to be small.

52. The Sum-Total of Conscience.—The sum-total of our conscience is all that has regularly been demanded of us, without reason, in the days of our childhood, by people whom we respected or feared. From conscience comes that feeling of obligation ("This I must do, this omit") which does not ask, Why must I?—In all cases where a thing is done with "because" and "why," man acts without conscience, but not necessarily on that account against conscience.—The belief in authority is the source of conscience; which is therefore not the voice of God in the heart of man, but the voice of some men in man.

53. Conquest of the Passions.—The man who has overcome his passions has entered into possession of the most fruitful soil, like the colonist who has become lord over bogs and forests. To sow the seed of spiritual good works on the soil of the vanquished passions is the next and most urgent task. The conquest itself is a means, not an end: if it be not so regarded, all kind of weeds and devil's crop quickly spring up upon the fertile soil that has been cleared, and soon the growth is all wilder and more luxuriant than before.

54. Skill in Service.—All so-called practical men have skill in service, whether it be serving others or themselves; this is what makes them practical. Robinson owned a servant even better than Friday—his name was Crusoe.

55. Danger in Speech to Intellectual Freedom.—Every word is a preconceived judgment.

56. Intellect and Boredom.—The proverb, "The Hungarian is far too lazy to feel bored," gives food for thought. Only the highest and most active animals are capable of being bored.—The boredom of God on the seventh day of Creation would be a subject for a great poet.

57. Intercourse with Animals.—The origin of our morality may still be observed in our relations with animals. Where advantage or the reverse do not come into play, we have a feeling of complete irresponsibility. For example, we kill or wound insects or let them live, and as a rule think no more about it. We are so clumsy that even our gracious acts towards flowers and small animals are almost always murderous: this does not in the least detract from our pleasure in them.—To-day is the festival of the small animals, the most sultry day of the year. There is a swarming and crawling around us, and we, without intention, but also without reflection, crush here and there a little fly or winged beetle.—If animals do us harm, we strive to annihilate them in every possible way. The means are often cruel enough, even without our really intending them to be so—it is the cruelty of thoughtlessness. If they are useful, we turn them to advantage, until a more refined wisdom teaches us that certain animals amply reward a different mode

of treatment, that of tending and breeding. Here responsibility first arises. Torturing is avoided in the case of the domestic animal. One man is indignant if another is cruel to his cow, quite in accordance with the primitive communal morality, which sees the commonwealth in danger whenever an individual does wrong. He who perceives any transgression in the community fears indirect harm to himself. Thus we fear in this case for the quality of meat, agriculture, and means of communication if we see the domestic animals ill-treated. Moreover, he who is harsh to animals awakens a suspicion that he is also harsh to men who are weak, inferior, and incapable of revenge. He is held to be ignoble and deficient in the finer form of pride. Thus arises a foundation of moral judgments and sentiments, but the greatest contribution is made by superstition. Many animals incite men by glances, tones, and gestures to transfer themselves into them in imagination, and some religions teach us, under certain circumstances, to see in animals the dwelling-place of human and divine souls: whence they recommend a nobler caution or even a reverential awe in intercourse with animals. Even after the disappearance of this superstition the sentiments awakened by it continue to exercise their influence, to ripen and to blossom.—Christianity, as is well known, has shown itself in this respect a poor and retrograde religion.

58. New Actors.—Among human beings there is no greater banality than death. Second in order, because it is possible to die without being born, comes birth, and next comes marriage. But these hackneyed little tragi-comedies are always presented, at each of their unnumbered and innumerable performances, by new actors, and accordingly do not cease to find interested spectators: whereas we might well believe that the whole audience of the world-theatre had long since hanged themselves to every tree from sheer boredom at these performances. So much depends on new actors, so little on the piece.

59. What is "Being Obstinate"?—The shortest way is not the straightest possible, but that wherein favourable winds swell our sails. So says the wisdom of seamen. Not to follow his course is obstinate, firmness of character being then adulterated by stupidity.

60. The Word "Vanity."—It is annoying that certain words, with which we moralists positively cannot dispense, involve in themselves a kind of censorship of morals, dating from the times when the most ordinary and natural impulses were denounced. Thus that fundamental conviction that on the waves of society we either find navigable waters or suffer shipwreck far more through what we appear than through what we are (a conviction that must act as guiding principle of all action in relation to society) is branded with the general word "vanity." In other words, one of the most weighty and significant of qualities is branded with an expression which denotes it as essentially empty and negative: a great thing is

designated by a diminutive, ay, even slandered by the strokes of caricature. There is no help for it; we must use such words, but then we must shut our ears to the insinuations of ancient habits.

61. The Fatalism of the Turk.—The fatalism of the Turk has this fundamental defect, that it contrasts man and fate as two distinct things. Man, says this doctrine, may struggle against fate and try to baffle it, but in the end fate will always gain the victory. Hence the most rational course is to resign oneself or to live as one pleases. As a matter of fact, every man is himself a piece of fate. When he thinks that he is struggling against fate in this way, fate is accomplishing its ends even in that struggle. The combat is a fantasy, but so is the resignation in fate—all these fantasies are included in fate.—The fear felt by most people of the doctrine that denies the freedom of the will is a fear of the fatalism of the Turk. They imagine that man will become weakly resigned and will stand before the future with folded hands, because he cannot alter anything of the future. Or that he will give a free rein to his caprices, because the predestined cannot be made worse by that course. The follies of men are as much a piece of fate as are his wise actions, and even that fear of belief in fate is a fatality. You yourself, you poor timid creature, are that indomitable Moira, which rules even the Gods; whatever may happen, you are a curse or a blessing, and in any case the fetters wherein the strongest lies bound: in you the whole future of the human world is predestined, and it is no use for you to be frightened of yourself.

62. The Advocate of the Devil.—"Only by our own suffering do we become wise, only by others' suffering do we become good"—so runs that strange philosophy which derives all morality from pity and all intellectuality from the isolation of the individual. Herein this philosophy is the unconscious pleader for all human deterioration. For pity needs suffering, and isolation contempt of others.

63. The Moral Character-Masks.—In ages when the character-masks of different classes are definitely fixed, like the classes themselves, moralists will be seduced into holding the moral character-masks, too, as absolute, and in delineating them accordingly. Thus Molière is intelligible as the contemporary of the society of Louis XIV.: in our society of transitions and intermediate stages he would seem an inspired pedant.

64. The Most Noble Virtue.—In the first era of the higher humanity courage is accounted the most noble virtue, in the next justice, in the third temperance, in the fourth wisdom. In which era do we live? In which do you live?

65. A Necessary Preliminary.—A man who will not become master of his irritability, his venomous and vengeful feelings, and his lust, and attempts to

become master in anything else, is as stupid as the farmer who lays out his field beside a torrent without guarding against that torrent.

66. What is Truth?–Schwarzert (Melanchthon): We often preach our faith when we have lost it, and leave not a stone unturned to find it–and then we often do not preach worst!

Luther: Brother, you are really speaking like an angel to-day.

Schwarzert: But that is the idea of your enemies, and they apply it to you.

Luther: Then it would be a lie from the devil's hind-quarters.

67. The Habit of Contrasts.–Superficial, inexact observation sees contrasts everywhere in nature (for instance, "hot and cold"), where there are no contrasts, only differences of degree. This bad habit has induced us to try to understand and interpret even the inner nature, the intellectual and moral world, in accordance with such contrasts. An infinite amount of cruelty, arrogance, harshness, estrangement, and coldness has entered into human emotion, because men imagined they saw contrasts where there were only transitions.

68. Can We Forgive?–How can we forgive them at all, if they know not what they do? We have nothing to forgive. But does a man ever fully know what he is doing? And if this point at least remains always debatable, men never have anything to forgive each other, and indulgence is for the reasonable man an impossible thing. Finally, if the evil-doers had really known what they did, we should still only have a right to forgive if we had a right to accuse and to punish. But we have not that right.

69. Habitual Shame.–Why do we feel shame when some virtue or merit is attributed to us which, as the saying goes, "we have not deserved"? Because we appear to have intruded upon a territory to which we do not belong, from which we should be excluded, as from a holy place or holy of holies, which ought not to be trodden by our foot. Through the errors of others we have, nevertheless, penetrated to it, and we are now swayed partly by fear, partly by reverence, partly by surprise; we do not know whether we ought to fly or to enjoy the blissful moment with all its gracious advantages. In all shame there is a mystery, which seems desecrated or in danger of desecration through us. All favour begets shame.–But if it be remembered that we have never really "deserved" anything, this feeling of shame, provided that we surrender ourselves to this point of view in a spirit of Christian contemplation, becomes habitual, because upon such a one God seems continually to be conferring his blessing and his favours. Apart from this Christian interpretation, the state of habitual shame will be possible even to the entirely godless sage, who clings firmly to the basic non-responsibility and non-meritoriousness of all action and being. If he be treated as if he had deserved this or that, he will seem to have won his way into a higher order of

beings, who do actually deserve something, who are free and can really bear the burden of responsibility for their own volition and capacity. Whoever says to him, "You have deserved it," appears to cry out to him, "You are not a human being, but a God."

70. The Most Unskilful Teacher.—In one man all his real virtues are implanted on the soil of his spirit of contradiction, in another on his incapacity to say "no"—in other words, on his spirit of acquiescence. A third has made all his morality grow out of his pride as a solitary, a fourth from his strong social instinct. Now, supposing that the seeds of the virtues in these four cases, owing to mischance or unskilful teachers, were not sown on the soil of their nature, which provides them with the richest and most abundant mould, they would become weak, unsatisfactory men (devoid of morality). And who would have been the most unskilful of teachers, the evil genius of these men? The moral fanatic, who thinks that the good can only grow out of the good and on the soil of the good.

71. The Cautious Style.—A. But if this were known to all, it would be injurious to the majority. You yourself call your opinions dangerous to those in danger, and yet you make them public?

B. I write so that neither the mob, nor the populi, nor the parties of all kinds can read me. So my opinions will never be "public opinions."

A. How do you write, then?

B. Neither usefully nor pleasantly—for the three classes I have mentioned.

72. Divine Missionaries.—Even Socrates feels himself to be a divine missionary, but I am not sure whether we should not here detect a tincture of that Attic irony and fondness for jesting whereby this odious, arrogant conception would be toned down. He talks of the fact without unction—his images of the gadfly and the horse are simple and not sacerdotal. The real religious task which he has set himself—to test God in a hundred ways and see whether he spoke the truth—betrays a bold and free attitude, in which the missionary walked by the side of his God. This testing of God is one of the most subtle compromises between piety and free-thinking that has ever been devised.—Nowadays we do not even need this compromise any longer.

73. Honesty in Painting.—Raphael, who cared a great deal for the Church (so far as she could pay him), but, like the best men of his time, cared little for the objects of the Church's belief, did not advance one step to meet the exacting, ecstatic piety of many of his patrons. He remained honest even in that exceptional picture which was originally intended for a banner in a procession—the Sistine Madonna. Here for once he wished to paint a vision, but such a vision as even noble youths without "faith" may and will have—the vision of the future wife, a wise, high-souled, silent, and very beautiful woman, carrying

her first-born in her arms. Let men of an older generation, accustomed to prayer and devotion, find here, like the worthy elder on the left, something superhuman to revere. We younger men (so Raphael seems to call to us) are occupied with the beautiful maiden on the right, who says to the spectator of the picture, with her challenging and by no means devout look, "The mother and her child—is not that a pleasant, inviting sight?" The face and the look are reflected in the joy in the faces of the beholders. The artist who devised all this enjoys himself in this way, and adds his own delight to the delight of the art-lover. As regards the "messianic" expression in the face of the child, Raphael, honest man, who would not paint any state of soul in which he did not believe, has amiably cheated his religious admirers. He painted that freak of nature which is very often found, the man's eye in the child's face, and that, too, the eye of a brave, helpful man who sees distress. This eye should be accompanied by a beard. The fact that a beard is wanting, and that two different ages are seen in one countenance, is the pleasing paradox which believers have interpreted in accordance with their faith in miracles. The artist could only expect as much from their art of exposition and interpretation.

74. Prayer.—On two hypotheses alone is there any sense in prayer, that not quite extinct custom of olden times. It would have to be possible either to fix or alter the will of the godhead, and the devotee would have to know best himself what he needs and should really desire. Both hypotheses, axiomatic and traditional in all other religions, are denied by Christianity. If Christianity nevertheless maintained prayer side by side with its belief in the all-wise and all-provident divine reason (a belief that makes prayer really senseless and even blasphemous), it showed here once more its admirable "wisdom of the serpent." For an outspoken command, "Thou shalt not pray," would have led Christians by way of boredom to the denial of Christianity. In the Christian ora et labora ora plays the rôle of pleasure. Without ora what could those unlucky saints who renounced labora have done? But to have a chat with God, to ask him for all kinds of pleasant things, to feel a slight amusement at one's own folly in still having any wishes at all, in spite of so excellent a father—all that was an admirable invention for saints.

75. A Holy Lie.—The lie that was on Arria's lips when she died (Paete, non dolet[19]) obscures all the truths that have ever been uttered by the dying. It is the only holy lie that has become famous, whereas elsewhere the odour of sanctity has clung only to errors.

76. The Most Necessary Apostle.—Among twelve apostles one must always be hard as stone, in order that upon him the new church may be built.

77. Which is more Transitory, the Body or the Spirit?—In legal, moral, and religious institutions the external and concrete elements—in other words, rites, gestures, and ceremonies—are the most permanent. They are the body to which a new spirit is constantly being superadded. The cult, like an unchangeable text, is ever interpreted anew. Concepts and emotions are fluid, customs are solid.

78. The Belief in Disease qua Disease.—Christianity first painted the devil on the wall of the world. Christianity first brought the idea of sin into the world. The belief in the remedies, which is offered as an antidote, has gradually been shaken to its very foundations. But the belief in the disease, which Christianity has taught and propagated, still exists.

79. Speech and Writings of Religious Men.—If the priest's style and general expression, both in speaking and writing, do not clearly betray the religious man, we need no longer take his views upon religion and his pleading for religion seriously. These opinions have become powerless for him if, judging by his style, he has at command irony, arrogance, malice, hatred, and all the changing eddies of mood, just like the most irreligious of men—how far more powerless will they be for his hearers and readers! In short, he will serve to make the latter still more irreligious.

80. The Danger in Personality.—The more God has been regarded as a personality in himself, the less loyal have we been to him. Men are far more attached to their thought-images than to their best beloved. That is why they sacrifice themselves for State, Church, and even for God—so far as he remains their creation, their thought, and is not too much looked upon as a personality. In the latter case they almost always quarrel with him. After all, it was the most pious of men who let slip that bitter cry: "My God, why hast thou forsaken me?"

81. Worldly Justice.—It is possible to unhinge worldly justice with the doctrine of the complete non-responsibility and innocence of every man. An attempt has been made in the same direction on the basis of the opposite doctrine of the full responsibility and guilt of every man. It was the founder of Christianity who wished to abolish worldly justice and banish judgment and punishment from the world. For he understood all guilt as "sin"—that is, an outrage against God and not against the world. On the other hand, he considered every man in a broad sense, and almost in every sense, a sinner. The guilty, however, are not to be the judges of their peers—so his rules of equity decided. Thus all dispensers of worldly justice were in his eyes as culpable as those they condemned, and their air of guiltlessness appeared to him hypocritical and pharisaical. Moreover, he looked to the motives and not to the results of actions, and thought that only one was keen-sighted enough to give a verdict on motives—himself or, as he expressed it, God.

82. An Affectation in Parting.—He who wishes to sever his connection with a party or a creed thinks it necessary for him to refute it. This is a most arrogant notion. The only thing necessary is that he should clearly see what tentacles hitherto held him to this party or creed and no longer hold him, what views impelled him to it and now impel him in some other directions. We have not joined the party or creed on strict grounds of knowledge. We should not affect this attitude on parting from it either.

83. Saviour and Physician.—In his knowledge of the human soul the founder of Christianity was, as is natural, not without many great deficiencies and prejudices, and, as physician of the soul, was addicted to that disreputable, laical belief in a universal medicine. In his methods he sometimes resembles that dentist who wishes to heal all pain by extracting the tooth. Thus, for example, he assails sensuality with the advice: "If thine eye offend thee, pluck it out."—Yet there still remains the distinction   that the dentist at least attains his object—painlessness for the patient—although in so clumsy a fashion that he becomes ridiculous; whereas the Christian who follows that advice and thinks he has killed his sensuality, is wrong, for his sensuality still lives in an uncanny, vampire form, and torments him in hideous disguises.

84. Prisoners.—One morning the prisoners entered the yard for work, but the warder was not there. Some, as their manner was, set to work at once; others stood idle and gazed defiantly around. Then one of them strode forward and cried, "Work as much as you will or do nothing, it all comes to the same. Your secret machinations have come to light; the warder has been keeping his eye on you of late, and will cause a terrible judgment to be passed upon you in a few days' time. You know him—he is of a cruel and resentful disposition. But now, listen: you have mistaken me hitherto. I am not what I seem, but far more—I am the son of the warder, and can get anything I like out of him. I can save you—nay, I will save you. But remember this: I will only save those of you who believe that I am the son of the prison warder. The rest may reap the fruits of their unbelief." "Well," said an old prisoner after an interval of silence, "what can it matter to you whether we believe you or not? If you are really the son, and can do what you say, then put in a good word for us all. That would be a real kindness on your part. But have done with all talk of belief and unbelief!" "What is more," cried a younger man, "I don't believe him: he has only got a bee in his bonnet. I'll wager that in a week's time we shall find ourselves in the same place as we are to-day, and the warder will know nothing." "And if the warder ever knew anything, he knows it no longer," said the last of the prisoners, coming down into the yard at that moment, "for he has just died suddenly." "Ah ha!" cried several in confusion, "ah ha! Sir Son, Sir Son, how stands it now with your title? Are we by

any chance your prisoners now?" "I told you," answered the man gently, "I will set free all who believe in me, as surely as my father still lives."—The prisoners did not laugh, but shrugged their shoulders and left him to himself.

85. The Persecutors of God.—Paul conceived and Calvin followed up the idea that countless creatures have been predestined to damnation from time immemorial, and that this fair world was made in order that the glory of God might be manifested therein. So heaven and hell and mankind merely exist to satisfy the vanity of God! What a cruel, insatiable vanity must have smouldered in the soul of the first or second thinker of such a thought!—Paul, then, after all, remained Saul—the persecutor of God.

86. Socrates.—If all goes well, the time will come when, in order to advance themselves on the path of moral reason, men will rather take up the Memorabilia of Socrates than the Bible, and when Montaigne and Horace will be used as pioneers and guides for the understanding of Socrates, the simplest and most enduring of interpretative sages. In him converge the roads of the most different philosophic modes of life, which are in truth the modes of the different temperaments, crystallised by reason and habit and all ultimately directed towards the delight in life and in self. The apparent conclusion is that the most peculiar thing about Socrates was his share in all the temperaments. Socrates excels the founder of Christianity by virtue of his merry style of seriousness and by that wisdom of sheer roguish pranks which constitutes the best state of soul in a man. Moreover, he had a superior intelligence.

87. Learning to Write Well.—The age of good speaking is over, because the age of city-state culture is over. The limit allowed by Aristotle to the great city—in which the town-crier must be able to make himself heard by the whole assembled community—troubles us as little as do any city-communities, us who even wish to be understood beyond the boundaries of nations. Therefore every one who is of a good European turn of mind must learn to write well, and to write better and better. He cannot help himself, he must learn that: even if he was born in Germany, where bad writing is looked upon as a national privilege. Better writing means better thinking; always to discover matter more worthy of communication; to be able to communicate it properly; to be translateable into the tongues of neighbouring nations; to make oneself comprehensible to foreigners who learn our language; to work with the view of making all that is good common property, and of giving free access everywhere to the free; finally, to pave the way for that still remote state of things, when the great task shall come for good Europeans—guidance and guardianship of the universal world-culture.—Whoever preaches the opposite doctrine of not troubling about good writing and good reading (both virtues grow together and decline together)

is really showing the peoples a way of becoming more and more national. He is intensifying the malady of this century, and is a foe to good Europeans, a foe to free spirits.

88. The Theory of the Best Style.—The theory of the best style may at one time be the theory of finding the expression by which we transfer every mood of ours to the reader and the listener. At another, it may be the theory of finding expressions for the more desirable human moods, the communication and transference of which one desires most—for the mood of a man moved from the depth of his heart, intellectually cheerful, bright, and sincere, who has conquered his passions. This will be the theory of the best style, a theory that corresponds to the good man.

89. Paying Attention to Movement.—The movement of the sentences shows whether the author be tired. Individual expressions may nevertheless be still strong and good, because they were invented earlier and for their own sake, when the thought first flashed across the author's mind. This is frequently the case with Goethe, who too often dictated when he was tired.

90. "Already" and "Still."—A. German prose is still very young. Goethe declares that Wieland is its father.

B. So young and already so ugly!

C. But, so far as I am aware, Bishop Ulfilas already wrote German prose, which must therefore be fifteen hundred years old.

B. So old and still so ugly!

91. Original German.—German prose, which is really not fashioned on any pattern and must be considered an original creation of German taste, should give the eager advocate of a future original German culture an indication of how real German dress, German society, German furniture, German meals would look without the imitation of models.—Some one who had long reflected on these vistas finally cried in great horror, "But, Heaven help us, perhaps we already have that original culture—only we don't like to talk about it!"

92. Forbidden Books.—One should never read anything written by those arrogant wiseacres and puzzle-brains who have the detestable vice of logical paradox. They apply logical formulæ just where everything is really improvised at random and built in the air. ("Therefore" with them means, "You idiot of a reader, this 'therefore' does not exist for you, but only for me." The answer to this is: "You idiot of a writer, then why do you write?")

93. Displaying One's Wit.—Every one who wishes to display his wit thereby proclaims that he has also a plentiful lack of wit. That vice which clever Frenchmen have of adding a touch of dédain to their best ideas arises from a

desire to be considered richer than they really are. They wish to be carelessly generous, as if weary of continual spending from overfull treasuries.

94. French and German Literature.—The misfortune of the French and German literature of the last hundred years is that the Germans ran away too early from the French school, and the French, later on, went too early to the German school.

95. Our Prose.—None of the present-day cultured nations has so bad a prose as the German. When clever, blasé Frenchmen say, "There is no German prose," we ought really not to be angry, for this criticism is more polite than we deserve. If we look for reasons, we come at last to the strange phenomenon that the German knows only improvised prose and has no conception of any other. He simply cannot understand the Italian, who says that prose is as much harder than poetry as the representation of naked beauty is harder to the sculptor than that of draped beauty. Verse, images, rhythm, and rhyme need honest effort—that even the German realises, and he is not inclined to set a very high value on extempore poetry. But the notion of working at a page of prose as at a statue sounds to him like a tale from fairyland.

96. The Grand Style.—The grand style comes into being when the beautiful wins a victory over the monstrous.

97. Dodging.—We do not realise, in the case of distinguished minds, wherein lies the excellence of their expression, their turn of phrase, until we can say what word every mediocre writer would inevitably have hit upon in expressing the same idea. All great artists, in steering their car, show themselves prone to dodge and leave the track, but never to fall over.

98. Something like Bread.—Bread neutralises and takes out the taste of other food, and is therefore necessary to every long meal. In all works of art there must be something like bread, in order that they may produce divers effects. If these effects followed one another without occasional pauses and intervals, they would soon make us weary and provoke disgust—in fact, a long meal of art would then be impossible.

99. Jean Paul.—Jean Paul knew a great deal, but had no science; understood all manner of tricks of art, but had no art; found almost everything enjoyable, but had no taste; possessed feeling and seriousness, but in dispensing them poured over them a nauseous sauce of tears; had even wit, but, unfortunately for his ardent desire for it, far too little—whence he drives the reader to despair by his very lack of wit. In short, he was the bright, rank-smelling weed that shot up overnight in the fair pleasaunces of Schiller and Goethe. He was a good, comfortable man, and yet a destiny, a destiny in a dressing-gown.[20]

100. Palate for Opposites.—In order to enjoy a work of the past as its contemporaries enjoyed it, one must have a palate for the prevailing taste of the age which it attacked.

101. Spirits-of-Wine Authors.—Many writers are neither spirit nor wine, but spirits of wine. They can flare up, and then they give warmth.

102. The Interpretative Sense.—The sense of taste, as the true interpretative sense, often talks the other senses over to its point of view and imposes upon them its laws and customs. At table one can receive disclosures about the most subtle secrets of the arts; it suffices to observe what tastes good and when and after what and how long it tastes good.

103. Lessing.—Lessing had a genuine French talent, and, as writer, went most assiduously to the French school. He knows well how to arrange and display his wares in his shop-window. Without this true art his thoughts, like the objects of them, would have remained rather in the dark, nor would the general loss be great. His art, however, has taught many (especially the last generation of German scholars) and has given enjoyment to a countless number. It is true his disciples had no need to learn from him, as they often did, his unpleasant tone with its mingling of petulance and candour.—Opinion is now unanimous on Lessing as "lyric poet," and will some day be unanimous on Lessing as "dramatic poet."

104. Undesirable Readers.—How an author is vexed by those stolid, awkward readers who always fall at every place where they stumble, and always hurt themselves when they fall!

105. Poets' Thoughts.—Real thoughts of real poets always go about with a veil on, like Egyptian women; only the deep eye of thought looks out freely through the veil.—Poets' thoughts are as a rule not of such value as is supposed. We have to pay for the veil and for our own curiosity into the bargain.

106. Write Simply and Usefully.—Transitions, details, colour in depicting the passions—we make a present of all these to the author because we bring them with us and set them down to the credit of his book, provided he makes us some compensation.

107. Wieland.—Wieland wrote German better than any one else, and had the genuine adequacies and inadequacies of the master. His translations of the letters of Cicero and Lucian are the best in the language. His ideas, however, add nothing to our store of thought. We can endure his cheerful moralities as little as his cheerful immoralities, for both are very closely connected. The men who enjoyed them were at bottom better men than we are, but also a good deal heavier. They needed an author of this sort. The Germans did not need Goethe, and therefore cannot make proper use of him. We have only to consider the best

of our statesmen and artists in this light. None of them had or could have had Goethe as their teacher.

108. Rare Festivals.—Pithy conciseness, repose, and maturity—where you find these qualities in an author, cry halt and celebrate a great festival in the desert. It will be long before you have such a treat again.

109. The Treasure of German Prose.—Apart from Goethe's writings and especially Goethe's conversations with Eckermann (the best German book in existence), what German prose literature remains that is worth reading over and over again? Lichtenberg's Aphorisms, the first book of Jung-Stilling's Story of My Life, Adalbert Stifter's St. Martin's Summer and Gottfried Keller's People of Seldwyla—and there, for the time being, it comes to an end.

110. Literary and Colloquial Style.—The art of writing demands, first and foremost, substitutions for the means of expression which speech alone possesses—in other words, for gestures, accent, intonation, and look. Hence literary style is quite different from colloquial style, and far more difficult, because it has to make itself as intelligible as the latter with fewer accessaries. Demosthenes delivered his speeches differently from what we read; he worked them up for reading purposes.—Cicero's speeches ought to be "demosthenised" with the same object, for at present they contain more of the Roman Forum than we can endure.

111. Caution in Quotation.—Young authors do not know that a good expression or idea only looks well among its peers; that an excellent quotation may spoil whole pages, nay the whole book; for it seems to cry warningly to the reader, "Mark you, I am the precious stone, and round about me is lead—pale, worthless lead!" Every word, every idea only desires to live in its own company—that is the moral of a choice style.

112. How should Errors be Enunciated?—We may dispute whether it be more injurious for errors to be enunciated badly or as well as the best truths. It is certain that in the former case they are doubly harmful to the brain and are less easily removed from it. But, on the other hand, they are not so certain of effect as in the latter case. They are, in fact, less contagious.

113. Limiting and Widening.—Homer limited and diminished the horizon of his subject, but allowed individual scenes to expand and blossom out. Later, the tragedians are constantly renewing this process. Each takes his material in ever smaller and smaller fragments than his predecessor did, but each attains a greater wealth of blooms within the narrow hedges of these sequestered garden enclosures.

114. Literature and Morality Mutually Explanatory.—We can show from Greek literature by what forces the Greek spirit developed, how it entered upon

different channels, and where it became enfeebled. All this also depicts to us how Greek morality proceeded, and how all morality will proceed: how it was at first a constraint and displayed cruelty, then became gradually milder; how a pleasure in certain actions, in certain forms and conventions arose, and from this again a propensity for solitary exercise, for solitary possession; how the track becomes crowded and overcrowded with competitors; how satiety enters in, new objects of struggle and ambition are sought, and forgotten aims are awakened to life; how the drama is repeated, and the spectators become altogether weary of looking on, because the whole gamut seems to have been run through—and then comes a stoppage, an expiration, and the rivulets are lost in the sand. The end, or at any rate an end, has come.

115. What Landscapes give Permanent Delight.—Such and such a landscape has features eminently suited for painting, but I cannot find the formula for it; it remains beyond my grasp as a whole. I notice that all landscapes which please me permanently have a simple geometrical scheme of lines underneath all their complexity. Without such a mathematical substratum no scenery becomes artistically pleasing. Perhaps this rule may be applied symbolically to human beings.

116. Reading Aloud.—The ability to read aloud involves of necessity the ability to declaim. Everywhere we must apply pale tints, but we must determine the degree of pallor in close relation to the richly and deeply coloured background, that always hovers before our eyes and acts as our guide—in other words, in accordance with the way in which we should declaim the same passages. That is why we must be able to declaim.

117. The Dramatic Sense.—He who has not the four subtler senses of art tries to understand everything with the fifth sense, which is the coarsest of all—the dramatic sense.

118. Herder.—Herder fails to be all that he made people think he was and himself wished to think he was. He was no great thinker or discoverer, no newly fertile soil with the unexhausted strength of a virgin forest. But he possessed in the highest degree the power of scenting the future, he saw and picked the first-fruits of the seasons earlier than all others, and they then believed that he had made them grow. Between darkness and light, youth and age, his mind was like a hunter on the watch, looking everywhere for transitions, depressions, convulsions, the outward and visible signs of internal growth. The unrest of spring drove him to and fro, but he was himself not the spring.—At times, indeed, he had some inkling of this, and yet would fain not have believed it—he, the ambitious priest, who would have so gladly been the intellectual pope of his epoch! This is his despair. He seems to have lived long as a pretender to several

kingdoms or even to a universal monarchy. He had his following which believed in him, among others the young Goethe. But whenever crowns were really distributed, he was passed over. Kant, Goethe, and then the first true German historians and scholars robbed him of what he thought he had reserved for himself (although in silence and secret he often thought the reverse). Just when he doubted in himself, he gladly clothed himself in dignity and enthusiasm: these were often in him mere garments, which had to hide a great deal and also to deceive and comfort him. He really had fire and enthusiasm, but his ambition was far greater! It blew impatiently at the fire, which flickered, crackled, and smoked—his style flickers, crackles, and smokes—but he yearned for the great flame which never broke out. He did not sit at the table of the genuine creators, and his ambition did not admit of his sitting modestly among those who simply enjoy. Thus he was a restless spirit, the taster of all intellectual dishes, which were collected by the Germans from every quarter and every age in the course of half a century. Never really happy and satisfied, Herder was also too often ill, and then at times envy sat by his bed, and hypocrisy paid her visit as well. He always had an air of being scarred and crippled, and he lacked simple, stalwart manliness more completely than any of the so-called "classical writers."

119. Scent of Words.—Every word has its scent; there is a harmony and discord of scents, and so too of words.

120. The Far-Fetched Style.—The natural style is an offence to the lover of the far-fetched style.

121. A Vow.—I will never again read an author of whom one can suspect that he wanted to make a book, but only those writers whose thoughts unexpectedly became a book.

122. The Artistic Convention.—Three-fourths of Homer is convention, and the same is the case with all the Greek artists, who had no reason for falling into the modern craze for originality. They had no fear of convention, for after all convention was a link between them and their public. Conventions are the artistic means acquired for the understanding of the hearer; the common speech, learnt with much toil, whereby the artist can really communicate his ideas. All the more when he wishes, like the Greek poets and musicians, to conquer at once with each of his works (since he is accustomed to compete publicly with one or two rivals), the first condition is that he must be understood at once, and this is only possible by means of convention. What the artist devises beyond convention he offers of his own free will and takes a risk, his success at best resulting in the setting-up of a new convention. As a rule originality is marvelled at, sometimes even worshipped, but seldom understood. A stubborn avoidance of convention

means a desire not to be understood. What, then, is the object of the modern craze for originality?

123. Artists' Affectation of Scientific Method.—Schiller, like other German artists, fancied that if a man had intellect he was entitled to improvise even with the pen on all difficult subjects. So there we see his prose essays—in every way a model of how not to attack scientific questions of æsthetics and ethics, and a danger for young readers who, in their admiration for Schiller the poet, have not the courage to think meanly of Schiller the thinker and author.—The temptation to traverse for once the forbidden paths, and to have his say in science as well, is easy and pardonable in the artist. For even the ablest artist from time to time finds his handicraft and his workshop unendurable. This temptation is so strong that it makes the artist show all the world what no one wishes to see, that his little chamber of thought is cramped and untidy. Why not, indeed? He does not live there. He proceeds to show that the storeroom of his knowledge is partly empty, partly filled with lumber. Why not, indeed? This condition does not really become the artist-child badly. In particular, the artist shows that for the very easiest exercises of scientific method, which are accessible even to beginners, his joints are too stiff and untrained. Even of that he need not really be ashamed! On the other hand, he often develops no mean art in imitating all the mistakes, vices, and base pedantries that are practised in the scientific community, in the belief that these belong to the appearance of the thing, if not to the thing itself. This is the very point that is so amusing in artists' writing, that the artist involuntarily acts as his vocation demands: he parodies the scientific and inartistic natures. Towards science he should show no attitude but that of parody, in so far as he is an artist and only an artist.

124. The Faust-Idea.—A little sempstress is seduced and plunged into despair: a great scholar of all the four Faculties is the evil-doer. That cannot have happened in the ordinary course, surely? No, certainly not! Without the aid of the devil incarnate, the great scholar would never have achieved the deed.—Is this really destined to be the greatest German "tragic idea," as one hears it said among Germans?—But for Goethe even this idea was too terrible. His kind heart could not avoid placing the little sempstress, "the good soul that forgot itself but once," near to the saints, after her involuntary death. Even the great scholar, "the good man" with "the dark impulse," is brought into heaven in the nick of time, by a trick which is played upon the devil at the decisive moment. In heaven the lovers find themselves again. Goethe once said that his nature was too conciliatory for really tragic subjects.

125. Are there "German Classics"?—Sainte-Beuve observes somewhere that the word "classic" does not suit the genius of certain literatures. For instance, nobody

could talk seriously of "German classics."—What do our German publishers, who are about to add fifty more to the fifty German classics we are told to accept, say to that? Does it not almost seem as if one need only have been dead for the last thirty years, and lie a lawful prey to the public,[21] in order to hear suddenly and unexpectedly the trumpet of resurrection as a "Classic"? And this in an age and a nation where at least five out of the six great fathers of its literature are undoubtedly antiquated or becoming antiquated—without there being any need for the age or the nation to be ashamed of this. For those writers have given way before the strength of our time—let that be considered in all fairness!—Goethe, as I have indicated, I do not include. He belongs to a higher species than "national literatures": hence life, revival, and decay do not enter into the reckoning in his relations with his countrymen. He lived and now lives but for the few; for the majority he is nothing but a flourish of vanity which is trumpeted from time to time across the border into foreign ears. Goethe, not merely a great and good man, but a culture, is in German history an interlude without a sequel. Who, for instance, would be able to point to any trace of Goethe's influence in German politics of the last seventy years (whereas the influence, certainly of Schiller, and perhaps of Lessing, can be traced in the political world)? But what of those five others? Klopstock, in a most honourable way, became out of date even in his own lifetime, and so completely that the meditative book of his later years, The Republic of Learning, has never been taken seriously from that day to this. Herder's misfortune was that his writings were always either new or antiquated. Thus for stronger and more subtle minds (like Lichtenberg) even Herder's masterpiece, his Ideas for the History of Mankind, was in a way antiquated at the very moment of its appearance. Wieland, who lived to the full and made others live likewise, was clever enough to anticipate by death the waning of his influence. Lessing, perhaps, still lives to-day—but among a young and ever younger band of scholars. Schiller has fallen from the hands of young men into those of boys, of all German boys. It is a well-known sign of obsolescence when a book descends to people of less and less mature age.—Well, what is it that has thrust these five into the background, so that well-educated men of affairs no longer read them? A better taste, a riper knowledge, a higher reverence for the real and the true: in other words, the very virtues which these five (and ten or twenty others of lesser repute) first re-planted in Germany, and which now, like a mighty forest, cast over their graves not only the shadow of awe, but something of the shadow of oblivion.—But classical writers are not planters of intellectual and literary virtues. They bring those virtues to perfection and are their highest luminous peaks, and being brighter, freer, and purer than all that surrounds them, they remain shining above the nations when the nations themselves perish. There may come an elevated stage of humanity, in which the Europe of the peoples is a dark, forgotten thing, but Europe lives on in thirty books, very old but never antiquated—in the classics.

126. Interesting, but not Beautiful.—This countryside conceals its meaning, but it has one that we should like to guess. Everywhere that I look, I read words and hints of words, but I do not know where begins the sentence that solves the riddle of all these hints. So I get a stiff neck in trying to discover whether I should start reading from this or that point.

127. Against Innovators in Language.—The use of neologisms or archaisms, the preference for the rare and the bizarre, the attempt to enrich rather than to limit the vocabulary, are always signs either of an immature or of a corrupted taste. A noble poverty but a masterly freedom within the limits of that modest wealth distinguishes the Greek artists in oratory. They wish to have less than the people has—for the people is richest in old and new—but they wish to have that little better. The reckoning up of their archaic and exotic forms is soon done, but we never cease marvelling if we have an eye for their light and delicate manner in handling the commonplace and apparently long outworn elements in word and phrase.

128. Gloomy and Serious Authors.—He who commits his sufferings to paper becomes a gloomy author, but he becomes a serious one if he tells us what he has suffered and why he is now enjoying a pleasurable repose.

129. Healthiness of Taste.—How is it that health is less contagious than disease—generally, and particularly in matters of taste? Or are there epidemics of health?

130. A Resolution.—Never again to read a book that is born and christened (with ink) at the same moment.

131. Improving our Ideas.—Improving our style means improving our ideas, and nothing else. He who does not at once concede this can never be convinced of the point.

132. Classical Books.—The weakest point in every classical book is that it is written too much in the mother tongue of its author.

133. Bad Books.—The book should demand pen, ink, and desk, but usually it is pen, ink, and desk that demand the book. That is why books are of so little account at present.

134. Presence of Sense.—When the public reflects on paintings, it becomes a poet; when on poems, an investigator. At the moment when the artist summons it it is always lacking in the right sense, and accordingly in presence of sense, not in presence of mind.

135. Choice Ideas.—The choice style of a momentous period does not only select its words but its ideas—and both from the customary and prevailing usage. Venturesome ideas, that smell too fresh, are to the maturer taste no less repugnant than new and reckless images and phrases. Later on both choice ideas and choice words soon smack of mediocrity, because the scent of the choice vanishes quickly, and then nothing but the customary and commonplace element is tasted.

136. Main Reason for Corruption of Style.—The desire to display more sentiment than one really feels for a thing corrupts style, in language and in all art. All great art shows rather the opposite tendency. Like every man of moral significance, it loves to check emotion on its way and not let it run its course to the very end. This modesty of letting emotion but half appear is most clearly to be observed, for example, in Sophocles. The features of sentiment seem to become beautified when sentiment feigns to be more shy than it really is.

137. An Excuse for the Heavy Style.—The lightly uttered phrase seldom falls on the ear with the full weight of the subject. This is, however, due to the bad training of the ear, which by education must pass from what has hitherto been called music to the school of the higher harmony—in other words, to conversation.

138. Bird's-Eye Views.—Here torrents rush from every side into a ravine: their movement is so swift and stormy, and carries the eye along so quickly, that the bare or wooded mountain slopes around seem not to sink down but to fly down. We are in an agonised tension at the sight, as if behind all this were hidden some hostile element, before which all must fly, and against which the abyss alone gave protection. This landscape cannot be painted, unless we hover above it like a bird in the open air. Here for once the so-called bird's-eye view is not an artistic caprice, but the sole possibility.

139. Rash Comparisons.—If rash comparisons are not proofs of the wantonness of the writer, they are proofs of the exhaustion of his imagination. In any case they bear witness to his bad taste.

140. Dancing in Chains.—In the case of every Greek artist, poet, or writer we must ask: What is the new constraint which he imposes upon himself and makes attractive to his contemporaries, so as to find imitators? For the thing called "invention" (in metre, for example) is always a self-imposed fetter of this kind. "Dancing in chains"—to make that hard for themselves and then to spread a false notion that it is easy—that is the trick that they wish to show us. Even in Homer we may perceive a wealth of inherited formulæ and laws of epic narration, within the circle of which he had to dance, and he himself created new conventions for them that came after. This was the discipline of the Greek poets: first to impose

upon themselves a manifold constraint by means of the earlier poets; then to invent in addition a new constraint, to impose it upon themselves and cheerfully to overcome it, so that constraint and victory are perceived and admired.

141. Authors' Copiousness.—The last quality that a good author acquires is copiousness: whoever has it to begin with will never become a good author. The noblest racehorses are lean until they are permitted to rest from their victories.

142. Wheezing Heroes.—Poets and artists who suffer from a narrow chest of the emotions generally make their heroes wheeze. They do not know what easy breathing means.

143. The Short-Sighted.[22]—The short-sighted are the deadly foes of all authors who let themselves go. These authors should know the wrath with which these people shut the book in which they observe that its creator needs fifty pages to express five ideas. And the cause of their wrath is that they have endangered what remains of their vision almost without compensation. A short-sighted person said, "All authors let themselves go." "Even the Holy Ghost?" "Even the Holy Ghost." But he had a right to, for he wrote for those who had lost their sight altogether.

144. The Style of Immortality.—Thucydides and Tacitus both imagined immortal life for their works when they executed them. That might be guessed (if not known otherwise) from their style. The one thought to give permanence to his ideas by salting them, the other by boiling them down; and neither, it seems, made a miscalculation.

145. Against Images and Similes.—By images and similes we convince, but we do not prove. That is why science has such a horror of images and similes. Science does not want to convince or make plausible, and rather seeks to provoke cold distrust by its mode of expression, by the bareness of its walls. For distrust is the touchstone for the gold of certainty.

146. Caution.—In Germany, he who lacks thorough knowledge should beware of writing. The good German does not say in that case "he is ignorant," but "he is of doubtful character."—This hasty conclusion, by the way, does great credit to the Germans.

147. Painted Skeletons.—Painted skeletons are those authors who try to make up for their want of flesh by artistic colourings.

148. The Grand Style and Something Better.—It is easier to learn how to write the grand style than how to write easily and simply. The reasons for this are inextricably bound up with morality.

149. Sebastian Bach.—In so far as we do not hear Bach's music as perfect and experienced connoisseurs of counterpoint and all the varieties of the fugal style (and accordingly must dispense with real artistic enjoyment), we shall feel in listening to his music—in Goethe's magnificent phrase—as if "we were present at

God's creation of the world." In other words, we feel here that something great is in the making but not yet made—our mighty modern music, which by conquering nationalities, the Church, and counterpoint has conquered the world. In Bach there is still too much crude Christianity, crude Germanism, crude scholasticism. He stands on the threshold of modern European music, but turns from thence to look at the Middle Ages.

150. Händel.—Händel, who in the invention of his music was bold, original, truthful, powerful, inclined to and akin to all the heroism of which a nation is capable, often proved stiff, cold, nay even weary of himself in composition. He applied a few well-tried methods of execution, wrote copiously and quickly, and was glad when he had finished—but that joy was not the joy of God and other creators in the eventide of their working day.

151. Haydn.—So far as genius can exist in a man who is merely good, Haydn had genius. He went just as far as the limit which morality sets to intellect, and only wrote music that has "no past."

152. Beethoven and Mozart.—Beethoven's music often appears like a deeply emotional meditation on unexpectedly hearing once more a piece long thought to be forgotten, "Tonal Innocence": it is music about music. In the song of the beggar and child in the street, in the monotonous airs of vagrant Italians, in the dance of the village inn or in carnival nights he discovers his melodies. He stores them together like a bee, snatching here and there some notes or a short phrase. To him these are hallowed memories of "the better world," like the ideas of Plato.—Mozart stands in quite a different relation to his melodies. He finds his inspiration not in hearing music but in gazing at life, at the most stirring life of southern lands. He was always dreaming of Italy, when he was not there.

153. Recitative.—Formerly recitative was dry, but now we live in the age of moist recitative. It has fallen into the water, and the waves carry it whithersoever they list.

154. "Cheerful" Music.—If for a long time we have heard no music, it then goes like a heavy southern wine all too quickly into the blood and leaves behind it a soul dazed with narcotics, half-awake, longing for sleep. This is particularly the case with cheerful music, which inspires in us bitterness and pain, satiety and home-sickness together, and forces us to sip again and again as at a sweetened draught of poison. The hall of gay, noisy merriment then seems to grow narrow, the light to lose its brightness and become browner. At last we feel as if this music were penetrating to a prison where a poor wretch cannot sleep for home-sickness.

155. Franz Schubert.—Franz Schubert, inferior as an artist to the other great musicians, had nevertheless the largest share of inherited musical wealth. He spent it with a free hand and a kind heart, so that for a few centuries musicians

will continue to nibble at his ideas and inspirations. In his works we find a store of unused inventions; the greatness of others will lie in making use of those inventions. If Beethoven may be called the ideal listener for a troubadour, Schubert has a right to be called the ideal troubadour.

156. Modern Musical Execution.—Great tragic or dramatic execution of music acquires its character by imitating the gesture of the great sinner, such as Christianity conceives and desires him: the slow-stepping, passionately brooding man, distracted by the agonies of conscience, now flying in terror, now clutching with delight, now standing still in despair—and all the other marks of great sinfulness. Only on the Christian assumption that all men are great sinners and do nothing but sin could we justify the application of this style of execution to all music. So far, music would be the reflection of all the actions and impulses of man, and would continually have to express by gestures the language of the great sinner. At such a performance, a listener who was not enough of a Christian to understand this logic might indeed cry out in horror, "For the love of Heaven, how did sin find its way into music?"

157. Felix Mendelssohn.—Felix Mendelssohn's music is the music of the good taste that enjoys all the good things that have ever existed. It always points behind. How could it have much "in front," much of a future?—But did he want it to have a future? He possessed a virtue rare among artists, that of gratitude without arrière-pensée. This virtue, too, always points behind.

158. A Mother of Arts.—In our sceptical age, real devotion requires almost a brutal heroism of ambition. Fanatical shutting of the eyes and bending of the knee no longer suffice. Would it not be possible for ambition—in its eagerness to be the last devotee of all the ages—to become the begetter of a final church music, as it has been the begetter of the final church architecture? (They call it the Jesuit style.)

159. Freedom in Fetters—a Princely Freedom.—Chopin, the last of the modern musicians, who gazed at and worshipped beauty, like Leopardi; Chopin, the Pole, the inimitable (none that came before or after him has a right to this name)—Chopin had the same princely punctilio in convention that Raphael shows in the use of the simplest traditional colours. The only difference is that Chopin applies them not to colour but to melodic and rhythmic traditions. He admitted the validity of these traditions because he was born under the sway of etiquette. But in these fetters he plays and dances as the freest and daintiest of spirits, and, be it observed, he does not spurn the chain.

160. Chopin's Barcarolle.—Almost all states and modes of life have a moment of rapture, and good artists know how to discover that moment. Such a moment there is even in life by the seashore—that dreary, sordid, unhealthy existence,

dragged out in the neighbourhood of a noisy and covetous rabble. This moment of rapture Chopin in his Barcarolle expressed in sound so supremely that Gods themselves, when they heard it, might yearn to lie long summer evenings in a boat.

161. Robert Schumann.—"The Stripling," as the romantic songsters of Germany and France of the first three decades of this century imagined him—this stripling was completely translated into song and melody by Robert Schumann, the eternal youth, so long as he felt himself in full possession of his powers. There are indeed moments when his music reminds one of the eternal "old maid."

162. Dramatic Singers.—"Why does this beggar sing?" "Probably he does not know how to wail." "Then he does right." But our dramatic singers, who wail because they do not know how to sing—are they also in the right?

163. Dramatic Music.—For him who does not see what is happening on the stage, dramatic music is a monstrosity, just as the running commentary to a lost text is a monstrosity. Such music requires us to have ears where our eyes are. This, however, is doing violence to Euterpe, who, poor Muse, wants to have her eyes and ears where the other Muses have theirs.

164. Victory and Reasonableness.—Unfortunately in the æsthetic wars, which artists provoke by their works and apologias for their works, just as is the case in real war, it is might and not reason that decides. All the world now assumes as a historical fact that, in his dispute with Piccini, Gluck was in the right. At any rate, he was victorious, and had might on his side.

165. Of the Principle of Musical Execution.—Do the modern musical performers really believe that the supreme law of their art is to give every piece as much high-relief as is possible, and to make it speak at all costs a dramatic language? Is not this principle, when applied for example to Mozart, a veritable sin against the spirit—the gay, sunny, airy, delicate spirit—of Mozart, whose seriousness was of a kindly and not awe-inspiring order, whose pictures do not try to leap from the wall and drive away the beholder in panic? Or do you think that all Mozart's music is identical with the statue-music in Don Juan? And not only Mozart's, but all music?—You reply that the advantage of your principle lies in its greater effect. You would be right if there did not remain the counter-question, "On whom has the effect operated, and on whom should an artist of the first rank desire to produce his effect?" Never on the populace! Never on the immature! Never on the morbidly sensitive! Never on the diseased! And above all—never on the blasé!

166. The Music of To-Day.—This ultra-modern music, with its strong lungs and weak nerves, is frightened above all things of itself.

167. Where Music is at Home.—Music reaches its high-water mark only among men who have not the ability or the right to argue. Accordingly, its chief promoters are princes, whose aim is that there should be not much criticism nor even much thought in their neighbourhood. Next come societies which, under some pressure or other (political or religious), are forced to become habituated to silence, and so feel all the greater need of spells to charm away emotional ennui—these spells being generally eternal love-making and eternal music. Thirdly, we must reckon whole nations in which there is no "society," but all the greater number of individuals with a bent towards solitude, mystical thinking, and a reverence for all that is inexpressible; these are the genuine "musical souls." The Greeks, as a nation delighting in talking and argument, accordingly put up with music only as an hors d'œuvre to those arts which really admit of discussion and dispute. About music one can hardly even think clearly. The Pythagoreans, who in so many respects were exceptional Greeks, are said to have been great musicians. This was the school that invented a five-years' silence,[23] but did not invent a dialectic.

168. Sentimentality in Music.—We may be ever so much in sympathy with serious and profound music, yet nevertheless, or perhaps all the more for that reason, we shall at occasional moments be overpowered, entranced, and almost melted away by its opposite—I mean, by those simple Italian operatic airs which, in spite of all their monotony of rhythm and childishness of harmony, seem at times to sing to us like the very soul of music. Admit this or not as you please, you Pharisees of good taste, it is so, and it is my present task to propound the riddle that it is so, and to nibble a little myself at the solution.—In childhood's days we tasted the honey of many things for the first time. Never was honey so good as then; it seduced us to life, into abundant life, in the guise of the first spring, the first flower, the first butterfly, the first friendship. Then—perhaps in our ninth year or so—we heard our first music, and this was the first that we understood; thus the simplest and most childish tunes, that were not much more than a sequel to the nurse's lullaby and the strolling fiddler's tune, were our first experience. (For even the most trifling "revelations" of art need preparation and study; there is no "immediate" effect of art, whatever charming fables the philosophers may tell.) Our sensation on hearing these Italian airs is associated with those first musical raptures, the strongest of our lives. The bliss of childhood and its flight, the feeling that our most precious possession can never be brought back, all this moves the chords of the soul more strongly than the most serious and profound music can move them.—This mingling of æsthetic pleasure with moral pain, which nowadays it is customary to call (rather too haughtily, I think) "sentimentality"—it is the mood of Faust at the end of the first scene—this

"sentimentality" of the listener is all to the advantage of Italian music. It is a feeling which the experienced   connoisseurs in art, the pure "æsthetes," like to ignore.—Moreover, almost all music has a magical effect only when we hear it speak the language of our own past. Accordingly, it seems to the layman that all the old music is continually growing better, and that all the latest is of little value. For the latter arouses no "sentimentality," that most essential element of happiness, as aforesaid, for every man who cannot approach this art with pure æsthetic enjoyment.

169. As Friends of Music.—Ultimately we are and remain good friends with music, as we are with the light of the moon. Neither, after all, tries to supplant the sun: they only want to illumine our nights to the best of their powers. Yet we may jest and laugh at them, may we not? Just a little, at least, and from time to time? At the man in the moon, at the woman in the music?

170. Art in an Age of Work.—We have the conscience of an industrious epoch. This debars us from devoting our best hours and the best part of our days to art, even though that art be the greatest and worthiest. Art is for us a matter of leisure, of recreation, and we consecrate to it the residue of our time and strength. This is the cardinal fact that has altered the relation of art to life. When art makes its great demands of time and strength upon its recipients, it has to battle against the conscience of the industrious and efficient, it is relegated to the idle and conscienceless, who, by their very nature, are not exactly suited to great art, and consider its claims arrogant. It might, therefore, be all over with art, since it lacks air and the power to breathe. But perhaps the great art attempts, by a sort of coarsening and disguising, to make itself at home in that other atmosphere, or at least to put up with it—an atmosphere which is really a natural element only for petty art, the art of recreation, of pleasant distraction. This happens nowadays almost everywhere. Even the exponents of great art promise recreation and distraction; even they address themselves to the exhausted; even they demand from him the evening hours of his working-day—just like the artists of the entertaining school, who are content to smooth the furrowed brow and brighten the lack-lustre eye. What, then, are the devices of their mightier brethren? These have in their medicine-chests the most powerful excitants, which might give a shock even to a man half-dead: they can deafen you, intoxicate you, make you shudder, or bring tears to your eyes. By this means they overpower the exhausted man and stimulate him for one night to an over-lively condition, to an ecstasy of terror and delight. This great art, as it now lives in opera, tragedy, and music—have we a right to be angry with it, because of its perilous fascination, as we should be angry with a cunning courtesan? Certainly not. It would far rather live in the pure element of morning calm, and would far rather make its appeal

to the fresh, expectant, vigorous morning-soul of the beholder or listener. Let us be thankful that it prefers living thus to vanishing altogether. But let us also confess that an era that once more introduces free and complete high-days and holidays into life will have no use for our great art.

171. The Employees of Science and the Others.—Really efficient and successful men of science might be collectively called "The Employees." If in youth their acumen is sufficiently practised, their memory is full, and hand and eye have acquired sureness, they are appointed by an older fellow-craftsman to a scientific position where their qualities may prove useful. Later on, when they have themselves gained an eye for the gaps and defects in their science, they place themselves in whatever position they are needed. These persons all exist for the sake of science. But there are rarer spirits, spirits that seldom succeed or fully mature—"for whose sake science exists"—at least, in their view. They are often unpleasant, conceited, or cross-grained men, but almost always prodigies to a certain extent. They are neither employees nor employers; they make use of what those others have worked out and established, with a certain princely carelessness and with little and rare praise—just as if the others belonged to a lower order of beings. Yet they possess the same qualities as their fellow-workers, and that sometimes in a less developed form. Moreover, they have a peculiar limitation, from which the others are free; this makes it impossible to put them into a place and to see in them useful tools. They can only live in their own air and on their own soil. This limitation suggests to them what elements of a science "are theirs"—in other words, what they can carry home into their house and atmosphere: they think that they are always collecting their scattered "property." If they are prevented from building at their own nest, they perish like shelterless birds. The loss of freedom causes them to wilt away. If they show, like their colleagues, a fondness for certain regions of science, it is always only regions where the fruits and seeds necessary to them can thrive. What do they care whether science, taken as a whole, has untilled or badly tilled regions? They lack all impersonal interest in a scientific problem. As they are themselves personal through and through, all their knowledge and ideas are remoulded into a person, into a living complexity, with its parts interdependent, overlapping, jointly nurtured, and with a peculiar atmosphere and scent as a whole.—Such natures, with their system of personal knowledge, produce the illusion that a science (or even the whole of philosophy) is finished and has reached its goal. The life in their system works this magic, which at times has been fatal to science and deceptive to the really efficient workers above described, and at other times, when drought and exhaustion prevailed, has acted as a kind of restorative, as if it were

the air of a cool, refreshing resting-place.—These men are usually called philosophers.

172. Recognition of Talent.—As I went through the village of S., a boy began to crack his whip with all his might—he had made great progress in this art, and he knew it. I threw him a look of recognition—in reality it hurt me cruelly. We do the same in our recognition of many of the talents. We do good to them when they hurt us.

173. Laughing and Smiling.—The more joyful and assured the mind becomes, the more man loses the habit of loud laughter. In compensation, there is an intellectual smile continually bubbling up in him, a sign of his astonishment at the innumerable concealed delights of a good existence.

174. The Talk of Invalids.—Just as in spiritual grief we tear our hair, strike our foreheads, lacerate our cheeks or even (like Œdipus) gouge our eyes out, so against violent physical pain we call to our aid a bitter, violent emotion, through the recollection of slanderous and malignant people, through the denigration of our future, through the sword-pricks and acts of malice which we mentally direct against the absent. And at times it is true that one devil drives out another—but then we have the other.—Hence a different sort of talk, tending to alleviate pain, should be recommended invalids: reflections upon the kindnesses and courtesies that can be performed towards friend and foe.

175. Mediocrity as a Mask.—Mediocrity is the happiest mask which the superior mind can wear, because it does not lead the great majority—that is, the mediocre—to think that there is any disguise. Yet the superior mind assumes the mask just for their sake—so as not to irritate them, nay, often from a feeling of pity and kindness.

176. The Patient.—The pine tree seems to listen, the fir tree to wait, and both without impatience. They do not give a thought to the petty human being below who is consumed by his impatience and his curiosity.

177. The Best Joker.—My favourite joke is the one that takes the place of a heavy and rather hesitating idea, and that at once beckons with its finger and winks its eye.

178. The Accessaries of all Reverence.—Wherever the past is revered, the over-cleanly and over-tidy people should not be admitted. Piety does not feel content without a little dust, dirt, and dross.

179. The Great Danger of Savants.—It is just the most thorough and profound savants who are in peril of seeing their life's goal set ever lower and lower, and, with a feeling of this in their minds, to become ever more discouraged and more unendurable in the latter half of their lives. At first they plunge into their science with spacious hopes and set themselves daring tasks, the ends of which are

already anticipated by their imaginations. Then there are moments as in the lives of the great maritime discoverers—knowledge, presentiment, and power raise each other higher and higher, until a new shore first dawns upon the eye in the far distance. But now the stern man recognises more and more how important it is that the individual task of the inquirer should be limited as far as possible, so that it may be entirely accomplished and the intolerable waste of force from which earlier periods of science suffered may be avoided. In those days everything was done ten times over, and then the eleventh always had the last and best word. Yet the more the savant learns and practises this art of solving riddles in their entirety, the more pleasure he finds in so doing. But at the same time his demands upon what is here called "entirety" grow more exacting. He sets aside everything that must remain in this sense incomplete, he acquires a disgust and an acute scent for the half-soluble—for all that can only give a kind of certainty in a general and indefinite form. His youthful plans crumble away before his eyes. There remains scarcely anything but a few little knots, in untying which the master now takes his pleasure and shows his strength. Then, in the midst of all this useful, restless activity, he, now grown old, is suddenly then often overcome by a deep misgiving, a sort of torment of conscience. He looks upon himself as one changed, as if he were diminished, humbled, transformed into a dexterous dwarf; he grows anxious as to whether mastery in small matters be not a convenience, an escape from the summons to greatness in life and form. But he cannot pass beyond any longer—the time for that has gone by.

180. Teachers in the Age of Books.—Now that self-education and mutual education are becoming more widespread, the teacher in his usual form must become almost unnecessary. Friends eager to learn, who wish to master some branch of knowledge together, find in our age of books a shorter and more natural way than "school" and "teachers."

181. Vanity as the Greatest Utility.—Originally the strong individual uses not only Nature but even societies and weaker individuals as objects of rapine. He exploits them, so far as he can, and then passes on. As he lives from hand to mouth, alternating between hunger and superfluity, he kills more animals than he can eat, and robs and maltreats men more than is necessary. His manifestation of power is at the same time one of revenge against his cramped and worried existence. Furthermore, he wishes to be held more powerful than he is, and thus misuses opportunities; the accretion of fear that he begets being an accretion of power. He soon observes that he stands or falls not by what he is but by what he is thought to be. Herein lies the origin of vanity. The man of power seeks by every means to increase others' faith in his power.—The thralls who tremble before him and serve him know, for their part, that they are worth just so much as they

appear to him to be worth, and so they work with an eye to this valuation rather than to their own self-satisfaction. We know vanity only in its most weakened forms, in its idealisations and its small doses, because we live in a late and very emasculated state of society. Originally vanity is the great utility, the strongest means of preservation. And indeed vanity will be greater, the cleverer the individual, because an increase in the belief in power is easier than an increase in the power itself, but only for him who has intellect or (as must be the case under primitive conditions) who is cunning and crafty.

182. Weather-Signs of Culture.—There are so few decisive weather-signs of culture that we must be glad to have at least one unfailing sign at hand for use in house and garden. To test whether a man belongs to us (I mean to the free spirits) or not, we must test his sentiments regarding Christianity. If he looks upon Christianity with other than a critical eye, we turn our backs to him, for he brings us impure air and bad weather.—It is no longer our task to teach such men what a sirocco wind is. They have Moses and the prophets of weather and of enlightenment.[24] If they will not listen to these, then——

183. There is a Proper Time for Wrath and Punishment.—Wrath and punishment are our inheritance from the animals. Man does not become of age until he has restored to the animals this gift of the cradle.—Herein lies buried one of the mightiest ideas that men can have, the idea of a progress of all progresses.—Let us go forward together a few millenniums, my friends! There is still reserved for mankind a great deal of joy, the very scent of which has not yet been wafted to the men of our day! Indeed, we may promise ourselves this joy, nay summon and conjure it up as a necessary thing, so long as the development of human reason does not stand still. Some day we shall no longer be reconciled to the logical sin that lurks in all wrath and punishment, whether exercised by the individual or by society—some day, when head and heart have learnt to live as near together as they now are far apart. That they no longer stand so far apart as they did originally is fairly palpable from a glance at the whole course of humanity. The individual who can review a life of introspective work will become conscious of the rapprochement arrived at, with a proud delight at the distance he has bridged, in order that he may thereupon venture upon more ample hopes.

184. Origin of Pessimists.—A snack of good food often decides whether we are to look to the future with hollow eye or in hopeful mood. The same influence extends to the very highest and most intellectual states. Discontent and reviling of the world are for the present generation an inheritance from starveling ancestors. Even in our artists and poets we often notice that, however exuberant their life, they are not of good birth, and have often, from oppressed and ill-nourished ancestors, inherited in their blood and brain much that comes out

as the subject and even the conscious colouring of their work. The culture of the Greeks is a culture of men of wealth, in fact, inherited wealth. For a few centuries they lived better than we do (better in every sense, in particular far more simply in food and drink). Then the brain finally became so well-stored and subtle, and the blood flowed so quickly, like a joyous, clear wine, that the best in them came to light no longer as gloomy, distorted, and violent, but full of beauty and sunshine.

185. Of Reasonable Death.—Which is more reasonable, to stop the machine when the works have done the task demanded of them, or to let it run on until it stands still of its own accord—in other words, is destroyed? Is not the latter a waste of the cost of upkeep, a misuse of the strength and care of those who serve? Are men not here throwing away that which would be sorely needed elsewhere? Is not a kind of contempt of the machines propagated, in that many of them are so uselessly tended and kept up?—I am speaking of involuntary (natural) and voluntary (reasonable) death. Natural death is independent of all reason and is really an irrational death, in which the pitiable substance of the shell determines how long the kernel is to exist or not; in which, accordingly, the stunted, diseased and dull-witted jailer is lord, and indicates the moment at which his distinguished prisoner shall die. Natural death is the suicide of nature—in other words, the annihilation of the most rational being through the most irrational element that is attached thereto. Only through religious illumination can the reverse appear; for then, as is equitable, the higher reason (God) issues its orders, which the lower reason has to obey. Outside religious thought natural death is not worth glorifying. The wise dispensation and disposal of death belongs to that now quite incomprehensible and immoral-sounding morality of the future, the dawn of which it will be an ineffable delight to behold.

186. Retrograde Influences.—All criminals force society back to earlier stages of culture than that in which they are placed for the time being. Their influence is retrograde. Let us consider the tools that society must forge and maintain for its defence: the cunning detectives, the jailers, the hangmen. Nor should we forget the public counsel for prosecution and defence. Finally we may ask ourselves whether the judge himself and punishment and the whole legal procedure are not oppressive rather than elevating in their reaction upon all who are not law-breakers. For we shall never succeed in arraying self-defence and revenge in the garb of innocence, and so long as men are used and sacrificed as a means to the end of society, all loftier humanity will deplore this necessity.

187. War as a Remedy.—For nations that are growing weak and contemptible war may be prescribed as a remedy, if indeed they really want to go on living. National consumption as well as individual admits of a brutal cure. The eternal

will to live and inability to die is, however, in itself already a sign of senility of emotion. The more fully and thoroughly we live, the more ready we are to sacrifice life for a single pleasurable emotion. A people that lives and feels in this wise has no need of war.

188. Intellectual and Physical Transplantation as Remedies.—The different cultures are so many intellectual climates, every one of which is peculiarly harmful or beneficial to this or that organism. History as a whole, as the knowledge of different cultures, is the science of remedies, but not the science of the healing art itself. We still need a physician who can make use of these remedies, in order to send every one—temporarily or permanently—to the climate that just suits him. To live in the present, within the limits of a single culture, is insufficient as a universal remedy: too many highly useful kinds of men, who cannot breathe freely in this atmosphere, would perish. With the aid of history we must give them air and try to preserve them: even men of lower cultures have their value.—Add to this cure of intellects that humanity, on considerations of bodily health, must strive to discover by means of a medical geography what kinds of degeneration and disease are caused by each region of the earth, and conversely, what ingredients of health the earth affords: and then, gradually, nations, families, and individuals must be transplanted long and permanently enough for them to become masters of their inherited physical infirmities. The whole world will finally be a series of sanatoria.

189. Reason and the Tree of Mankind.—What you all fear in your senile short-sightedness, regarding the over-population of the world, gives the more hopeful a mighty task. Man is some day to become a tree overshadowing the whole earth, with millions upon millions of buds that shall all grow to fruits side by side, and the earth itself shall be prepared for the nourishment of this tree. That the shoot, tiny as yet, may increase in sap and strength; that the sap may flow in countless channels for the nutrition of the whole and the parts—from these and similar tasks we must derive our standard for measuring whether a man of to-day is useful or worthless. The task is unspeakably great and adventurous: let us all contribute our share to prevent the tree from rotting before its time! The historically trained mind will no doubt succeed in calling up the human activities of all the ages before its eyes, as the community of ants with its cunningly wrought mounds stands before our eyes. Superficially judged, mankind as a whole, like ant-kind, might admit of our speaking of "instinct." On a closer examination we observe how whole nations, nay whole centuries, take pains to discover and test new means of benefiting the great mass of humanity, and thus finally the great common fruit-tree of the world. Whatever injury the individual nations or periods may suffer in this testing process, they have each become wise

through this injury, and from them the tide of wisdom slowly pours over the principles of whole races and whole epochs. Ants too go astray and make blunders. Through the folly of its remedies, mankind may well go to rack and ruin before the proper time. There is no sure guiding instinct for the former or the latter. Rather must we boldly face the great task of preparing the earth for a plant of the most ample and joyous fruitfulness—a task set by reason to reason!

190. The Praise of Disinterestedness and its Origin.—Between two neighbouring chieftains there was a long-standing quarrel: they laid waste each other's territories, stole cattle, and burnt down houses, with an indecisive result on the whole, because their power was fairly equal. A third, who from the distant situation of his property was able to keep aloof from these feuds, yet had reason to dread the day when one of the two neighbours should gain a decisive preponderance, at last intervened between the combatants with ceremonial goodwill. Secretly he lent a heavy weight to his peace proposal by giving either to understand that he would henceforth join forces with the other against the one who strove to break the peace. They met in his presence, they hesitatingly placed into his hand the hands that had hitherto been the tools and only too often the causes of hatred—and then they really and seriously tried to keep the peace. Either saw with astonishment how suddenly his prosperity and his comfort increased; how he now had as neighbour a dealer ready to buy and sell instead of a treacherous or openly scornful evil-doer; how even, in unforeseen troubles, they could reciprocally save each other from distress, instead of, as before, making capital out of this distress of his neighbour and enhancing it to the highest degree. It even seemed as if the human type had improved in both countries, for the eyes had become brighter, the forehead had lost its wrinkles; all now felt confidence in the future—and nothing is more advantageous for the souls and bodies of men than this confidence. They saw each other every year on the anniversary of the alliance, the chieftains as well as their retinue, and indeed before the eyes of the mediator, whose mode of action they admired and revered more and more, the greater the profit that they owed to him became. Then his mode of action was called disinterested. They had looked far too fixedly at the profit they had reaped themselves hitherto to see anything more of their neighbour's method of dealing than that his condition in consequence of this had not altered so much as their own; he had rather remained the same: and thus it appeared that the former had not had his profit in view. For the first time people said to themselves that disinterestedness was a virtue. It is true that in minor private matters similar circumstances had arisen, but men only had eyes for this virtue when it was depicted on the walls in a large script that was legible to the whole community. Moral qualities are not recognised as virtues, endowed

with names, held in esteem, and recommended as worthy of acquisition until the moment when they have visibly decided the happiness and destiny of whole societies. For then the loftiness of sentiment and the excitation of the inner creative forces is in many so great, that offerings are brought to this quality, offerings from the best of what each possesses. At its feet the serious man lays his seriousness, the dignified man his dignity, women their gentleness, the young all the wealth of hope and futurity that in them lies; the poet lends it words and names, sets it marching in the procession of similar beings, gives it a pedigree, and finally, as is the way of artists, adores the picture of his fancy as a new godhead—he even teaches others to adore. Thus in the end, with the co-operation of universal love and gratitude, a virtue becomes, like a statue, a repository of all that is good and honourable, a sort of temple and divine personage combined. It appears thenceforward as an individual virtue, as an absolute entity, which it was not before, and exercises the power and privileges of a sanctified super-humanity.—In the later days of Greece the cities were full of such deified human abstractions (if one may so call them). The nation, in its own fashion, had set up a Platonic "Heaven of Ideas" on earth, and I do not think that its inhabitants were felt to be less alive than any of the old Homeric divinities.

191. Days of Darkness.—"Days of Darkness" is the name given in Norway to the period when the sun remains below the horizon the whole day long. The temperature then falls slowly but continually.—A fine simile for all thinkers for whom the sun of the human future is temporarily eclipsed.

192. The Philosophy of Luxury.—A garden, figs, a little cheese, and three or four good friends—that was the luxury of Epicurus.

193. The Epochs of Life.—The real epochs of life are those brief periods of cessation midway between the rise and decline of a dominating idea or emotion. Here once again there is satisfaction: all the rest is hunger and thirst—or satiety.

194. Dreams.—Our dreams, if for once in a way they succeed and are complete—generally a dream is a bungled piece of work—are symbolic concatenations of scenes and images in place of a narrative poetical language. They paraphrase our experiences or expectations or relations with poetic boldness and definiteness, so that in the morning we are always astonished at ourselves when we remember the nature of our dream. In dreams we use up too much artistry—and hence are often too poor in artistry in the daytime.

195. Nature and Science.—As in nature, so in science the worse and less fertile soils are first cultivated—because the means that science in its early stages has at command are fairly sufficient for this purpose. The working of the most fertile soils requires an enormous, carefully developed, persevering method, tangible

individual results, and an organised body of well-trained workers. All these are found together only at a late stage.—Impatience and ambition often grasp too early at these most fertile soils, but the results are then from the first null and void. In nature such losses would usually be avenged by the starvation of the settlers.

196. The Simple Life.—A simple mode of life is nowadays difficult, requiring as it does far more reflection and gift for invention than even very clever people possess. The most honourable will perhaps still say, "I have not the time for such lengthy reflection. The simple life is for me too lofty a goal: I will wait till those wiser than I have discovered it."

197. Peaks and Needle-Points.—The poor fertility, the frequent celibacy, and in general the sexual coldness of the highest and most cultivated spirits, as that of the classes to which they belong, is essential in human economy. Intelligence recognises and makes use of the fact that at an acme of intellectual development the danger of a neurotic offspring is very great. Such men are the peaks of mankind—they ought no longer to run out into needle-points.

198. Natura non facit saltum.—However strongly man may develop upwards and seem to leap from one contradiction to another, a close observation will reveal the dovetails where the new building grows out of the old. This is the biographer's task: he must reflect upon his subject on the principle that nature takes no jumps.

199. Clean, but—He who clothes himself with rags washed clean dresses cleanly, to be sure, but is still ragged.

200. The Solitary Speaks.—In compensation for much disgust, disheartenment, boredom—such as a lonely life without friends, books, duties, and passions must involve—we enjoy those short spans of deep communion with ourselves and with Nature. He who fortifies himself completely against boredom fortifies himself against himself too. He will never drink the most powerful elixir from his own innermost spring.

201. False Renown.—I hate those so-called natural beauties which really have significance only through science, especially geographical science, but are insignificant in an æsthetic sense: for example, the view of Mont Blanc from Geneva. This is an insignificant thing without the auxiliary mental joy of science: the nearer mountains are all more beautiful and fuller of expression, but "not nearly so high," adds that absurd depreciatory science. The eye here contradicts science: how can it truly rejoice in the contradiction?

202. Those that Travel for Pleasure.—Like animals, stupid and perspiring, they climb mountains: people forgot to tell them that there were fine views on the way.

203. Too Much and Too Little.—Men nowadays live too much and think too little. They have hunger and dyspepsia together, and become thinner and thinner, however much they eat. He who now says "Nothing has happened to me" is a blockhead.

204. End and Goal.—Not every end is the goal. The end of a melody is not its goal, and yet if a melody has not reached its end, it has also not reached its goal. A parable.

205. Neutrality of Nature on a Grand Scale.—The neutrality of Nature on a grand scale (in mountain, sea, forest, and desert) is pleasing, but only for a brief space. Afterwards we become impatient. "Have they all nothing to say to us? Do we not exist so far as they are concerned?" There arises a feeling that a lèse-majesté is committed against humanity.

206. Forgetting our Purpose.—In a journey we commonly forget its goal. Almost every vocation is chosen and entered upon as means to an end, but is continued as the ultimate end. Forgetting our purpose is the most frequent form of folly.

207. Solar Orbit of an Idea.—When an idea is just rising on the horizon, the soul's temperature is usually very low. Gradually the idea develops in warmth, and is hottest (that is to say, exerts its greatest influence) when belief in the idea is already on the wane.

208. How to have every Man against You.—If some one now dared to say, "He that is not for me is against me," he would at once have all against him.—This sentiment does credit to our era.

209. Being Ashamed of Wealth.—Our age endures only a single species of rich men—those who are ashamed of their wealth. If we hear it said of any one that he is very rich, we at once feel a similar sentiment to that experienced at the sight of a repulsively swollen invalid, one suffering from diabetes or dropsy. We must with an effort remember our humanity, in order to go about with this rich man in such a way that he does not notice our feeling of disgust. But as soon as he prides himself at all on his wealth, our feelings are mingled with an almost compassionate surprise at such a high degree of human unreason. We would fain raise our hands to heaven and cry, "Poor deformed and overburdened creature, fettered a hundredfold, to whom every hour brings or may bring something unpleasant, in whose frame twitches every event that occurs in scores of countries, how can you make us believe that you feel at ease in your position? If you appear anywhere in public, we know that it is a sort of running the gauntlet amid countless glances that have for you only cold hate or importunity or silent scorn. You may earn more easily than others, but it is only a superfluous earning, which brings little joy, and the guarding of what you have earned is now, at any rate, a more troublesome business than any toilsome process of earning. You are

continually suffering, because you are continually losing. What avails it you that they are always injecting you with fresh artificial blood? That does not relieve the pain of those cupping-glasses that are fixed, for ever fixed, on your neck!—But, to be quite fair to you, it is difficult or perhaps impossible for you not to be rich. You must guard, you must earn more; the inherited bent of your character is the yoke fastened upon you. But do not on that account deceive us—be honestly and visibly ashamed of the yoke you wear, as in your soul you are weary and unwilling to wear it. This shame is no disgrace."

210. Extravagant Presumptions.—There are men so presumptuous that they can only praise a greatness which they publicly admire by representing it as steps and bridges that lead to themselves.

211. On the Soil of Insult.—He who wishes to deprive men of a conception is generally not satisfied with refuting it and drawing out of it the illogical worm that resides within. Rather, when the worm has been killed, does he throw the whole fruit as well into the mire, in order to make it ignoble in men's sight and to inspire disgust. Thus he thinks that he has found a means of making the usual "third-day resurrection" of conceptions an impossibility.—He is wrong, for on the very soil of insult, in the midst of the filth, the kernel of the conception soon produces new seeds.—The right thing then, is not to scorn and bespatter what one wishes finally to remove, but to lay it tenderly on ice again and again, having regard to the fact that conceptions are very tenacious of life. Here we must act according to the maxim: "One refutation is no refutation."

212. The Lot of Morality.—Since spiritual bondage is being relaxed, morality (the inherited, traditional, instinctive mode of action in accordance with moral sentiments) is surely also on the decline. This, however, is not the case with the individual virtues, moderation, justice, repose; for the greatest freedom of the conscious intellect leads at some time, even unconsciously, back to these virtues, and then enjoins their practice as expedient.

213. The Fanatic of Distrust and His Surety.—

The Elder: You wish to make the tremendous venture and instruct mankind in the great things? What is your surety?

Pyrrho: It is this: I intend to warn men against myself; I intend to confess all the defects of my character quite openly, and reveal to the world my hasty conclusions, my contradictions, and my foolish blunders. "Do not listen to me," I will say to them, "until I have become equal to the meanest among you, nay am even less than he. Struggle against truth as long as you can, from your disgust with her advocate. I shall be your seducer and betrayer if you find in me the slightest glimmering of respectability and dignity."

The Elder: You promise too much; you cannot bear this burden.

Pyrrho: Then I will tell men even that, and say that I am too weak, and cannot keep my promise. The greater my unworthiness, the more will they mistrust the truth, when it passes through my lips.

The Elder: You propose to teach distrust of truth?

Pyrrho: Yes; distrust as it never was yet on earth, distrust of anything and everything. This is the only road to truth. The right eye must not trust the left eye, and for some time light must be called darkness: this is the path that you must tread. Do not imagine that it will lead you to fruit trees and fair pastures. You will find on this road little hard grains—these are truths. For years and years you will have to swallow handfuls of lies, so as not to die of hunger, although you know that they are lies. But those grains will be sown and planted, and perhaps, perhaps some day will come the harvest. No one may promise that day, unless he be a fanatic.

The Elder: Friend, friend! Your words too are those of a fanatic!

Pyrrho: You are right! I will be distrustful of all words.

The Elder: Then you will have to be silent.

Pyrrho: I shall tell men that I have to be silent, and that they are to mistrust my silence.

The Elder: So you draw back from your undertaking?

Pyrrho: On the contrary—you have shown me the door through which I must pass.

The Elder: I don't know whether we yet completely understand each other?

Pyrrho: Probably not.

The Elder: If only you understand yourself!

(Pyrrho turns round and laughs.)

The Elder: Ah, friend! Silence and laughter—is that now your whole philosophy?

Pyrrho: There might be a worse.

214. European Books.—In reading Montaigne, La Rochefoucauld, La Bruyère, Fontenelle (especially the Dialogues des Morts), Vauvenargues, and Chamfort we are nearer to antiquity than in any group of six authors of other nations. Through these six the spirit of the last centuries before Christ has once more come into being, and they collectively form an important link in the great and still continuous chain of the Renaissance. Their books are raised above all changes of national taste and philosophical nuances from which as a rule every book takes and must take its hue in order to become famous. They contain more real ideas than all the books of German philosophers put together: ideas of the sort that breed ideas——I am at a loss how to define to the end: enough to say that they appear to me writers who wrote neither for children nor for visionaries, neither

for virgins nor for Christians, neither for Germans nor for—I am again at a loss how to finish my list. To praise them in plain terms, I may say that had they been written in Greek, they would have been understood by Greeks. How much, on the other hand, would even a Plato have understood of the writings of our best German thinkers—Goethe and Schopenhauer, for instance—to say nothing of the repugnance that he would have felt to their style, particularly to its obscure, exaggerated, and occasionally dry-as-dust elements? And these are defects from which these two among German thinkers suffer least and yet far too much (Goethe as thinker was fonder than he should have been of embracing the cloud, and Schopenhauer almost constantly wanders, not with impunity, among symbols of objects rather than among the objects themselves).—On the other hand, what clearness and graceful precision there is in these Frenchmen! The Greeks, whose ears were most refined, could not but have approved of this art, and one quality they would even have admired and reverenced—the French verbal wit: they were extremely fond of this quality, without being particularly strong in it themselves.

215. Fashion and Modernity.—Wherever ignorance, uncleanness, and superstition are still rife, where communication is backward, agriculture poor, and the priesthood powerful, national costumes are still worn. Fashion, on the other hand, rules where the opposite conditions prevail. Fashion is accordingly to be found next to the virtues in modern Europe. Are we to call it their seamy side?—Masculine dress that is fashionable and no longer national proclaims of its wearer: firstly, that he does not wish to appear as an individual or as member of a class or race; that he has made an intentional suppression of these kinds of vanity a law unto himself: secondly, that he is a worker, and has little time for dressing and self-adornment, and moreover regards anything expensive or luxurious in material and cut as out of harmony with his work: lastly, that by his clothes he indicates the more learned and intellectual callings as those to which he stands or would like to stand nearest as a European—whereas such national costumes as still exist would exhibit the occupations of brigand, shepherd, and soldier as the most desirable and distinguished. Within this general character of masculine fashion exist the slight fluctuations demanded by the vanity of young men, the dandies and dawdlers of our great cities—in other words, Europeans who have not yet reached maturity.—European women are as yet far less mature, and for this reason the fluctuations with them are much greater. They also will not have the national costume, and hate to be recognised by their dress as German, French, or Russian. They are, however, very desirous of creating an impression as individuals. Then, too, their dress must leave no one in doubt that they belong to one of the more reputable classes of society (to "good" or "high"

or "great" society), and on this score their pretensions are all the greater if they belong scarcely or not at all to that class. Above all, the young woman does not want to wear what an older woman wears, because she thinks she loses her market value if she is suspected of being somewhat advanced in years. The older woman, on the other hand, would like to deceive the world as long as possible by a youthful garb. From this competition must continually arise temporary fashions, in which the youthful element is unmistakably and inimitably apparent. But after the inventive genius of the young female artists has run riot for some time in such indiscreet revelations of youth (or rather, after the inventive genius of older, courtly civilisations and of still existing peoples—in fact, of the whole world of dress—has been pressed into the service, and, say, the Spaniards, Turks, and ancient Greeks have been yoked together for the glorification of fair flesh), then they at last discover, time and again, that they have not been good judges of their own interest; that if they wish to have power over men, the game of hide-and-seek with the beautiful body is more likely to win than naked or half-naked honesty. And then the wheel of taste and vanity turns once more in an opposite direction. The rather older young women find that their kingdom has come, and the competition of the dear, absurd creatures rages again from the beginning.—But the more women advance mentally, and no longer among themselves concede the pre-eminence to an unripe age, the smaller their fluctuations of costume grow and the less elaborate their adornment. A just verdict in this respect must not be based on ancient models—in other words, not on the standard of the dress of women who dwell on the shores of the Mediterranean—but must have an eye to the climatic conditions of the central and northern regions, where the intellectual and creative spirit of Europe now finds its most natural home.—Generally speaking, therefore, it is not change that will be the characteristic mark of fashion and modernity, for change is retrograde, and betokens the still unripened men and women of Europe; but rather the repudiation of national, social, and individual vanity. Accordingly, it is commendable, because involving a saving of time and strength, if certain cities and districts of Europe think and invent for all the rest in the matter of dress, in view of the fact that a sense of form does not seem to have been bestowed upon all. Nor is it really an excessive ambition, so long as these fluctuations still exist, for Paris, for example, to claim to be the sole inventor and innovator in this sphere. If a German, from hatred of these claims on the part of a French city, wishes to dress differently,—as, for example, in the Dürer style,—let him reflect that he then has a costume which the Germans of olden times wore, but which the Germans have not in the slightest degree invented. For there has never been a style of dress that characterised the German as a German. Moreover, let him observe how he looks in his costume, and whether his altogether modern face, with all its hues and wrinkles, does not raise a protest against a Dürer fashion of dress.—Here, where the concepts "modern" and "European" are almost identical, we understand by "Europe" a far wider region than is embraced by the Europe of geography, the little peninsula of Asia. In particular, we must include America, in so far as America is the daughter of our civilisation. On the other hand, not all Europe falls under the heading of cultured "Europe," but only those nations and divisions of nations which have their common past in Greece, Rome, Judaism, and Christianity.

216. "German Virtue."—There is no denying that from the end of the eighteenth century a current of moral awakening flowed through Europe. Then only Virtue found again the power of speech. She learnt to discover the unrestrained gestures of exaltation and emotion, she was no longer ashamed of herself, and she created philosophies and poems for her own glorification. If we look for the sources of this current, we come upon Rousseau, but the mythical Rousseau, the phantom formed from the impression left by his writings (one might almost say again, his mythically interpreted writings) and by the indications that he provided himself. He and his public constantly worked at the fashioning of this ideal figure. The other origin lies in the resurrection of the Stoical side of Rome's greatness, whereby the French so nobly carried on the task of the Renaissance. With striking success they proceeded from the reproduction of antique forms to the reproduction of antique characters. Thus they may always claim a title to the highest honours, as the nation which has hitherto given the modern world its best books and its best men. How this twofold archetype, the mythical Rousseau and the resurrected spirit of Rome, affected France's weaker neighbours, is particularly noticeable in Germany, which, in consequence of her novel and quite unwonted impulse to seriousness and loftiness in will and self-control, finally came to feel astonishment at her own newfound virtue, and launched into the world the concept "German virtue," as if this were the most original and hereditary of her possessions. The first great men who transfused into their own blood that French impulse towards greatness and consciousness of the moral will were more honest, and more grateful. Whence comes the moralism of Kant? He is continually reminding us: from Rousseau and the revival of Stoic Rome. The moralism of Schiller has the same source and the same glorification of the source. The moralism of Beethoven in notes is a continual song in praise of Rousseau, the antique French, and Schiller. "Young Germany" was the first to forget its gratitude, because in the meantime people had listened to the preachers of hatred of the French. The "young German" came to the fore with more consciousness than is generally allowed to youths. When he

investigated his paternity, he might well think of the proximity of Schiller, Schleiermacher, and Fichte. But he should have looked for his grandfathers in Paris and Geneva, and it was very short-sighted of him to believe what he believed: that virtue was not more than thirty years old. People became used to demanding that the word "German" should connote "virtue," and this process has not been wholly forgotten to this day.—Be it observed further that this moral awakening, as may almost be guessed, has resulted only in drawbacks and obstacles to the recognition of moral phenomena. What is the entire German philosophy, starting from Kant, with all its French, English, and Italian offshoots and by-products? A semi-theological attack upon Helvetius, a rejection of the slowly and laboriously acquired views and signposts of the right road, which in the end he collected and expressed so well. To this day Helvetius is the best-abused of all good moralists and good men in Germany.

217. Classic and Romantic.—Both classically and romantically minded spirits—two species that always exist—cherish a vision of the future; but the former derive their vision from the strength of their time, the latter from its weakness.

218. The Machine as Teacher.—Machinery teaches in itself the dovetailed working of masses of men, in activities where each has but one thing to do. It is the model of party organisations and of warfare. On the other hand, it does not teach individual self-glorification, for it makes of the many a machine, and of each individual a tool for one purpose. Its most general effect is to teach the advantage of centralisation.

219. Unable to Settle.—One likes to live in a small town. But from time to time just this small town drives us out into bare and lonely Nature, especially when we think we know it too well. Finally, in order to refresh ourselves from Nature, we go to the big town. A few draughts from this cup and we see its dregs, and the circle begins afresh, with the small town as starting-point.—So the moderns live; they are in all things rather too thorough to be able to settle like the men of other days.

220. Reaction against the Civilisation of Machinery.—The machine, itself a product of the highest mental powers, sets in motion hardly any but the lower, unthinking forces of the men who serve it. True, it unfetters a vast quantity of force which would otherwise lie dormant. But it does not communicate the impulse to climb higher, to improve, to become artistic. It creates activity and monotony, but this in the long-run produces a counter-effect, a despairing ennui of the soul, which through machinery has learnt to hanker after the variety of leisure.

221. The Danger of Enlightenment.—All the half-insane, theatrical, bestially cruel, licentious, and especially sentimental and self-intoxicating elements which

go to form the true revolutionary substance, and became flesh and spirit, before the revolution, in Rousseau—all this composite being, with factitious enthusiasm, finally set even "enlightenment" upon its fanatical head, which thereby began itself to shine as in an illuminating halo. Yet, enlightenment is essentially foreign to that phenomenon, and, if left to itself, would have pierced silently through the clouds like a shaft of light, long content to transfigure individuals alone, and thus only slowly transfiguring national customs and institutions as well. But now, bound hand and foot to a violent and abrupt monster, enlightenment itself became violent and abrupt. Its danger has therefore become almost greater than its useful quality of liberation and illumination, which it introduced into the great revolutionary movement. Whoever grasps this will also know from what confusion it has to be extricated, from what impurities to be cleansed, in order that it may then by itself continue the work of enlightenment and also nip the revolution in the bud and nullify its effects.

222. Passion in the Middle Ages.—The Middle Ages are the period of great passions. Neither antiquity nor our period possesses this widening of the soul. Never was the capacity of the soul greater or measured by larger standards. The physical, primeval sensuality of the barbarian races and the over-soulful, over-vigilant, over-brilliant eyes of Christian mystics, the most childish and youthful and the most over-ripe and world-weary, the savageness of the beast of prey and the effeminacy and excessive refinement of the late antique spirit—all these elements were then not seldom united in one and the same person. Thus, if a man was seized by a passion, the rapidity of the torrent must have been greater, the whirl more confused, the fall deeper than ever before.—We modern men may be content to feel that we have suffered a loss here.

223. Robbing and Saving.—All intellectual movements whereby the great may hope to rob and the small to save are sure to prosper. That is why, for instance, the German Reformation made progress.

224. Gladsome Souls.—When even a remote hint of drink, drunkenness, and an evil-smelling kind of jocularity was given, the souls of the old Germans waxed gladsome. Otherwise they were depressed, but here they found something they really understood.

225. Debauchery at Athens.—Even when the fish-market of Athens acquired its thinkers and poets, Greek debauchery had a more idyllic and refined appearance than Roman or German debauchery ever had. The voice of Juvenal would have sounded there like a hollow trumpet, and would have been answered by a good-natured and almost childish outburst of laughter.

226. Cleverness of the Greek.—As the desire for victory and pre-eminence is an ineradicable trait of human nature, older and more primitive than any respect of

or joy in equality, the Greek State sanctioned gymnastic and artistic competitions among equals. In other words, it marked out an arena where this impulse to conquer would find a vent without jeopardising the political order. With the final decline of gymnastic and artistic contests the Greek State fell into a condition of profound unrest and dissolution.

227. The "Eternal Epicurus."—Epicurus has lived in all periods, and lives yet, unbeknown to those who called and still call themselves Epicureans, and without repute among philosophers. He has himself even forgotten his own name—that was the heaviest luggage that he ever cast off.

228. The Style of Superiority.—"University slang," the speech of the German students, has its origin among the students who do not study. The latter know how to acquire a preponderance over their more serious fellows by exposing all the farcical elements of culture, respectability, erudition, order, and moderation, and by having words taken from these realms always on their lips, like the better and more learned students, but with malice in their glance and an accompanying grimace. This language of superiority—the only one that is original in Germany—is nowadays unconsciously used by statesmen and newspaper critics as well. It is a continual process of ironical quotation, a restless, cantankerous squinting of the eye right and left, a language of inverted commas and grimaces.

229. The Recluse.—We retire into seclusion, but not from personal misgivings, as if the political and social conditions of the day did not satisfy us; rather because by our retirement we try to save and collect forces which will some day be urgently needed by culture, the more this present is this present, and, as such, fulfils its task. We form a capital and try to make it secure, but, as in times of real danger, our method is to bury our hoard.

230. Tyrants of the Intellect.—In our times, any one who expressed a single moral trait so thoroughly as the characters of Theophrastus and Molière do, would be considered ill, and be spoken of as possessing "a fixed idea." The Athens of the third century, if we could visit it, would appear to us populated by fools. Nowadays the democracy of ideas rules in every brain—there the multitude collectively is lord. A single idea that tried to be lord is now called, as above stated, "a fixed idea." This is our method of murdering tyrants—we hint at the madhouse.

231. A Most Dangerous Emigration.—In Russia there is an emigration of the intelligence. People cross the frontier in order to read and write good books. Thus, however, they are working towards turning their country, abandoned by the intellect, into a gaping Asiatic maw, which would fain swallow our little Europe.

232. Political Fools.—The almost religious love of the king was transferred by the Greeks, when the monarchy was abolished, to the polis. An idea can be loved more than a person, and does not thwart the lover so often as a beloved human being (for the more men know themselves to be loved, the less considerate they usually become, until they are no longer worthy of love, and a rift really arises). Hence the reverence for State and polis was greater than the reverence for princes had ever been. The Greeks are the political fools of ancient history—today other nations boast that distinction.

233. Against Neglect of the Eyes.—Might one not find among the cultured classes of England, who read the Times, a decline in their powers of sight every ten years?

234. Great Works and Great Faith.—One man had great works, but his comrade had great faith in these works. They were inseparable, but obviously the former was entirely dependent upon the latter.

235. The Sociable Man.—"I don't get on well with myself," said some one in explanation of his fondness for society. "Society has a stronger digestion than I have, and can put up with me."

236. Shutting the Mind's Eyes.—If we are practised and accustomed to reflect upon our actions, we must nevertheless close the inner eye while performing an action (be this even only writing letters or eating or drinking). Even in conversation with average people we must know how to obscure our own mental vision in order to attain and grasp average thinking. This shutting of the eyes is a conscious act and can be achieved by the will.

237. The Most Terrible Revenge.—If we wish to take a thorough revenge upon an opponent, we must wait until we have our hand quite full of truths and equities, and can calmly use the whole lot against him. Hence the exercise of revenge may be identified with the exercise of equity. It is the most terrible kind of revenge, for there is no higher court to which an appeal can be made. Thus did Voltaire revenge himself on Piron, with five lines that sum up Piron's whole life, work, and character: every word is a truth. So too he revenged himself upon Frederick the Great in a letter to him from Ferney.

238. Taxes of Luxury.—In shops we buy the most necessary and urgent things, and have to pay very dear, because we pay as well for what is also to be had there cheap, but seldom finds a customer—articles of luxury that minister to pleasure. Thus luxury lays a constant tax upon the man of simple life who does without luxuries.

239. Why Beggars still Live.—If all alms were given only out of compassion, the whole tribe of beggars would long since have died of starvation.

240. Why Beggars still Live.—The greatest of almsgivers is cowardice.

241. How the Thinker Makes Use of a Conversation.—Without being eavesdroppers, we can hear a good deal if we are able to see well, and at the same time to let ourselves occasionally get out of our own sight. But people do not know how to make use of a conversation. They pay far too much attention to what they want to say and reply, whereas the true listener is often contented to make a provisional answer and to say something merely as a payment on account of politeness, but on the other hand, with his memory lurking in ambush, carries away with him all that the other said, together with his tones and gestures in speaking.—In ordinary conversation every one thinks he is the leader, just as if two ships, sailing side by side and giving each other a slight push here and there, were each firmly convinced that the other ship was following or even being towed.

242. The Art of Excusing Oneself.—If some one excuses himself to us, he has to make out a very good case, otherwise we readily come to feel ourselves the culprits, and experience an unpleasant emotion.

243. Impossible Intercourse.—The ship of your thoughts goes too deep for you to be able to travel with it in the waters of these friendly, decorous, obliging people. There are too many shallows and sandbanks: you would have to tack and turn, and would find yourself continually at your wits' end, and they would soon also be in perplexity as to your perplexity, the reason for which they cannot divine.

244. The Fox of Foxes.—A true fox not only calls sour the grapes he cannot reach, but also those he has reached and snatched from the grasp of others.

245. In Intimate Intercourse.—However closely men are connected, there are still all the four quarters of the heavens in their common horizon, and at times they become aware of this fact.

246. The Silence of Disgust.—Behold! some one undergoes a thorough and painful transformation as thinker and human being, and makes a public avowal of the change. And those who hear him see nothing, and still believe he is the same as before! This common experience has already disgusted many writers. They had rated the intellectuality of mankind too highly, and made a vow to be silent as soon as they became aware of their mistake.

247. Business Seriousness.—The business of many rich and eminent men is their form of recreation from too long periods of habitual leisure. They then become as serious and impassioned as other people do in their rare moments of leisure and amusement.

248. The Eye's Double Sense.—Just as a sudden scaly ripple runs over the waters at your feet, so there are similar sudden uncertainties and ambiguities in the human eye. They lead to the question: is it a shudder, or a smile, or both?

249. Positive and Negative.—This thinker needs no one to refute him—he is quite capable of doing that himself.

250. The Revenge of the Empty Nets.—Above all we should beware of those who have the bitter feeling of the fisherman who after a hard day's work comes home in the evening with nets empty.

251. Non-Assertion of our Rights.—The exertion of power is laborious and demands courage. That is why so many do not assert their most valid rights, because their rights are a kind of power, and they are too lazy or too cowardly to exercise them. Indulgence and patience are the names given to the virtues that cloak these faults.

252. Bearers of Light.—In Society there would be no sunshine if the born flatterers (I mean the so-called amiable people) did not bring some in with them.

253. When most Benevolent.—When a man has been highly honoured and has eaten a little, he is most benevolent.

254. To the Light.—Men press forward to the light not in order to see better but to shine better.—The person before whom we shine we gladly allow to be called a light.

255. The Hypochondriac.—The hypochondriac is a man who has just enough intellect and pleasure in the intellect to take his sorrows, his losses, and his mistakes seriously. But the field on which he grazes is too small: he crops it so close that in the end he has to look for single stalks. Thus he finally becomes envious and avaricious—and only then is he unbearable.

256. Giving in Return.—Hesiod advises us to give the neighbour who has helped us good measure and, if possible, fuller measure in return, as soon as we have the power. For this is where the neighbour's pleasure comes in, since his former benevolence brings him interest. Moreover, he who gives in return also has his pleasure, inasmuch as, by giving a little more than he got, he redeems the slight humiliation of being compelled to seek aid.

257. More subtle than Is Necessary.—Our sense of observation for how far others perceive our weaknesses is far more subtle than our sense of observation for the weaknesses of others. It follows that the first-named sense is more subtle than is necessary.

258. A Kind of Bright Shadows.—Close to the nocturnal type of man we almost regularly find, as if bound up with him, a bright soul. This is, as it were, the negative shadow cast by the former.

259. Not to take Revenge.—There are so many subtle sorts of revenge that one who has occasion to take revenge can really do or omit to do what he likes. In any case, the whole world will agree, after a time, that he has avenged himself. Hence the avoidance of revenge is hardly within man's power. He must not even so

much as say that he does not want to do so, since the contempt for revenge is interpreted and felt as a sublime and exquisite form of revenge.—It follows that we must do nothing superfluous.

260. The Mistake of Those who Pay Homage.—Every one thinks he is paying a most agreeable compliment to a thinker when he says that he himself hit upon exactly the same idea and even upon the same expression. The thinker, however, is seldom delighted at hearing such news, nay, rather, he often becomes distrustful of his own thoughts and expressions. He silently resolves to revise both some day. If we wish to pay homage to any one, we must beware of expressing our agreement, for this puts us on the same level.—Often it is a matter of social tact to listen to an opinion as if it were not ours or even travelled beyond the limits of our own horizon—as, for example, when an old man once in a while opens the storehouse of his acquired knowledge.

261. Letters.—A letter is an unannounced visit, and the postman is the intermediary of impolite surprises. Every week we ought to have one hour for receiving letters, and then go and take a bath.

262. Prejudiced.—Some one said: I have been prejudiced against myself from childhood upwards, and hence I find some truth in every censure and some absurdity in every eulogy. Praise I generally value too low and blame too high.

263. The Path to Equality.—A few hours of mountain-climbing make a blackguard and a saint two rather similar creatures. Weariness is the shortest path to equality and fraternity—and finally liberty is bestowed by sleep.

264. Calumny.—If we begin to trace to its source a real scandalous misrepresentation, we shall rarely look for its origin in our honourable and straightforward enemies; for if they invented anything of the sort about us, they, as being our enemies, would gain no credence. Those, however, to whom for a time we have been most useful, but who, from some reason or other, may be secretly sure that they will obtain no more from us—such persons are in a position to start the ball of slander rolling. They gain credence, firstly, because it is assumed that they would invent nothing likely to do them damage; secondly, because they have learnt to know us intimately.—As a consolation, the much-slandered man may say to himself: Calumnies are diseases of others that break out in your body. They prove that Society is a (moral) organism, so that you can prescribe to yourself the cure that will in the end be useful to others.

265. The Child's Kingdom of Heaven.—The happiness of a child is as much of a myth as the happiness of the Hyperboreans of whom the Greeks fabled. The Greeks supposed that, if indeed happiness dwells anywhere on our earth, it must certainly dwell as far as possible from us, perhaps over yonder at the edge of the world. Old people have the same thought—if man is at all capable of being happy,

he must be happy as far as possible from our age, at the frontiers and beginnings of life. For many a man the sight of children, through the veil of this myth, is the greatest happiness that he can feel. He enters himself into the forecourt of heaven when he says, "Suffer the little children to come unto me, for of them is the kingdom of heaven." The myth of the child's kingdom of heaven holds good, in some way or other, wherever in the modern world some sentimentality exists.

266. The Impatient.—It is just the growing man who does not want things in the growing stage. He is too impatient for that. The youth will not wait until, after long study, suffering, and privation, his picture of men and things is complete. Accordingly, he confidently accepts another picture that lies ready to his hand and is recommended to him, and pins his faith to that, as if it must give him at once the lines and colours of his own painting. He presses a philosopher or a poet to his bosom, and must from that time forth perform long stretches of forced labour and renounce his own self. He learns much in the process, but he often forgets what is most worth learning and knowing—his self. He remains all his life a partisan. Ah, a vast amount of tedious work has to be done before you find your own colours, your own brush, your own canvas!—Even then you are very far from being a master in the art of life, but at least you are the boss in your own workshop.

267. There are no Teachers.—As thinkers we ought only to speak of self-teaching. The instruction of the young by others is either an experiment performed upon something as yet unknown and unknowable, or else a thorough levelling process, in order to make the new member of society conform to the customs and manners that prevail for the time being. In both cases the result is accordingly unworthy of a thinker—the handiwork of parents and teachers, whom some valiantly honest person[25] has called "nos ennemis naturels." One day, when, as the world thinks, we have long since finished our education, we discover ourselves. Then begins the task of the thinker, and then is the time to summon him to our aid—not as a teacher, but as a self-taught man who has experience.

268. Sympathy with Youth.—We are sorry when we hear that some one who is still young is losing his teeth or growing blind. If we knew all the irrevocable and hopeless feelings hidden in his whole being, how great our sorrow would be! Why do we really suffer on this account? Because youth has to continue the work we have undertaken, and every flaw and failing in its strength is likely to injure our work, that will fall into its hands. It is the sorrow at the imperfect guarantee of our immortality: or, if we only feel ourselves as executors of the human mission, it is the sorrow that this mission must pass to weaker hands than ours.

269. The Ages of Life.—The comparison of the four ages of life with the four seasons of the year is a venerable piece of folly. Neither the first twenty nor the

last twenty years of a life correspond to a season of the year, assuming that we are not satisfied with drawing a parallel between white hair and snow and similar colour-analogies. The first twenty years are a preparation for life in general, for the whole year of life, a sort of long New Year's Day. The last twenty review, assimilate, bring into union and harmony all that has been experienced till then: as, in a small degree, we do on every New Year's Eve with the whole past year. But in between there really lies an interval which suggests a comparison with the seasons—the time from the twentieth to the fiftieth year (to speak here of decades in the lump, while it is an understood thing that every one must refine for himself these rough outlines). Those three decades correspond to three seasons—summer, spring, and autumn. Winter human life has none, unless we like to call the (unfortunately) often intervening hard, cold, lonely, hopeless, unfruitful periods of disease the winters of man. The twenties, hot, oppressive, stormy, impetuous, exhausting years, when we praise the day in the evening, when it is over, as we wipe the sweat from our foreheads—years in which work seems to us cruel but necessary—these twenties are the summer of life. The thirties, on the other hand, are its spring-time, with the air now too warm, now too cold, ever restless and stimulating, bubbling sap, bloom of leaves, fragrance of buds everywhere, many delightful mornings and evenings, work to which the song of birds awakens us, a true work of the heart, a kind of joy in our own robustness, strengthened by the savour of hopeful anticipation. Lastly the forties, mysterious like all that is stationary, like a high, broad plateau, traversed by a fresh breeze, with a clear, cloudless sky above it, which always has the same gentle look all day and half the night—the time of harvest and cordial gaiety—that is the autumn of life.

270. Women's Intellect in Modern Society.—What women nowadays think of men's intellect may be divined from the fact that in their art of adornment they think of anything but of emphasising the intellectual side of their faces or their single intellectual features. On the contrary, they conceal such traits, and understand, for example by an arrangement of their hair over their forehead, how to give themselves an appearance of vivid, eager sensuality and materialism, just when they but slightly possess those qualities. Their conviction that intellect in women frightens men goes so far that they even gladly deny the keenness of the most intellectual sense and purposely invite the reputation of short-sightedness. They think they will thereby make men more confiding. It is as if a soft, attractive twilight were spreading itself around them.

271. Great and Transitory.—What moves the observer to tears is the rapturous look of happiness with which a fair young bride gazes upon her husband. We feel

all the melancholy of autumn in thinking of the greatness and of the transitoriness of human happiness.

272. Sense and Sacrifice.—Many a woman has the intelletto del sacrifizio,[26] and no longer enjoys life when her husband refuses to sacrifice her. With all her wit, she then no longer knows—whither? and without perceiving it, is changed from sacrificial victim to sacrificial priest.

273. The Unfeminine.—"Stupid as a man," say the women; "Cowardly as a woman," say the men. Stupidity in a woman is unfeminine.

274. Masculine and Feminine Temperament and Mortality.—That the male sex has a worse temperament than the female follows from the fact that male children have a greater mortality than female, clearly because they "leap out of their skins" more easily. Their wildness and unbearableness soon make all the bad stuff in them deadly.

275. The Age of Cyclopean Building.—The democratisation of Europe is a resistless force. Even he who would stem the tide uses those very means that democratic thought first put into men's hands, and he makes these means more handy and workable. The most inveterate enemies of democracy (I mean the spirits of upheaval) seem only to exist in order, by the fear that they inspire, to drive forward the different parties faster and faster on the democratic course. Now we may well feel sorry for those who are working consciously and honourably for this future. There is something dreary and monotonous in their faces, and the grey dust seems to have been wafted into their very brains. Nevertheless, posterity may possibly some day laugh at our anxiety, and see in the democratic work of several generations what we see in the building of stone dams and walls—an activity that necessarily covers clothes and face with a great deal of dust, and perhaps unavoidably makes the workmen, too, a little dull-witted; but who would on that account desire such work undone? It seems that the democratisation of Europe is a link in the chain of those mighty prophylactic principles which are the thought of the modern era, and whereby we rise up in revolt against the Middle Ages. Now, and now only, is the age of Cyclopean building! A final security in the foundations, that the future may build on them without danger! Henceforth, an impossibility of the orchards of culture being once more destroyed overnight by wild, senseless mountain torrents! Dams and walls against barbarians, against plagues, against physical and spiritual serfdom! And all this understood at first roughly and literally, but gradually in an ever higher and more spiritual sense, so that all the principles here indicated may appear as the intellectual preparation of the highest artist in horticulture, who can only apply himself to his own task when the other is fully accomplished!—True, if we consider the long intervals of time that here lie

between means and end, the great, supreme labour, straining the powers and brains of centuries, that is necessary in order to create or to provide each individual means, we must not bear too hardly upon the workers of the present when they loudly proclaim that the wall and the fence are already the end and the final goal. After all, no one yet sees the gardener and the fruit, for whose sake the fence exists.

276. The Right of Universal Suffrage.—The people has not granted itself universal suffrage but, wherever this is now in force, it has received and accepted it as a temporary measure. But in any case the people has the right to restore the gift, if it does not satisfy its anticipations. This dissatisfaction seems universal nowadays, for when, at any occasion where the vote is exercised, scarce two-thirds, nay perhaps not even the majority of all voters, go to the polls, that very fact is a vote against the whole suffrage system.—On this point, in fact, we must pronounce a much sterner verdict. A law that enacts that the majority shall decide as to the welfare of all cannot be built up on the foundation that it alone has provided, for it is bound to require a far broader foundation, namely the unanimity of all. Universal suffrage must not only be the expression of the will of a majority, but of the whole country. Thus the dissent of a very small minority is already enough to set aside the system as impracticable; and the abstention from voting is in fact a dissent of this kind, which ruins the whole institution. The "absolute veto" of the individual, or—not to be too minute—the veto of a few thousands, hangs over the system as the consequence of justice. On every occasion when it is employed, the system must, according to the variety of the division, first prove that it has still a right to exist.

277. False Conclusions.—What false conclusions are drawn in spheres where we are not at home, even by those of us who are accustomed as men of science to draw right conclusions! It is humiliating! Now it is clear that in the great turmoil of worldly doings, in political affairs, in all sudden and urgent matters such as almost every day brings up, these false conclusions must decide. For no one feels at home with novelties that have sprung up in the night. All political work, even with great statesmen, is an improvisation that trusts to luck.

278. Premisses of the Age of Machinery.—The press, the machine, the railway, the telegraph are premisses of which no one has yet dared to draw the conclusions that will follow in a thousand years.

279. A Drag upon Culture.—When we are told that here men have no time for productive occupations, because military manœuvres and processions take up their days, and the rest of the population must feed and clothe them, their dress, however, being striking, often gay and full of absurdities; that there only a few distinguished qualities are recognised, individuals resemble each other more than

elsewhere, or at any rate are treated as equals, yet obedience is exacted and yielded without reasoning, for men command and make no attempt to convince; that here punishments are few, but these few cruel and likely to become the final and most terrible; that there treason ranks as the capital offence, and even the criticism of evils is only ventured on by the most audacious; that there, again, human life is cheap, and ambition often takes the form of setting life in danger—when we hear all this, we at once say, "This is a picture of a barbarous society that rests on a hazardous footing." One man perhaps will add, "It is a portrait of Sparta." But another will become meditative and declare that this is a description of our modern military system, as it exists in the midst of our altogether different culture and society, a living anachronism, the picture, as above said, of a community resting on a hazardous footing; a posthumous work of the past, which can only act as a drag upon the wheels of the present.—Yet at times even a drag upon culture is vitally necessary—that is to say, when culture is advancing too rapidly downhill or (as perhaps in this case) uphill.

280. More Reverence for Them that Know.—In the competition of production and sale the public is made judge of the product. But the public has no special knowledge, and judges by the appearance of the wares. In consequence, the art of appearance (and perhaps the taste for it) must increase under the dominance of competition, while on the other hand the quality of every product must deteriorate. The result will be—so far as reason does not fall in value—that one day an end will be put to that competition, and a new principle will win the day. Only the master of the craft should pronounce a verdict on the work, and the public should be dependent on the belief in the personality of the judge and his honesty. Accordingly, no anonymous work! At least an expert should be there as guarantor and pledge his name if the name of the creator is lacking or is unknown. The cheapness of an article is for the layman another kind of illusion and deceit, since only durability can decide that a thing is cheap and to what an extent. But it is difficult, and for a layman impossible, to judge of its durability.—Hence that which produces an effect on the eye and costs little at present gains the advantage—this being naturally machine-made work. Again, machinery—that is to say, the cause of the greatest rapidity and facility in production—favours the most saleable kind of article. Otherwise it involves no tangible profit; it would be too little used and too often stand idle. But as to what is most saleable, the public, as above said, decides: it must be the most exchangeable—in other words, the thing that appears good and also appears cheap. Thus in the domain of labour our motto must also hold good: "More respect for them that know!"

281. The Danger of Kings.—Democracy has it in its power, without any violent means, and only by a lawful pressure steadily exerted, to make kingship and emperorship hollow, until only a zero remains, perhaps with the significance of every zero in that, while nothing in itself, it multiplies a number tenfold if placed on the right side. Kingship and emperorship would remain a gorgeous ornament upon the simple and appropriate dress of democracy, a beautiful superfluity that democracy allows itself, a relic of all the historically venerable, primitive ornaments, nay the symbol of history itself, and in this unique position a highly effective thing if, as above said, it does not stand alone, but is put on the right side.—In order to avoid the danger of this nullification, kings hold by their teeth to their dignity as war-lords. To this end they need wars, or in other words exceptional circumstances, in which that slow, lawful pressure of the democratic forces is relaxed.

282. The Teacher a Necessary Evil.—Let us have as few people as possible between the productive minds and the hungry and recipient minds! The middlemen almost unconsciously adulterate the food which they supply. For their work as middlemen they want too high a fee for themselves, and this is drawn from the original, productive spirits—namely, interest, admiration, leisure, money, and other advantages.—Accordingly, we should always look upon the teacher as a necessary evil, just like the merchant; as an evil that we should make as small as possible.—Perhaps the prevailing distress in Germany has its main cause in the fact that too many wish to live and live well by trade (in other words, desiring as far as possible to diminish prices for the producer and raise prices for the consumer, and thus to profit by the greatest possible loss to both). In the same way, we may certainly trace a main cause of the prevailing intellectual poverty in the superabundance of teachers. It is because of teachers that so little is learnt, and that so badly.

283. The Tax of Homage.—Him whom we know and honour,—be he physician, artist, or artisan,—who does and produces something for us, we gladly pay as highly as we can, often a fee beyond our means. On the other hand, we pay the unknown as low a price as possible; here is a contest in which every one struggles and makes others struggle for a foot's breadth of land. In the work of the known there is something that cannot be bought, the sentiment and ingenuity put into his work for our own sake. We think we cannot better express our sense of obligation than by a sort of sacrifice on our part.—The heaviest tax is the tax of homage. The more competition prevails, the more we buy for the unknown and work for the unknown, the lower does this tax become, whereas it is really the standard for the loftiness of man's spiritual intercourse.

284. The Means towards Genuine Peace.—No government will nowadays admit that it maintains an army in order to satisfy occasionally its passion for conquest. The army is said to serve only defensive purposes. This morality, which justifies self-defence, is called in as the government's advocate. This means, however, reserving morality for ourselves and immorality for our neighbour, because he must be thought eager for attack and conquest if our state is forced to consider means of self-defence.—At the same time, by our explanation of our need of an army (because he denies the lust of attack just as our state does, and ostensibly also maintains his army for defensive reasons), we proclaim him a hypocrite and cunning criminal, who would fain seize by surprise, without any fighting, a harmless and unwary victim. In this attitude all states face each other to-day. They presuppose evil intentions on their neighbour's part and good intentions on their own. This hypothesis, however, is an inhuman notion, as bad as and worse than war. Nay, at bottom it is a challenge and motive to war, foisting as it does upon the neighbouring state the charge of immorality, and thus provoking hostile intentions and acts. The doctrine of the army as a means of self-defence must be abjured as completely as the lust of conquest. Perhaps a memorable day will come when a nation renowned in wars and victories, distinguished by the highest development of military order and intelligence, and accustomed to make the heaviest sacrifice to these objects, will voluntarily exclaim, "We will break our swords," and will destroy its whole military system, lock, stock, and barrel. Making ourselves defenceless (after having been the most strongly defended) from a loftiness of sentiment—that is the means towards genuine peace, which must always rest upon a pacific disposition. The so-called armed peace that prevails at present in all countries is a sign of a bellicose disposition, of a disposition that trusts neither itself nor its neighbour, and, partly from hate, partly from fear, refuses to lay down its weapons. Better to perish than to hate and fear, and twice as far better to perish than to make oneself hated and feared—this must some day become the supreme maxim of every political community!—Our liberal representatives of the people, as is well known, have not the time for reflection on the nature of humanity, or else they would know that they are working in vain when they work for "a gradual diminution of the military burdens." On the contrary, when the distress of these burdens is greatest, the sort of God who alone can help here will be nearest. The tree of military glory can only be destroyed at one swoop, with one stroke of lightning. But, as you know, lightning comes from the cloud and from above.

285. Whether Property can be squared with Justice.—When the injustice of property is strongly felt (and the hand of the great clock is once more at this place), we formulate two methods of relieving this injustice: either an equal

distribution, or an abolition of private possession and a return to State ownership. The latter method is especially dear to the hearts of our Socialists, who are angry with that primitive Jew for saying, "Thou shalt not steal." In their view the eighth[27] commandment should rather run, "Thou shalt not possess."—The former method was frequently tried in antiquity, always indeed on a small scale, and yet with poor success. From this failure we too may learn. "Equal plots of land" is easily enough said, but how much bitterness is aroused by the necessary division and separation, by the loss of time-honoured possessions, how much piety is wounded and sacrificed! We uproot the foundation of morality when we uproot boundary-stones. Again, how much fresh bitterness among the new owners, how much envy and looking askance! For there have never been two really equal plots of land, and if there were, man's envy of his neighbour would prevent him from believing in their equality. And how long would this equality, unhealthy and poisoned at the very roots, endure? In a few generations, by inheritance, here one plot would come to five owners, there five plots to one. Even supposing that men acquiesced in such abuses through the enactment of stern laws of inheritance, the same equal plots would indeed exist, but there would also be needy malcontents, owning nothing but dislike of their kinsmen and neighbours, and longing for a general upheaval.—If, however, by the second method we try to restore ownership to the community and make the individual but a temporary tenant, we interfere with agriculture. For man is opposed to all that is only a transitory possession, unblessed with his own care and sacrifice. With such property he behaves in freebooter fashion, as robber or as worthless spendthrift. When Plato declares that self-seeking would be removed with the abolition of property, we may answer him that, if self-seeking be taken away, man will no longer possess the four cardinal virtues either; as we must say that the most deadly plague could not injure mankind so terribly as if vanity were one day to disappear. Without vanity and self-seeking what are human virtues? By this I am far from meaning that these virtues are but varied names and masks for these two qualities. Plato's Utopian refrain, which is still sung by Socialists, rests upon a deficient knowledge of men. He lacked the historical science of moral emotions, the insight into the origin of the good and useful characteristics of the human soul. He believed, like all antiquity, in good and evil as in black and white—that is to say, in a radical difference between good and bad men and good and bad qualities.—In order that property may henceforth inspire more confidence and become more moral, we should keep open all the paths of work for small fortunes, but should prevent the effortless and sudden acquisition of wealth. Accordingly, we should take all the branches of transport and trade which favour the accumulation of large fortunes—especially, therefore, the money market—out of the hands of private persons or private companies, and look upon those who own too much, just as upon those who own nothing, as types fraught with danger to the community.

286. The Value of Labour.—If we try to determine the value of labour by the amount of time, industry, good or bad will, constraint, inventiveness or laziness, honesty or make-believe bestowed upon it, the valuation can never be a just one. For the whole personality would have to be thrown into the scale, and this is impossible. Here the motto is, "Judge not!" But after all the cry for justice is the cry we now hear from those who are dissatisfied with the present valuation of labour. If we reflect further we find every person non-responsible for his product, the labour; hence merit can never be derived therefrom, and every labour is as good or as bad as it must be through this or that necessary concatenation of forces and weaknesses, abilities and desires. The worker is not at liberty to say whether he shall work or not, or to decide how he shall work. Only the standpoints of usefulness, wider and narrower, have created the valuation of labour. What we at present call justice does very well in this sphere as a highly refined utility, which does not only consider the moment and exploit the immediate opportunity, but looks to the permanence of all conditions, and thus also keeps in view the well-being of the worker, his physical and spiritual contentment: in order that he and his posterity may work well for our posterity and become trustworthy for longer periods than the individual span of human life. The exploitation of the worker was, as we now understand, a piece of folly, a robbery at the expense of the future, a jeopardisation of society. We almost have the war now, and in any case the expense of maintaining peace, of concluding treaties and winning confidence, will henceforth be very great, because the folly of the exploiters was very great and long-lasting.

287. Of the Study of the Social Body.—The worst drawback for the modern student of economics and political science in Europe, and especially in Germany, is that the actual conditions, instead of exemplifying rules, illustrate exceptions or stages of transition and extinction. We must therefore learn to look beyond actually existing conditions and, for example, turn our eyes to distant North America, where we can still contemplate and investigate, if we will, the initial and normal movement of the social body. In Germany such a study requires arduous and historical research, or, as I have suggested, a telescope.

288. How far Machinery Humiliates.—Machinery is impersonal; it robs the piece of work of its pride, of the individual merits and defects that cling to all work that is not machine-made—in other words, of its bit of humanity. Formerly, all buying from handicraftsmen meant a mark of distinction for their personalities, with whose productions people surrounded themselves. Furniture

and dress accordingly became the symbols of mutual valuation and personal connection. Nowadays, on the other hand, we seem to live in the midst of anonymous and impersonal serfdom.—We must not buy the facilitation of labour too dear.

289. Century-old Quarantine.—Democratic institutions are centres of quarantine against the old plague of tyrannical desires. As such they are extremely useful and extremely tedious.

290. The Most Dangerous Partisan.—The most dangerous partisan is he whose defection would involve the ruin of the whole party—in other words, the best partisan.

291. Destiny and the Stomach.—A piece more or less of bread and butter in the jockey's body is occasionally the decisive factor in races and bets, and thus in the good and bad luck of thousands.—So long as the destiny of nations depends upon diplomats, the stomachs of diplomats will always be the object of patriotic misgivings. Quousque tandem....

292. The Victory of Democracy.—All political powers nowadays attempt to exploit the fear of Socialism for their own strengthening. Yet in the long run democracy alone gains the advantage, for all parties are now compelled to flatter "the masses" and grant them facilities and liberties of all kinds, with the result that the masses finally become omnipotent. The masses are as far as possible removed from Socialism as a doctrine of altering the acquisition of property. If once they get the steering-wheel into their hands, through great majorities in their Parliaments, they will attack with progressive taxation the whole dominant system of capitalists, merchants, and financiers, and will in fact slowly create a middle class which may forget Socialism like a disease that has been overcome.—The practical result of this increasing democratisation will next be a European league of nations, in which each individual nation, delimited by the proper geographical frontiers, has the position of a canton with its separate rights. Small account will be taken of the historic memories of previously existing nations, because the pious affection for these memories will be gradually uprooted under the democratic régime, with all its craze for novelty and experiment. The corrections of frontiers that will prove necessary will be so carried out as to serve the interests of the great cantons and at the same time that of the whole federation, but not that of any venerable memories. To find the standpoints for these corrections will be the task of future diplomats, who will have to be at the same time students of civilisation, agriculturists, and commercial experts, with no armies but motives and utilities at their back. Then only will foreign and home politics be inseparably connected, whereas to-day the latter follows its haughty dictator, and gleans in sorry baskets the stubble that is left over from the harvest of the former.

293. Goal and Means of Democracy.—Democracy tries to create and guarantee independence for as many as possible in their opinions, way of life, and occupation. For this purpose democracy must withhold the political suffrage both from those who have nothing and from those who are really rich, as being the two intolerable classes of men. At the removal of these classes it must always work, because they are continually calling its task in question. In the same way democracy must prevent all measures that seem to aim at party organisation. For the three great foes of independence, in that threefold sense, are the have-nots, the rich, and the parties.—I speak of democracy as of a thing to come. What at present goes by that name is distinguished from older forms of government only by the fact that it drives with new horses; the roads and the wheels are the same as of yore.—Has the danger really become less with these conveyances of the commonwealth?

294. Discretion and Success.—That great quality of discretion, which is fundamentally the virtue of virtues, their ancestress and queen, has in common life by no means always success on its side. The wooer would find himself deceived if he had wooed that virtue only for the sake of success. For it is rated by practical people as suspicious, and is confused with cunning and hypocrisy: he who obviously lacks discretion, the man who quickly grasps and sometimes misses his grasp, has prejudice on his side—he is an honest, trustworthy fellow. Practical people, accordingly, do not like the prudent man, thinking he is to them a danger. Moreover, we often assume the prudent man to be anxious, preoccupied, pedantic—unpractical, butterfly people find him uncomfortable, because he does not live in their happy-go-lucky way, without thinking of actions and duties; he appears among them as their embodied conscience, and the bright day is dimmed to their eyes before his gaze. Thus when success and popularity fail him, he may often say by way of private consolation, "So high are the taxes you have to pay for the possession of the most precious of human commodities—still it is worth the price!"

295. Et in Arcadia Ego.—I looked down, over waves of hills, to a milky-green lake, through firs and pines austere with age; rocky crags of all shapes about me, the soil gay with flowers and grasses. A herd of cattle moved, stretched, and expanded itself before me; single cows and groups in the distance, in the clearest evening light, hard by the forest of pines; others nearer and darker; all in calm and eventide contentment. My watch pointed to half-past six. The bull of the herd had stepped into the white foaming brook, and went forward slowly, now striving against, now giving way to his tempestuous course; thus, no doubt, he took his sort of fierce pleasure. Two dark brown beings, of Bergamasque origin, tended the herd, the girl dressed almost like a boy. On the left, overhanging cliffs

and fields of snow above broad belts of woodland; to the right, two enormous ice-covered peaks, high above me, shimmering in the veil of the sunny haze—all large, silent, and bright. The beauty of the whole was awe-inspiring and induced to a mute worship of the moment and its revelation. Unconsciously, as if nothing could be more natural, you peopled this pure, clear world of light (which had no trace of yearning, of expectancy, of looking forward or backward) with Greek heroes. You felt it all as Poussin and his school felt—at once heroic and idyllic.—So individual men too have lived, constantly feeling themselves in the world and the world in themselves, and among them one of the greatest men, the inventor of a heroico-idyllic form of philosophy—Epicurus.

296. Counting and Measuring.—The art of seeing many things, of weighing one with another, of reckoning one thing with another and constructing from them a rapid conclusion, a fairly correct sum—that goes to make a great politician or general or merchant. This quality is, in fact, a power of speedy mental calculation. The art of seeing one thing alone, of finding therein the sole motive for action, the guiding principle of all other action, goes to make the hero and also the fanatic. This quality means a dexterity in measuring with one scale.

297. Not to See too Soon.—As long as we undergo some experience, we must give ourselves up to the experience and shut our eyes—in other words, not become observers of what we are undergoing. For to observe would disturb good digestion of the experience, and instead of wisdom we should gain nothing but dyspepsia.

298. From the Practice of the Wise.—To become wise we must will to undergo certain experiences, and accordingly leap into their jaws. This, it is true, is very dangerous. Many a "sage" has been eaten up in the process.

299. Exhaustion of the Intellect.—Our occasional coldness and indifference towards people, which is imputed to us as hardness and defect of character, is often only an exhaustion of the intellect. In this state other men are to us, as we are to ourselves, tedious or immaterial.

300. "The One Thing Needful."—If we are clever, the one thing we need is to have joy in our hearts. "Ah," adds some one, "if we are clever, the best thing we can do is to be wise."

301. A Sign of Love.—Some one said, "There are two persons about whom I have never thought deeply. That is a sign of my love for them."

302. How we Seek to Improve Bad Arguments.—Many a man adds a bit of his personality to his bad arguments, as if they would thus go better and change into straight and good arguments. In the same way, players at skittles, even after a throw, try to give a direction to the ball by turns and gestures.

303. Honesty.—It is but a small thing to be a pattern sort of man with regard to rights and property—for instance (to name trifling points, which of course give a better proof of this sort of pattern nature than great examples), if as a boy one never steals fruit from another's orchard, and as a man never walks on unmown fields. It is but little; you are then still only a "law-abiding person," with just that degree of morality of which a "society," a group of human beings, is capable.

304. "Man!"—What is the vanity of the vainest individual as compared with the vanity which the most modest person feels when he thinks of his position in nature and in the world as "Man!"

305. The Most Necessary Gymnastic.—Through deficiency in self-control in small matters a similar deficiency on great occasions slowly arises. Every day on which we have not at least once denied ourselves some trifle is turned to bad use and a danger to the next day. This gymnastic is indispensable if we wish to maintain the joy of being our own master.

306. Losing Ourselves.—When we have first found ourselves, we must understand how from time to time to lose ourselves and then to find ourselves again.—This is true on the assumption that we are thinkers. A thinker finds it a drawback always to be tied to one person.

307. When it is Necessary to Part.—You must, for a time at least, part from that which you want to know and measure. Only when you have left a city do you see how high its towers rise above its houses.

308. At Noontide.—He to whom an active and stormy morning of life is allotted, at the noontide of life feels his soul overcome by a strange longing for a rest that may last for months and years. All grows silent around him, voices sound farther and farther in the distance, the sun shines straight down upon him. On a hidden woodland sward he sees the great God Pan sleeping, and with Pan Nature seems to him to have gone to sleep with an expression of eternity on their faces. He wants nothing, he troubles about nothing; his heart stands still, only his eye lives. It is a death with waking eyes. Then man sees much that he never saw before, and, so far as his eye can reach, all is woven into and as it were buried in a net of light. He feels happy, but it is a heavy, very heavy kind of happiness.—Then at last the wind stirs in the trees, noontide is over, life carries him away again, life with its blind eyes, and its tempestuous retinue behind it—desire, illusion, oblivion, enjoyment, destruction, decay. And so comes evening, more stormy and more active than was even the morning.—To the really active man these prolonged phases of cognition seem almost uncanny and morbid, but not unpleasant.

309. To Beware of One's Portrait-Painter.—A great painter, who in a portrait has revealed and put on canvas the fullest expression and look of which a man

is capable, will almost always think, when he sees the man later in real life, that he is only looking at a caricature.

310. The Two Principles of the New Life.—First Principle: to arrange one's life on the most secure and tangible basis, not as hitherto upon the most distant, undetermined, and cloudy foundation. Second Principle: to establish the rank of the nearest and nearer things, and of the more and less secure, before one arranges one's life and directs it to a final end.

311. Dangerous Irritability.—Talented men who are at the same time idle will always appear somewhat irritated when one of their friends has accomplished a thorough piece of work. Their jealousy is awakened, they are ashamed of their own laziness, or rather, they fear that their active friend will now despise them even more than before. In such a mood they criticise the new achievement, and, to the utter astonishment of the author, their criticism becomes a revenge.

312. Destructions of Illusions.—Illusions are certainly expensive amusements; but the destruction of illusions is still more expensive, if looked upon as an amusement, as it undoubtedly is by some people.

313. The Monotone of the "Sage."—Cows sometimes have a look of wondering which stops short on the path to questioning. In the eye of the higher intelligence, on the other hand, the nil admirari is spread out like the monotony of the cloudless sky.

314. Not to be Ill too Long.—We should beware of being ill too long. The lookers-on become impatient of their customary duty of showing sympathy, because they find it too much trouble to maintain the appearance of this emotion for any length of time. Then they immediately pass to suspicion of our character, with the conclusion: "You deserve to be ill, and we need no longer be at pains to show our sympathy."

315. A Hint to Enthusiasts.—He who likes to be carried away, and would fain be carried on high, must beware lest he become too heavy. For instance, he must not learn much, and especially not let himself be crammed with science. Science makes men ponderous—take care, ye enthusiasts!

316. Knowledge of how to Surprise Oneself.—He who would see himself as he is, must know how to surprise himself, torch in hand. For with the mind it is as with the body: whoever is accustomed to look at himself in the glass forgets his ugliness, and only recognises it again by means of the portrait-painter. Yet he even grows used to the picture and forgets his ugliness all over again.—Herein we see the universal law that man cannot endure unalterable ugliness, unless for a moment. He forgets or denies it in all cases.—The moralists must reckon upon that "moment" for bringing forward their truths.

317. Opinions and Fish.—We are possessors of our opinions as of fish—that is, in so far as we are possessors of a fish pond. We must go fishing and have luck—then we have our fish, our opinions. I speak here of live opinions, of live fish. Others are content to possess a cabinet of fossils—and, in their head, "convictions."

318. Signs of Freedom and Servitude.—To satisfy one's needs so far as possible oneself, even if imperfectly, is the path towards freedom in mind and personality. To satisfy many even superfluous needs, and that as fully as possible, is a training for servitude. The Sophist Hippias, who himself earned and made all that he wore within and without, is the representative of the highest freedom of mind and personality. It does not matter whether all is done equally well and perfectly—pride can repair the damaged places.

319. Belief in Oneself.—In our times we mistrust every one who believes in himself. Formerly this was enough to make people believe in one. The recipe for finding faith now runs: "Spare not thyself! In order to set thy opinion in a credible light, thou must first set fire to thy own hut!"

320. At Once Richer and Poorer.—I know a man who accustomed himself even in childhood to think well of the intellectuality of mankind—in other words, of their real devotion as regards things of the intellect, their unselfish preference for that which is recognised as true—but who had at the same time a modest or even depreciatory view of his own brain (judgment, memory, presence of mind, imagination). He set no value on himself when he compared himself with others. Now in the course of years he was compelled, first once and then in a hundred ways, to revise this verdict. One would have thought he would be thoroughly satisfied and delighted. Such, in fact, was to some extent the case, but, as he once said, "Yet a bitterness of the deepest dye is mingled with my feeling, such as I did not know in earlier life; for since I learnt to value men and myself more correctly, my intellect seems to me of less use. I scarcely think I can now do any good at all with it, because the minds of others cannot understand the good. I now always see before me the frightful gulf between those who could give help and those who need help. So I am troubled by the misfortune of having my intellect to myself and of being forced to enjoy it alone so far as it can give any enjoyment. But to give is more blessed than to possess, and what is the richest man in the solitude of a desert?"[28]

321. How we should Attack.—The reasons for which men believe or do not believe are in very few people as strong as they might be. As a rule, in order to shake a belief it is far from necessary to use the heaviest weapon of attack. Many attain their object by merely making the attack with some noise—in fact, pop-guns are often enough. In dealing with very vain persons, the semblance of a strong

attack is enough. They think they are being taken quite seriously, and readily give way.

322. Death.—Through the certain prospect of death a precious, fragrant drop of frivolity might be mixed with every life—and now, you singular druggist-souls, you have made of death a drop of poison, unpleasant to taste, which makes the whole of life hideous.

323. Repentance.—Never allow repentance free play, but say at once to yourself, "That would be adding a second piece of folly to the first." If you have worked evil, you must bethink yourself of doing good. If you are punished for your actions, submit to the punishment with the feeling that by this very submission you are somehow doing good, in that you are deterring others from falling into the same error. Every malefactor who is punished has a right to consider himself a benefactor to mankind.

324. Becoming a Thinker.—How can any one become a thinker if he does not spend at least a third part of the day without passions, men, and books?

325. The Best Remedy.—A little health on and off is the best remedy for the invalid.

326. Don't Touch.—There are dreadful people who, instead of solving a problem, complicate it for those who deal with it and make it harder to solve.[29] Whoever does not know how to hit the nail on the head should be entreated not to hit the nail at all.

327. Forgetting Nature.—We speak of Nature, and, in doing so, forget ourselves: we ourselves are Nature, quand même.—Consequently, Nature is something quite different from what we feel on hearing her name pronounced.

328. Profundity and Ennui.—In the case of profound men, as of deep wells, it takes a long time before anything that is thrown into them reaches the bottom. The spectators, who generally do not wait long enough, too readily look upon such a man as callous and hard—or even as boring.

329. When it is Time to Vow Fidelity to Oneself.—We sometimes go astray in an intellectual direction which does not correspond to our talents. For a time we struggle heroically against wind and tide, really against ourselves; but finally we become weary and we pant. What we accomplish gives us no real pleasure, since we think that we have paid too heavy a price for these successes. We even despair of our productivity, of our future, perhaps in the midst of victory.—Finally, finally we turn back—and then the wind swells our sails and bears us into our smooth water. What bliss! How certain of victory we feel! Only now do we know what we are and what we intend, and now we vow fidelity to ourselves, and have a right to do so—as men that know.

330. Weather Prophets.—Just as the clouds reveal to us the direction of the wind high above our heads, so the lightest and freest spirits give signs of future weather by their course. The wind in the valley and the market-place opinions of to-day have no significance for the future, but only for the past.

331. Continual Acceleration.—Those who begin slowly and find it hard to become familiar with a subject, sometimes acquire afterwards the quality of continual acceleration—so that in the end no one knows where the current will take them.

332. The Three Good Things.—Greatness, calm, sunlight—these three embrace all that a thinker desires and also demands of himself: his hopes and duties, his claims in the intellectual and moral sphere, nay even in his daily manner of life and the scenic background of his residence. Corresponding to these three things are, firstly thoughts that exalt, secondly thoughts that soothe, and thirdly thoughts that illuminate—but, fourthly, thoughts that share in all these three qualities, in which all earthly things are transfigured. This is the kingdom of the great trinity of joy.

333. Dying for "Truth."—We should not let ourselves be burnt for our opinions—we are not so certain of them as all that. But we might let ourselves be burnt for the right of possessing and changing our opinions.

334. Market Value.—If we wish to pass exactly for what we are, we must be something that has its market value. As, however, only objects in common use have a market value, this desire is the consequence either of shrewd modesty or of stupid immodesty.

335. Moral for Builders.—We must remove the scaffolding when the house has been built.

336. Sophocleanism.—Who poured more water into wine than the Greeks? Sobriety and grace combined—that was the aristocratic privilege of the Athenian in the time of Sophocles and after. Imitate that whoever can! In life and in work!

337. Heroism.—The heroic consists in doing something great (or in nobly not doing something) without feeling oneself to be in competition with or before others. The hero carries with him, wherever he goes, the wilderness and the holy land with inviolable precincts.

338. Finding our "Double" in Nature.—In some country places we rediscover ourselves, with a delightful shudder: it is the pleasantest way of finding our "double."—How happy must he be who has that feeling just here, in this perpetually sunny October air, in this happy elfin play of the wind from morn till eve, in this clearest of atmospheres and mildest of temperatures, in all the serious yet cheerful landscape of hill, lake, and forest on this plateau, which has encamped fearlessly next to the terrors of eternal snow: here, where Italy and

Finland have joined hands, and where the home of all the silver colour-tones of Nature seems to be established. How happy must he be who can say, "True, there are many grander and finer pieces of scenery, but this is so familiar and intimate to me, related by blood, nay even more to me!"

339. Affability of the Sage.—The sage will unconsciously be affable in his intercourse with other men, as a prince would be, and will readily treat them as equals, in spite of all differences of talent, rank, and character. For this characteristic, however, so soon as people notice it, he is most heavily censured.

340. Gold.—All that is gold does not glitter. A soft sheen characterises the most precious metal.

341. Wheel and Drag.—The wheel and the drag have different duties, but also one in common—that of hurting each other.

342. Disturbances of the Thinker.—All that interrupts the thinker in his thoughts (disturbs him, as people say) must be regarded by him calmly, as a new model who comes in by the door to offer himself to the artist. Interruptions are the ravens which bring food to the recluse.

343. Being very Clever.—Being very clever keeps men young, but they must put up with being considered, for that very reason, older than they are. For men read the handwriting of the intellect as signs of experience—that is, of having lived much and evilly, of suffering, error, and repentance. Hence, if we are very clever and show it, we appear to them older and wickeder than we are.

344. How we must Conquer.—We ought not to desire victory if we only have the prospect of overcoming our opponent by a hair's breadth. A good victory makes the vanquished rejoice, and must have about it something divine which spares humiliation.

345. An Illusion of Superior Minds.—Superior minds find it difficult to free themselves from an illusion; for they imagine that they excite envy among the mediocre and are looked upon as exceptions. As a matter of fact, however, they are looked upon as superfluous, as something that would not be missed if it did not exist.

346. Demanded by Cleanliness.—Changing opinions is in some natures as much demanded by cleanliness as changing clothes. In the case of other natures it is only demanded by vanity.

347. Also Worthy of a Hero.—Here is a hero who did nothing but shake the tree as soon as the fruits were ripe. Do you think that too small a thing? Well, just look at the tree that he shook.

348. A Gauge for Wisdom.—The growth of wisdom may be gauged exactly by the diminution of ill-temper.

349. Expressing an Error Disagreeably.—It is not to every one's taste to hear truth pleasantly expressed. But let no one at least believe that error will become truth if it is disagreeably expressed.

350. The Golden Maxim.—Man has been bound with many chains, in order that he may forget to comport himself like an animal. And indeed he has become more gentle, more intellectual, more joyous, more meditative than any animal. But now he still suffers from having carried his chains so long, from having been so long without pure air and free movement—these chains, however, are, as I repeat again and again, the ponderous and significant errors of moral, religious, and metaphysical ideas. Only when the disease of chains is overcome is the first great goal reached—the separation of man from the brute. At present we stand in the midst of our work of removing the chains, and in doing so we need the strictest precautions. Only the ennobled man may be granted freedom of spirit; to him alone comes the alleviation of life and heals his wounds; he is the first who can say that he lives for the sake of joy, with no other aim; in any other mouth, his motto of "Peace around me and goodwill towards all the most familiar things," would be dangerous.—In this motto for single individuals he is thinking of an ancient saying, magnificent and pathetic, which applied to all, and has remained standing above all mankind, as a motto and a beacon whereby shall perish all who adorn their banner too early—the rock on which Christianity foundered. It is not even yet time, it seems, for all men to have the lot of those shepherds who saw the heavens lit up above them and heard the words: "Peace on earth and goodwill to one another among men."—It is still the age of the individual.

The Shadow: Of all that you have enunciated, nothing pleased me more than one promise: "Ye want again to be good neighbours to the most familiar things." This will be to the advantage of us poor shadows too. For do but confess that you have hitherto been only too fond of reviling us.

The Wanderer: Reviling? But why did you never defend yourselves? After all, you were very close to our ears.

The Shadow: It seemed to us that we were too near you to have a right to talk of ourselves.

The Wanderer: What delicacy! Ah, you shadows are "better men"[30] than we, I can see that.

The Shadow: And yet you called us "importunate"—us, who know one thing at least extremely well: how to be silent and to wait—no Englishman knows it better. It is true we are very, very often in the retinue of men, but never as their bondsmen. When man shuns light, we shun man—so far, at least, we are free.

The Wanderer: Ah, light shuns man far oftener, and then also you abandon him.

The Shadow: It has often pained me to leave you. I am eager for knowledge, and much in man has remained obscure to me, because I cannot always be in his company. At the price of complete knowledge of man I would gladly be your slave.

The Wanderer: Do you know, do I know, whether you would not then unwittingly become master instead of slave? Or would remain a slave indeed, but would lead a life of humiliation and disgust because you despised your master? Let us both be content with freedom such as you have enjoyed up to now—you and I! For the sight of a being not free would embitter my greatest joys; all that is best would be repugnant to me if any one had to share it with me—I will not hear of any slaves about me. That is why I do not care for the dog, that lazy, tail-wagging parasite, who first became "doggish" as the slave of man, and of whom they still say that he is loyal to his master and follows him like—

The Shadow: Like his shadow, they say. Perhaps I have already followed you too long to-day? It has been the longest day, but we are nearing the end; be patient a little more! The grass is damp; I am feeling chilly.

The Wanderer: Oh, is it already time to part? And I had to hurt you in the end—I saw you became darker.

The Shadow: I blushed the only colour I have at command. I remembered that I had often lain at your feet like a dog, and that you then—

The Wanderer: Can I not with all speed do something to please you? Have you no wish?

The Shadow: None, except perhaps the wish that the philosophic "dog"[31] expressed to Alexander the Great—just move a little out of my light; I feel cold.

The Wanderer: What am I to do?

The Shadow: Walk under those fir-trees and look around you towards the mountains; the sun is sinking.

The Wanderer: Where are you? Where are you?

Footnotes:

[1]"Foreword" and "forword" would be the literal rendering of the play on words.—Tr.

[2]The allusion is to the ending of the Second Part of Goethe's Faust—"das Ewig Weibliche Zieht uns hinan!"—"The Eternal Feminine Draweth us on!"—Tr.

[3]It has been attempted to render the play on "Gewissen" and "Wissen."—Tr.

[4]Cf. John i. 1.—Tr.

[5]The German word Mitfreude, coined by Nietzsche in opposition to Mitleid (sympathy), is untranslateable.—Tr.

[6]Herostratus of Ephesus (in 356 b.c.) set fire to the temple of Diana in order (as he confessed on the rack) to gain notoriety.—Tr.

[7]Quotation from Schiller, Don Carlos, i. 5.—Tr.

[8]This, of course, refers to Jesus and Socrates.—Tr.

[9]Queen of the Amazons, slain by Achilles in the Trojan War.—Tr.

[10]From Schiller, Wallenstein's Lager: "Wer den Besten seiner Zeit genug gethan, der hat gelebt für alle Zeiten" ("He that has satisfied the best men of his time has lived for all time").

[11]In German Barockstil, i.e. the degenerate post-Renaissance style in art and literature, which spread from Italy in the seventeenth century.—Tr.

[12]The original word, Freizügig, means, in the modern German Empire, possessing the free right of migration, without pecuniary burdens or other restrictions, from one German state to another. The play on words in Zug zur Freiheit ("impulse to freedom") is untranslateable.—Tr.

[13]Nietzsche seems to allude to his own case, for he ultimately contracted a myopia which bordered on blindness.—Tr.

[14]The play on bergen (shelter) and verbergen (hide) is untranslateable.—Tr.

[15]Allusion to German proverb: "Where there is nothing, the Emperor has lost his rights."—Tr.

[16]Genesis xiii. 9.—Tr.

[17]Luke viii. 33.—Tr.

[18]The play on Freudenschaften (i.e. pleasure-giving passions) and Leidenschaften (i.e. pain-giving passions) is often used by Nietzsche, and is untranslateable.—Tr.

[19]The wife of the Stoic Thrasea Paetus, when their complicity in the great conspiracy of 65 a.d. against Nero was discovered, is reported to have said as she committed suicide, "It doesn't hurt, Paetus."—Tr.

[20]It is interesting to compare this judgment with Carlyle's praise of Jean Paul. The dressing-gown is an allusion to Jean Paul's favourite costume.—Tr.

[21]The German copyright expires thirty years after publication.—Tr.

[22]Nietzsche himself was extremely short-sighted.—Tr.

[23]In the sixth century b.c. Pythagoras founded at Croton a "school" somewhat resembling a monastic order. Among the ordeals for novitiates was enforced silence for five years.—Tr.

[24]In the German Aufklärung there is a play on the sense "clearing up" (of weather) and "enlightenment."—Tr.

[25]Stendhal.—Tr.

[26]A transposition of sacrifizio dell' intelletto, the Jesuit maxim.—Tr.

[27]The original, by a curious slip, has "seventh."—Tr.

[28]Clearly autobiographical. Nietzsche, like all great men, passed through a period of modesty and doubt.—Tr.

[29]Nietzsche here alludes to his own countrymen.—Tr.

[30]An allusion to the poem "Der Wilde" (The Savage) by Säume, which ends with the line, "Sehet, wir wilden sind doch bessere Menschen" (Behold, after all, we savages are better men).—Tr.

[31]Diogenes, founder of the Cynic school, which derived its name from κυ ν (dog).—Tr.

www.ingramcontent.com/pod-product-compliance
Lightning Source LLC
Chambersburg PA
CBHW051821040426
42447CB00006B/317